● 普通高校专业英语教程系列

人力资源管理英语

陈红美　司小侠　车艳菊　编著

清华大学出版社
北京

内 容 简 介

本书是为提高人力资源管理专业学生的英语能力而编写的教材，包括以下主题：人力资源管理、工作分析、人力资源规划、招聘、员工配置、培训需求分析、绩效管理、薪酬管理、激励劳动关系管理。

本书共有十个单元，每单元由以下几部分组成：课文——本单元所涉主题的基本理论、主要领域、常用方法；单词——课文中出现的新词，读者由此可以积累专业基础词汇；词组——课文中的常用词组；缩略语——课文中出现的、业内人士必须掌握的缩略语；习题——巩固所学知识；阅读材料——提供最新的行业资料，进一步扩大读者的视野。

本书既可作为高等院校人力资源管理专业英语教材，也可供相应的培训机构使用。相关从业人员使用本书"自我充电"，亦颇得当。

版权所有，侵权必究。举报：010-62782989，beiqinquan@tup.tsinghua.edu.cn。

图书在版编目（CIP）数据

人力资源管理英语 / 陈红美，司小侠，车艳菊编著 . —北京：清华大学出版社，2019（2023.8重印）
（普通高校专业英语教程系列）
ISBN 978-7-302-51994-2

Ⅰ.①人… Ⅱ.①陈…②司…③车… Ⅲ.①人力资源－英语－高等学校－教材 Ⅳ.①F243

中国版本图书馆 CIP 数据核字（2018）第 000137 号

责任编辑：徐博文
封面设计：子 一
责任校对：王凤芝
责任印制：刘海龙

出版发行：清华大学出版社
网　　址：http://www.tup.com.cn, http://www.wqbook.com
地　　址：北京清华大学学研大厦 A 座　　邮　编：100084
社 总 机：010-83470000　　邮　购：010-62786544
投稿与读者服务：010-62776969, c-service@tup.tsinghua.edu.cn
质量反馈：010-62772015, zhiliang@tup.tsinghua.edu.cn

印 装 者：三河市春园印刷有限公司
经　　销：全国新华书店
开　　本：185mm×260mm　　印　张：14.25　　字　数：345 千字
版　　次：2019 年 5 月第 1 版　　印　次：2023 年 8 月第 5 次印刷
定　　价：69.00 元

产品编号：077366-01

前　言
Preface

全球经济一体化的一个主要标志是组织的国际化，因此，组织中的人力资源管理人员必须有国际化的视野和理解的多元化，并要有面向全球的人力资源组织与管理能力。具备相关专业知识并精通外语的人员能处于竞争的优势地位，成为行业中的佼佼者。职场对从业人员的专业英语水平要求很高，这有力地促进了从业人员学习专业英语积极性的提升。许多大学也因此开设了"人力资源管理专业英语"课程，本书就是为了提高读者的专业英语能力而编写的行业英语教材。

结合学生情况，面对学生毕业后的就业环境，根据未来工作的实际要求，本书做了切合实际的精心编排，主要内容包括：人力资源管理基础、人力资源管理的重要性、人力资源管理历史、工作分析、工作设计、组织结构、人力资源规划、人力资源规划的流程、人力资源规划的重要因素、招聘、面试、员工配置、员工选择和安置、就业测试、培训需求分析、培训组织与实施、培训评估、绩效管理、绩效评估、激励理论、激励员工的策略、薪酬管理、薪酬结构设计、薪酬调查、员工福利、劳动关系管理、集体谈判以及劳动合同等。

本书每一单元由以下几部分组成：课文——本书所涉主题的基本理论、主要领域、常用方法；单词——课文中出现的新词，读者由此可以积累专业基础词汇；词组——课文中的常用词组；缩略语——课文中出现的、业内人士必须掌握的缩略语；习题——巩固所学知识；阅读材料——最新的行业资料，进一步扩大读者的视野。

本书配有教案和习题参考答案，读者可从出版社官网下载，在使用本书过程中如有任何问题，可以通过电子邮件与我们交流（邮箱地址：zqh3882355@163.com；cici12323@tom.com），邮件标题请注明姓名及"人力资源管理英语教程（清华大学出版社版）"。

由于编者水平有限，书中难免有疏漏和不足之处，恳请广大读者和同人提出宝贵意见，以便再版时进行修正。

编　者
2019 年 3 月

目录 Contents

Unit 1

Text A	Human Resource Management	1
Text B	Importance of Human Resource Management	8
Supplementary Reading	A History of Human Resource Management	12
参考译文（Text A）	人力资源管理	15

Unit 2

Text A	Job Analysis	17
Text B	Job Design	24
Supplementary Reading	Organizational Structure	30
参考译文（Text A）	工作分析	33

Unit 3

Text A	Human Resource Planning	37
Text B	The Process of Human Resource Planning	44
Supplementary Reading	Factors Affecting Human Resource Planning	49
参考译文（Text A）	人力资源规划	53

Unit 4

Text A	Recruitment	57
Text B	Recruitment Sources	65

| Supplementary Reading | Job Interview | 72 |
| 参考译文（Text A） | 招聘 | 78 |

Unit 5

Text A	An Overview of Employee Placement	83
Text B	Employee Selection and Placement	90
Supplementary Reading	Employment Testing	94
参考译文（Text A）	员工配置	98

Unit 6

Text A	Training Needs Analysis	103
Text B	Training Organization and Implementation	109
Supplementary Reading	Training Evaluation	116
参考译文（Text A）	培训需求分析	120

Unit 7

Text A	Performance Management	123
Text B	Performance Appraisal	131
Supplementary Reading	Motivational Theories	137
参考译文（Text A）	绩效管理	141

Unit 8

Text A	Compensation Management	145
Text B	Compensation Structure Design	153
Supplementary Reading	Compensation Surveys	160
参考译文（Text A）	薪酬管理	166

Unit 9

Text A	Incentives	171
Text B	Employee Benefits	179
Supplementary Reading	Strategies to Motivate Employees	186
参考译文（Text A）	激励	191

Unit 10

Text A	Labor Relations Management	195
Text B	Collective Bargaining	204
Supplementary Reading	Employment Contract	210
参考译文（Text A）	劳动关系管理	214

Unit 1

Text A

Human Resource Management

Undoubtedly, any organization's success depends on how it manages its resources. A firm's resources propel it toward its goals, just as an engine propels an automobile toward its destination. Many of an organization's resources are non-human, such as land, capital, and equipment. Although the management of these resources is very important, a business cannot succeed without also managing its human resources (i.e. its people) properly. Just as automobiles will not operate efficiently if they are not driven by capable people, and organizations will not operate successfully unless they too are "driven" by capable people. People determine the organization's objectives, and people run the operations that allow the organization to reach its objectives.

Human resource management, focusing on the people aspect of management, consists of practices that help the organization deal effectively with its people during the various phases of the employment cycle: pre-selection, selection, and post-selection.

The HRM pre-selection practices, which are human resource planning and job analysis, lay the foundation for the other HRM practices. The organization must decide what type of job openings will exist in the upcoming period and determine what qualifications are necessary to perform these jobs. In other words, firms must analyze and plan for their treatment of workers before they can carry out the remaining HRM practices.

Human resource planning helps managers anticipate and meet changing needs relating to the acquisition, deployment and utilization of its employees. The organization first maps out an overall plan (called a strategic plan). Then, through a process called demand and supply forecasting, it estimates the number and types of employees needed to successfully carry out overall plan. Such information enables a firm to plan its recruitment, selection, and training strategies. For example, let's say that a firm's HR plan estimates that 15 additional engineers will be needed during the next year. The firm typically hires recent engineering graduates to fill such positions. Because these majors are in high demand, the firm decides to begin its campus recruiting early in the academic year, before other companies can "snatch away" the best candidates.

Job analysis is a systematic procedure of gathering, analyzing, and documenting information about particular jobs. The analysis specifies what each worker does, the work conditions, and the worker's qualifications necessary to perform the job successfully. Job analysis information is used to plan and coordinate nearly all HRM practices, such as these: determining job qualifications for recruitment purposes, choosing the most appropriate selection techniques, developing training programs, helping to determine pay rates. For example, an organization may decide to use a mechanical aptitude test to screen applicants because a job analysis indicated that the nature of the work had recently changed and was then more demanding.

HRM selection practices are policies and procedures used by organizations to staff their positions, which include recruiting applicants, assessing their qualifications, and ultimately selecting those who are deemed to be the most qualified. Organizations use recruitment to locate and attract job applicants for particular positions. Organizations may recruit candidates internally or externally. The aim of recruitment practices is to identify a suitable pool of applicants quickly, cost efficiently and legally. Selection involves assessing and choosing among job candidates. To be effective, selection processes must be technically sound (i.e. accurate) and legal.

In the post-selection phase, the organization develops HRM practices for effectively managing people once they have "come through the door". These practices are designed to maximize the performance and satisfaction levels of a firm's employees by providing them with the necessary knowledge and skills to perform their jobs and by creating conditions that will energize, direct, and facilitate the employees' efforts toward meeting the organization's objectives.

Training and development are planned learning experiences that teach workers how to perform their current or future jobs effectively. Training focuses on present jobs, whereas development prepares employees for possible future jobs. Training and development practices are designed to improve organizational performance by enhancing the knowledge and skill levels of employees. Training and development is an ongoing process. Changes in technology and the environment, as well as in an organization's goals and strategies, often require organizational members to learn new techniques and ways of working.

Through the performance appraisal process, organizations measure the adequacy of their employees' job performances and communicate these evaluations to them. One aim of appraisal systems is to motivate employees to continue appropriate behaviors and correct inappropriate ones. Management may also use performance appraisals as tools for making HRM-related decisions, such as promotions, demotions, discharges and pay raises.

On the basis of performance appraisals, managers distribute pay to employees. By rewarding

Unit 1

high-performing organization members with pay raises, bonuses, and the like, managers increase the likelihood that an organization's most valuable human resources are motivated to continue their high levels of contribution to the organization. Moreover, by linking pay to performance, high-performing employees are more likely to stay with the organization, and managers are more likely to fill positions that become open with highly talented individuals. Benefits, such as health insurance or employee discounts, are important outcomes that employees receive by virtue of their membership in an organization.

Last but not least, labor relations encompass the steps that managers take to develop and maintain good working relationship with the labor unions that may represent their employees' interests.

Managers must ensure that all these practices fit together and complement their company's structure and control system. For example, if managers decide to decentralize authority and empower employees, they need to invest in training and development to ensure that lower level employees have the knowledge and expertise they need to make the decisions that top managers would make in a more centralized structure.

New Words

undoubtedly [ʌn'dautidli] *adv.* 毋庸置疑地，的确地
propel [prə'pel] *v.* 推进；驱使
destination [ˌdesti'neiʃən] *n.* 目的地；终点
non-human ['nɔn-'hju:mən] *adj.* 非人类的
capital ['kæpitəl] *n.* 首都；资本；大写字母 *adj.* 资本的；大写的；一流的；首要的
properly ['prɔpəli] *adv.* 适当地，完全地
equipment [i'kwipmənt] *n.* 装备，设备，器材
capable ['keipəbl] *adj.* 有能力的，能干的；有……的可能性
determine [di'tə:min] *v.* 决定；确定；测定
objective [əb'dʒektiv] *adj.* 客观的；真实的 *n.* 目标；目的
aspect ['æspekt] *n.* 方面；方位；外观；外貌

various ['vɛəriəs] *adj.* 各种各样的
phase [feiz] *n.* 阶段；时期 *v.* 逐步执行
pre-selection [pri-si'lekʃən] *n.* 预选择
upcoming ['ʌpˌkʌmiŋ] *adj.* 即将来临的；预定将要
qualification [ˌkwɔlifi'keiʃən] *n.* 资格，资历；限制；授权
perform [pə'fɔ:m] *v.* 执行，履行；表演；运转
treatment ['tri:tmənt] *n.* 处置，处理；治疗；对待
remaining [ri'meiniŋ] *adj.* 剩余的
anticipate [æn'tisipeit] *v.* 预期；提前使用
acquisition [ˌækwi'ziʃən] *n.* 获得；所获之物
deployment [di'plɔimənt] *n.* 部署；展开
utilization [ˌju:tilai'zeiʃən] *n.* 利用
overall ['əuvərɔ:l] *adj.* 全部的；总体的

strategic [strə'ti:dʒik] adj. 战略的；重要的；基本的
forecasting ['fɔ:kɑ:stiŋ] n. 预测，预报 v. 预测
estimate ['estimeit] n. 估价；估计 v. 估计；估价；评价
recruitment [ri'kru:tmənt] n. 征募新兵；补充；招聘
selection [si'lekʃn] n. 选拔，挑选
strategy ['strætədʒi] n. 政策，策略
additional [ə'diʃnl] adj. 另外的，附加的，额外的
candidate ['kændideit] n. 候选人，投考者
systematic [ˌsistə'mætik] adj. 系统的，体系的
document ['dɔkjumənt] v. 记载；（用文件等）证明 n. 文件；公文
procedure [prə'si:dʒə] n. 过程；程序；手续；步骤
specify ['spesifai] v. 指定，详细说明
coordinate [kəu'ɔ:dineit] v. （使）协调；（使）一致
purpose ['pə:pəs] n. 目的，意图；用途；效果；决心 v. 打算，企图
appropriate [ə'prəuprieit] adj. 适当的；相称的
mechanical [mi'kænikl] adj. 机械的；力学的
aptitude ['æptitju:d] n. 天资；资质；才能
policy ['pɔlisi] n. 政策，方针；手段；计谋；策略
staff [stɑ:f] v. 供给人员，充当职员 n. 工作人员
screen [skri:n] v. 筛；检查
applicant ['æplikənt] n. 申请人
indicate ['indikeit] v. 表明；指明

demanding [di'mændiŋ] adj. 要求多的；吃力的
position [pə'ziʃn] n. 位置；职位；立场
assess [ə'ses] v. 评定，评估，估算
ultimately ['ʌltimətli] adv. 最后，最终
deem [di:m] v. 认为，视作
qualified ['kwɔlifaid] adj. 有资格的，能胜任的
locate [ləu'keit] v. 确定；找出，找到
internally [in'tə:nəli] adv. 内部地；国内地
externally [eks'tə:nəli] adv. 外部地；外面地
identify [ai'dentifai] v. 鉴定；识别，辨认出
accurate ['ækjurət] adj. 准确的，精确的
legal ['li:gəl] adj. 法定的；法律的；合法的
maximize ['mæksimaiz] v. 使增加至最大限度；充分利用
performance [pə'fɔ:məns] n. 表演；表现；实行，履行
energize ['enədʒaiz] v. 使活跃；激励；使精力充沛
facilitate [fə'siliteit] v. 促进，帮助，使……容易
enhance [in'hɑ:ns] v. 提高；增加，加强
appraisal [ə'preizəl] n. 估计，评估
adequacy ['ædikwəsi] n. 足够；适当
evaluation [iˌvælju'eiʃn] n. 评价；评估
motivate ['məutiveit] v. 激发（兴趣或欲望）
promotion [prə'məuʃn] n. 提升；促进；晋升；促销
demotion [di:'məuʃn] n. 降级；降职
discharge [dis'tʃɑ:dʒ] v. 解雇；解除
distribute [di'stribju:t] v. 分配；散发；分布

Unit 1

bonus ['bəunəs] n. 红利；意外所得之物；奖金
contribution [ˌkɔntri'bju:ʃən] n. 贡献
discount ['diskaunt] n. 贴现率；折扣价
outcome ['autkʌm] n. 结果；后果
encompass [in'kʌmpəs] v. 围绕，包围；包括
develop [di'veləp] v. 培养；发展
maintain [mein'tein] v. 维持；维修；坚持；断言
represent [ˌrepri'zent] v. 代表；象征

ensure [in'ʃuə] v. 担保，保证，确保
complement ['kɔmplimənt] v. 相辅相成 n. 补足物
structure ['strʌktʃə] n. 结构；体系
decentralize [di:'sentrəlaiz] v. （使）权力下放
authority [ɔ:'θɔrəti] n. 权威；权利
empower [im'pauə] v. 授权；使能够
invest [in'vest] v. 投资；投入
expertise [ˌekspə'ti:z] n. 专门知识，专门技术

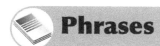
Phrases

depend on 依赖，依靠；取决于；随……而定
just as 正如，就好像
focus on 集中在
consist of 由……组成
deal with 对付，应付；处理
human resource planning 人力资源规划
job analysis 工作分析，职务分析
lay the foundation for 给奠定基础，给……打下基础
job opening 职务空缺
in other words 换句话说，也就是说
carry out 施行，实现
map out 筹划
overall plan 整体计划，总体规划
strategic plan 战略计划，战略规划
demand and supply forecasting 供求预测，供需预测
in high demand 需要量很大

campus recruiting 校园招聘
academic year 学年
snatch away 迅速拿走
pay rate 工资标准
aptitude test 能力倾向测验
a pool of 许多
come through 经历；成功
performance appraisal 绩效考核
pay raise 加薪
on the basis of 根据，在……的基础上
and the like 等等，诸如此类
link… to 把……与……联系
be likely to do sth. 可能做某事
health insurance 医疗保险，健康保险
employee discount 员工折扣
by virtue of 由于，因为；凭借，依靠
labor relation 劳资关系，劳动关系
labor union 工会

HRM (Human Resource Management) 人力资源管理
HR (Human Resources) 人力资源

EX. 1 Answer the following questions according to the text.

1. What does an organization's success depend on?
2. What are the phases of the employment cycle?
3. How important are the HRM pre-selection practices?
4. What does human resources planning help managers do?
5. What does job analysis specify?
6. What practices does HRM selection include?
7. How can the post-selection practices maximize the performance and satisfaction levels of a firm's employees?
8. Why are training and development necessary for employees?
9. What is the aim of appraisal systems?
10. On what basis do managers distribute pay to employees?

EX. 2 Translate the following terms or phrases from English into Chinese and vice versa.

1. aptitude test   1. _____
2. campus recruiting   2. _____
3. human resource planning 3. _____
4. job analysis   4. _____
5. labor relation   5. _____
6. 加薪，增加薪水，增加工资 6. _____
7. 工资标准   7. _____
8. 绩效考核   8. _____
9. n. 候选人   9. _____
10. v. 解雇；解除   10. _____

Unit 1

EX. 3 Translate the following text into Chinese.

Human resource management is the management of human resources. It is designed by the HR department to maximize employee performance in service of an employer's strategic objectives. HR departments are responsible for overseeing employee-benefits design, employee recruitment, training and development, performance appraisal, and rewarding. HR also concerns itself with organizational change and industrial relations. That is, the balancing of organizational practices with requirements arise from collective bargaining and from governmental laws.

HR is a product of the human relations movement of the early 20th century, when researchers began documenting ways of creating business value through the strategic management of the workforce. It was initially dominated by transactional work, such as payroll and benefits administration, but due to globalization, company consolidation, technological advances, and further research, HR as of 2015 focuses on strategic initiatives like mergers and acquisitions, talent management, succession planning, industrial and labor relations, and diversity and inclusion.

EX. 4 Fill in the blanks with the words given below.

adapting	asset	determine	budget	compensation
internal	motivated	strategies	attract	deliver

HRM System

An effective HRM system allows organizations to address human resource issues strategically. This helps the workforce __1__ high quality health services, despite __2__ and external challenges to the organization. A strong human resource management system helps organizations prioritize their organizational and business __3__ while effectively managing the changes inherent in health sector reform and decentralization. HRM helps __4__ and retains competent employees, assists employees and managers in __5__ to organizational change, and facilitates the use of technology to __6__ how and where work is done.

HRM is perhaps one of the most misunderstood, but most important management systems. Employees are an organization's most important __7__, as well as its most expensive: personnel costs often consume 70–80% of an organization's __8__. With a strong and equitable HRM system, employees receive __9__ that reflects their level of responsibility, feel more __10__ and understand how their work relates to the organization's mission and values.

Text B

Importance of Human Resource Management

In today's business world, human resources is an increasingly prominent field that is taking shape throughout industries and workplaces worldwide. Recognizing the fact that people are a company's greatest asset, business leaders across the globe are coming to rely more and more upon an effective management policy that applies specifically to the area of human resources.

Human resources management is the strategic and coherent approach to the management of an organization's most valued assets—the people working there who individually and collectively contribute to the achievement of the objectives of the business. Its goal is to help an organization to meet strategic goals by attracting, and maintaining employees and also to manage them effectively. The key word here perhaps is "fit", i.e. an HRM approach seeks to ensure a fit between the management of an organization's employees and the overall strategic direction of the company.

For small businesses and large conglomerates alike, the human resources management can be helpful for much more than simply processing payroll or handling the open enrollment season once a year. Human resources management plays an essential role in developing a company's strategy as well as handling the employee-centered activities of an organization. Here are ten reasons why the human resource management is important.

Human capital value. Having an in-house human resources function is important. An in-house human resources staff or a human resources expert on staff can increase the understanding of how important human capital is to the company's bottom line. For small businesses, in particular, human capital is critical because so many smaller firms have employees who perform cross-functional duties. With a smaller workforce, if just one person leaves, it leaves the company with a huge gap to fill and a potential threat to the company's profitability.

Budget control. Human resources management curbs excessive spending through developing methods for trimming workforce management costs, which include negotiating better rates for benefits such as health care coverage. In addition, human resources ensure competitive and realistic wage-setting based on studying the labor market, employment trends and salary analysis based on job functions. As some small businesses have budget constraints, this human resources function is especially helpful.

Conflict resolution. Workplace conflict is inevitable, given the diversity of personalities, work styles, backgrounds and levels of experience among employees. A human resources manager or a staff person specially trained to handle employee relation matters can identify and resolve conflict between two employees or a manager and an employee and restore positive working relationships.

Training and development. Human resources conduct needs assessments for the organization's current workforce to determine the type of skills training and employee development necessary for improving skills and qualifications. Companies in the beginning or growth phases can benefit from identifying training needs for existing staff. It's much less expensive than the cost to hire additional staff or more qualified candidates. In addition, it's a strategy that can also reduce turnover and improve employee retention.

Employee satisfaction. Human resources specialists usually are charged with the responsibility of determining the level of employee satisfaction—often an ambiguous measurement at best. With carefully designed employee surveys, focus groups and an exit interview strategy, human resources determine what underlies employee dissatisfaction and address those issues to motivate employees.

Cost savings. The cost to hire new or replacement workers, including training and rampup time, can be exorbitant for employers, especially for small businesses. With a well-constructed recruitment and selection process, the human resources function can minimize expenses regarding advertising job postings, training new employees and enrolling new employees in benefits plans.

Performance improvement. Human resources develop performance management systems. Without a human resources staff person to construct a plan that measures performance, employees can wind in jobs that aren't suitable for their skills and expertise. Additionally, employees whose performance falls below the employer's expectations can continue on the payroll, thereby creating wasted money on lowperforming employees.

Sustaining business. Through succession planning that human resources develop, the company identifies employees with the promise and requisite capabilities to eventually transition into leadership roles with the company. This is an important function as it can guarantee the organization's stability and future success.

Corporate image. Businesses want to be known as the "employer of choice". Employers of choice are the companies that receive recognition for the way they treat employees; they are the companies for whom people want to work. Becoming an employer of choice means human resources balance recruiting the most qualified applicants, selecting the most suitable candidates and retaining the most talented employees.

Steadfast principles. Human resource ensures the workforce embraces the company's philosophy and business principles. From the perspective of a small business, creating a cohesive work environment is imperative. The first opportunity human resource has to accomplish is through wise hiring decisions that identify desirable professional traits, as well as orientation and on-boarding programs.

Generally speaking, human resource management practices and policies can play a crucial role in fostering employee commitment and enabling the firm to function efficiently. However, as we'll see in a moment, intensified global competition, deregulation and technical advances have triggered an avalanche of change, which poses some great challenges to human resource management. For instance, as organizations become more diverse, employers have been adapting their human resource practices to reflect those changes. Many organizations today, such as Bank of America, have workforce diversity programs. They tend to hire, promote, and retain minorities, encourage vendor diversity, and provide diversity training for employees. Workforce diversity requires employers to be more sensitive to the differences that each group brings to the work setting. Employers may have to shift their philosophy from treating everyone alike to recognizing individual differences and responding to those differences in ways that will ensure employee retention and greater productivity. They must recognize and deal with the different values, needs, interests and expectations of employees. They must avoid any practice or action that can be interpreted as being sexist, racist, or offensive to any particular group and of course must not illegibly discriminate against any employee.

New Words

prominent ['prɔminənt] *adj.* 显著的；杰出的，突出的
coherent [kəu'hiərənt] *adj.* 连贯的，一致的；有条理的
asset ['æset] *n.* 资产；优点
collectively [kə'lektivli] *adv.* 共同地；集体地
achievement [ə'tʃi:vmənt] *n.* 成就，成绩；完成
conglomerate [kɔn'glɔmərət] *n.* 联合企业；密集体
payroll ['peirəul] *n.* 工资单；工薪总额
enrollment [in'rəulmənt] *n.* 登记，注册；入伍；入会
critical ['kritikəl] *adj.* 批评的，挑剔的；决定性的；危险的
potential [pə'tenʃəl] *adj.* 潜在的，可能的 *n.* 潜力，潜能
profitability [,prɔfitə'biləti] *n.* 收益性；盈利能力
curb [kə:b] *v.* 抑制；勒住
excessive [ik'sesiv] *adj.* 过分的；过多的
trim [trim] *v.* 修剪；削减；装饰
budget ['bʌdʒit] *n.* 预算 *v.* 为……做预算

conflict ['kɔnflikt] *n.* 冲突；战斗 *v.* 冲突；抵触；争执
resolution [,rezə'lu:ʃən] *n.* 解决；决议
inevitable [in'evitəbl] *adj.* 不可避免的，必然（发生）的
given ['givn] *prep.* 考虑到；如果
diversity [dai'və:səti] *n.* 多样性；差异
restore [ris'tɔ:] *v.* 恢复，复原；归还
current ['kʌrənt] *adj.* 现在的；流通的
satisfaction [,sætis'fækʃən] *n.* 满意；赔偿
ambiguous [æm'bigjuəs] *adj.* 模棱两可的；含糊不清的
underlie [,ʌndə'lai] *v.* 位于……之下；成为……的基础
dissatisfaction ['dis,sætis'fækʃən] *n.* 不满
address [ə'dres] *v.* 称呼；发表演说；处理
replacement [ri'pleismənt] *n.* 更换；接替者
exorbitant [ig'zɔ:bitənt] *adj.* （价格等）过高的；过分的；不合法的
minimize ['minimaiz] *v.* 将……减到最少；贬低
wind [waind] *v.* 使喘不过气来；缠绕；给……上发条

Unit 1

expectation [ˌekspek'teiʃən] n. 预料；期望
sustain [səs'tein] v. 支持；承受；维持
succession [sək'seʃən] n. 连续；继承权；继位
capability [ˌkeipə'biləti] n. 能力，才能；性能；容量
eventually [i'ventjuəli] adv. 最后；终于
transition [træn'ziʃən] n. 转变；过渡
stability [stə'biləti] n. 稳定性
retain [ri'tein] v. 保持；保留
steadfast ['stedfast] adj. 坚定的，毫不动摇的
embrace [im'breis] v. 拥抱；包含；包围；接受
cohesive [kəu'hi:siv] adj. 黏性的；有结合性的
imperative [im'perətiv] adj. 紧要的；必要的
desirable [di'zaiərəbl] adj. 令人满意的；有吸引力的
trait [treit] n. 特征；特点

orientation [ˌɔ:rien'teiʃən] n. 适应；定位；情况介绍
foster ['fɔstə] v. 领养；培养；促进
intensify [in'tensifai] v. 增强；强化；加剧
deregulation [di:ˌregju'leiʃən] n. 撤销管制规定，解除管制
trigger ['trigə] v. 使发生；触发；使运行 n. 扳机；起因
pose [pəuz] v. 摆姿势；提出；假装 n. 姿态，姿势
diverse [dai'və:s] adj. 不同的；多种多样的
adapt [ə'dæpt] v. 改编；使适应
reflect [ri'flekt] v. 反映；反射；反省
sexist ['seksist] n. 性别歧视者 adj. 性别歧视的
racist ['reisist] adj. 种族主义的 n. 种族主义者
offensive [ə'fensiv] adj. 令人不快的；冒犯的；侮辱的
illegibly [i'ledʒəbli] adv. 难读地
discriminate [dis'krimineit] v. 区分；区别对待

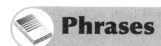

Phrases

take shape 形成；体现
apply to 适用于，运用于
contribute to 为……做贡献；有助于
human capital 人力资本；人力资源
bottom line 底线；结果
in particular 特别，尤其
health care coverage 医疗保险
be charged with 承担；被指控
job posting 公开招聘，招聘公告

benefits plan 福利方案
be suitable for 适合……的
global competition 国际竞争，全球竞争
an avalanche of 突然一阵的，蜂拥而来的
be sensitive to 对……敏感（易感受）
shift from... to... 从……转向
respond to 响应；对……起反应
be interpreted as 被解释为

EX. 5 Answer the following questions according to the text.

1. What is the goal of human resources management in an organization?
2. Why is human capital particularly critical for small businesses?
3. How can human resources ensure competitive and realistic wage-setting?
4. Why is workplace conflict inevitable?
5. What can companies benefit from training and developing existing staff?
6. How do human resources determine what underlies employee dissatisfaction?
7. What will happen to an organization if there is no performance management system within it?
8. What is the importance of succession planning?
9. What are employers of choice?
10. How can human resources create a cohesive work environment within a small business?

Supplementary Reading

Text	Notes
A History of Human Resource Management The history of human resource management started with providing welfare measures to apprentices[1] of the putting-out system. The first personnel department came in the early 20th century. Human resource management has evolved through the ages and gained importance with each passing age. **1. The Origins of Workforce Management** The earliest forms of human resource management were the working arrangements struck between craftsmen and their apprentices during the pre-industrial cottage-based guild[2] system. The apprentice lived in the workshop or home of his master, and the master took care of his health and welfare. The Industrial Revolution of the mid-18th century led to the emergence of large factories and the displacement of cottage-based guild manufacturing. The unhygienic[3] and arduous[4] work in factories led to many labor riots[5], and the government stepped in to provide basic rights and protections for workers. The need to comply with[6] such statutory[7] regulations	[1] apprentice [ə'prentis] *n.* 学徒，见习生 [2] guild [gild] *n.* 行会，协会 [3] unhygienic [ˌʌnhai'dʒi:nik] *adj.* 不卫生的；不健康的 [4] arduous ['ɑ:djuəs] *adj.* 努力的；辛勤的 [5] riot ['raiət] *n.* 暴乱，骚乱 [6] comply with: 服从，遵守 [7] statutory ['stætjut(ə)ri] *adj.* 法定的，法令的

forced factory owners to set up a formal mechanism to redress[8] issues concerning labor.

The National Cash Register Company (NCR) established the first personnel management department to look into issues such as grievances[9], safety, dismissals[10], court cases, and also record keeping and wage management, in the aftermath of a bitter strike and lockout in 1901. Many other factories soon set up similar personnel departments. The role of such labor departments in factories was a continuation of their previous commitment to monitor wages, safety, working hours, and related issues, but this change meant there were formal personnel departments that ensured statutory compliance[11].

2. Personnel Management (Early 20th Century)

By the early 1900s, increased competition and pressing demands to fulfill orders made factory owners take serious note of productivity, and issues such as employee absenteeism and high turnover came into focus. The dominant[12] philosophy during this time was that employees would accept rigid standards and work faster if provided training and more wages. This approach led to Frederick W. Taylor's scientific management theory that involved time studies in an attempt to establish the most productive way to undertake a process.

The personnel department during this time was an instrument in the hands of the employer to ensure maximum productivity. Side-by-side with providing training and wages, it broke strikes by blacklisting[13] union members and forcing workers to sign "yellow-dog" contracts or an agreement not to join unions.

Personnel management gained a more professional role in the aftermath of World War I and the Great Depression of the early 1930s. The demands of wartime production had led to enactment of several provisions[14] to ensure that issues related to wages or working conditions did not hinder[15] production. Among the social security measures initiated in the aftermath of the Great Depression were *the Norris-LaGuardia Act* that made "yellow-dog" contracts unenforceable and *the National Labor Relations Act* (NLRA) or *Wagner Act* (1935) that gave employees the right to form unions and bargain[16] collectively, and listed unfair labor practices.

---

[8] redress [ri'dres] v. 纠正；补偿；革除；惩罚

[9] grievance ['gri:vəns] n. 委屈，不平；冤情

[10] dismissal [dis'misl] n. 免职，解雇；摒弃

[11] compliance [kəm'plaiəns] n. 顺从，服从；遵守

[12] dominant ['dɔminənt] adj. 主要的；占优势的

[13] blacklist ['blæklist] v. 把……列入黑名单

[14] provision [prə'viʒən] n. 供应；规定

[15] hinder ['hində] v. 阻碍；打扰

[16] bargain ['bɑ:gin] v. 讨价还价，议价

Elton Mayo, the father of human relations, had conducted his famous Hawthorne Studies (1924—1932) and concluded that human factors or non-monetary rewards were more important than physical factors or monetary rewards in motivating employees. Trade unions now began to challenge the fairness of Taylor's scientific management theories, forcing employers to take a more behavior-oriented[17] approach. Personnel programs now expanded to include new benefits such as sick benefits, vaccinations[18], holidays, housing allowances, and similar measures, and to implement the new behavioral-oriented theories.

World War II increased the importance of keeping factories running, and with most workers away in war, the workforce now began to include the hitherto-absent women and native Americans. This laid the foundation for a multicultural[19] workforce, and along with it, new challenges for the human resource department.

The Labor-Management Relations Act (1947) or *the Taft-Hartley Act* banned the use of "closed shops" or hiring only workers from a union, and gave government the role of mediating[20] union and management disagreements.

3. Traditional Human Resource Management (Late 20th Century)

The post-World War II and post-Korean War era marked a distinct change in human resource management history. This era witnessed well educated baby boomers influenced by ideas such as human rights and self-actualization, taking the various behavioral oriented management philosophies to heart[21] and adopting management philosophies that encouraged incorporation[22] of worker ideas and initiatives[23].

The changes manifested[24] as a spate of labor legislations such as *the Equal Pay Act* (1963), *the Civl Rights Act* (1964), *Occupational Safety and Health Act* (1970), and *the Employee Retirement Income Security Act* (1974). The need to comply with such legislation increased the importance of the human resource function.

The Michigan Model or "Hard HRM" proposed by Fombrun, Tichy, and Devanna in 1984 encapsulated[25] the spirit of the age and became the basis for a traditional human resource approach. This model held employees as a valuable resource, to be obtained cost effectively, used sparingly, and developed and exploited to the maximum to further corporate interests.

---

[17] **behavior-oriented** [bɪˈheɪvjə(r)-ˈɔːrientɪd] *adj.* 以行为为导向的

[18] **vaccination** [ˌvæksɪˈneɪʃən] *n.* 接种疫苗；种痘

[19] **multicultural** [ˌmʌltɪˈkʌltʃər(ə)l] *adj.* （融合或具有）多种文化的

[20] **mediate** [ˈmiːdieɪt] *v.* 调停；斡旋

[21] **take… to heart**: 认真对待

[22] **incorporation** [ɪnˌkɔːpəˈreɪʃən] *n.* 包含；合并

[23] **initiative** [ɪˈnɪʃɪətɪv] *n.* 首创精神；主动权

[24] **manifest** [ˈmænɪfest] *v.* 显示；证实；表露

[25] **encapsulate** [ɪnˈkæpsjuleɪt] *v.* 压缩；概括

4. Strategic Human Resource Management (21st Century)

The new business environment in the post-Cold War age, combined with the widespread use of computers and Internet for commercial applications, radically altered ways of doing business, and workforce management was not immune to[26] the change. The increase of service-oriented firms, the infusion[27] of more and more women into the workforce, and other changes all made obsolete[28] the traditional paradigms[29] of people management.

In sharp contrast to the attitude of the early 1900s when workers were cogs[30] in the industrial machine, the highly skilled knowledgeable workers of today control the machines, and with technology freely available, the skill of such workers becomes the major source of competitive advantage for firms. The human resource department tries to retain such knowledgeable workers by facilitating a conducive[31] work environment, enriching the work, communicating objectives clearly, encouraging innovation, and many other behavioral interventions[32].

The "Harvard Model" of Beer et al. (1984), or Soft HRM, advocates[33] leading people through communication and motivation rather than managing them; it underlines[34] the strategic human resource management approach. This approach considers employees as assets, far more valuable than resources.

[26] be immune to: 不受……影响的；对……有免疫力的
[27] infusion [in'fju:ʒən] n. 灌输；激励
[28] obsolete ['ɔbsəli:t] adj. 已废弃的；过时的
[29] paradigm ['pærədaim] n. 范例，示范
[30] cog [kɔg] n. 轮齿；从属地位的人或物
[31] conducive [kən'dju:siv] adj. 有助的；有益的
[32] intervention [ˌintə(:)'venʃən] n. 介入；干预；调停
[33] advocate ['ædvəkit] v. 提倡；主张
[34] underline [ˌʌndə'lain] v. 在……下面画线；强调

参考译文（Text A）

人力资源管理

毋庸置疑，任何企业的成功都取决于它如何管理资源。企业资源驱动着企业去实现目标，就如同汽车要用发动机驱动才能到达目的地一样。企业的大多数资源都是非人的，如土地、资本和设备。尽管管理这些资源非常重要，但是企业必须恰当地管理其人力资源（如员工）才能取得成功。正如汽车不可能有效地驱动，除非有能力的人来驾驶；企业也不可能成功地运转，除非有能力的人来管理。人决定了企业的目标，也是通过人的有效运作，企业才能够实现其目标。

人力资源管理关注对人员的管理，包括对雇佣周期中不同阶段的人员进行的有效管理阶段，即挑选前阶段、挑选阶段，和挑选后阶段。

人力资源管理的挑选前阶段由人力资源规划和工作分析构成，它们为其他的人力资源管理阶段奠定了基础。企业要决定近期何种类型的工作职位有空缺，并决定胜任该工作需要何种资质。换言之，企业在实施其余的人力资源管理前，必须首先分析和规划如何对待

其员工。

人力资源规划帮助管理者预见并满足不断变化的、与员工获取、配置和使用相关的需求。首先，企业要制订一个整体计划（战略计划），然后，通过人力资源供求预测来估计顺利完成该计划所需要的员工数量和类型。这些信息能使企业合理规划其招聘、挑选和培训战略。例如，假设人力资源规划预计企业在下一年度需要增加15个工程师，那么企业通常会招聘工程专业的大学毕业生来填补职位空缺。由于这些专业的学生的市场需求较高，在其他公司"迅速抢走"最好的候选人之前，企业应决定在学年年初就启动校园招聘。

工作分析是收集、分析、记录特定工作信息的一个系统化流程。分析结果能详细地说明每位员工的工作内容、工作条件和成功完成该工作所必需的资格。工作分析信息被用于计划和协调几乎所有的人力资源管理实践，如确定任职资格、选择最恰当的挑选方法、开发培训项目、决定工资标准。例如，一个企业的工作分析显示，一项工作的性质最近已发生变化，对人员的要求更加严格，所以该企业可以决定用能力倾向测试来筛选应征者。

人力资源管理挑选阶段是企业用于员工安置的政策和程序，包括招募申请人、评价其资格，以及最终挑选出最胜任的申请人。企业通过招聘来搜寻和吸引那些申请特定职位的应征者，招聘既可在公司内部也可在公司外部进行。招聘的目的是快速、低成本、合法地识别出合适的应征者。挑选阶段包括对工作候选人的评价和选择。为了能够有效实施此阶段，挑选过程必须技术精确且符合法律要求。

在挑选后阶段，企业将通过人力资源管理实践来有效地管理那些顺利进入企业的员工。这些管理实践的设计目的是：通过向员工提供完成工作所必需的知识和技能，以及通过激发、指导、促进员工努力实现企业目标，使企业员工的绩效和满意度得到最大化。

培训和开发是有计划的学习体验，它教会员工如何有效地开展当前和未来的工作。培训关注当前的工作，而开发则是让员工为未来的工作做好准备。企业设计培训与开发实践的目的是通过提高员工的知识和技能水平，来提高企业绩效。培训与开发是一个持续不断的过程，技术和环境的变化，或组织目标和战略的变化常常会要求员工学习新的工作技术和方法。

企业通过绩效考核来测试员工是否能够胜任其工作，并将评价结果告诉员工。绩效考核系统的一个重要目的就是激励员工保持正确的行为并纠正不恰当的行为。管理层也可以以绩效考核为工具，做一些相关的人力资源管理决策，如晋升、降级、解雇和加薪。

企业管理者根据绩效考核结果给员工发放工资，并通过增加薪水、发放奖金等方式来奖励高绩效的企业员工。管理者以此激励企业中最具价值的人力资源，使他们继续为企业做出更大的贡献。而且，通过将薪酬与绩效挂钩，高绩效的员工继续留在本企业的可能性更大，管理者也更可能为空缺职位填补上高素质的人才。福利政策，如健康保险或员工折扣，都是员工作为企业成员所得到的重要回报。

最后，同样重要的是劳动关系管理，它包括企业管理者与代表员工利益的工会为发展和保持良好工作关系所采取的一系列措施。

管理者必须确保上述所有实践相互结合并能辅助完善公司的结构与控制系统。例如，如果管理者决定分散权力，对员工授权，那么他们必须在员工培训与开发上进行投资，使较低级别的员工掌握拥有决策权所必需的知识和专业技术，而这些决策在更加集权的企业结构下通常是由高层管理者负责的。

Unit 2

Text A

Job Analysis

Job analysis is a family of procedures to identify the content of a job in terms of activities involved and attributes or job requirements needed to perform the activities. Job analysis provides information to organizations, which helps to determine which employees are best fit for specific jobs. Through job analysis, the analyst needs to understand what the important tasks of the job are, how they are carried out, and the necessary human qualities needed to complete the job successfully.

Job analysis is crucial for helping individuals develop their careers, and for helping organizations develop their employees in order to maximize talent. The outcomes of job analysis are key influences in designing learning, developing performance interventions, and improving processes. The application of job analysis techniques makes an implicit assumption that information about a job as it presently exists may be used to develop programs to recruit, select, train, and appraise people for the job as it will exist in the future.

1. Purpose of Job Analysis

Job analysis involves collecting and recording job-related data such as knowledge and skills required to perform a job, duties and responsibilities involved, education qualifications and experience required and physical and emotional characteristics required to perform a job in a desired manner.

The main purpose of conducting a job analysis process is to use this particular information to create a right fit between jobs and employees, to assess the performance of an employee, to determine the worth of a particular task and to analyze training and development needs of an employee delivering that specific job.

Virtually, job analysis plays an important role in recruitment and selection, job evaluation, job designing, deciding compensation and benefits packages, performance appraisal, analyzing training and development needs, assessing the worth of a job and increasing personnel as well as organizational productivity.

Recruitment and selection. Job analysis helps in determining what kind of person is required to perform a particular job. It points out the educational qualifications, level of experience and technical, physical, emotional and personal skills required to carry out a job in a desired fashion. The objective is to fit a right person at a right place.

Performance analysis. Job analysis is done to check if goals and objectives of a particular job are met or not. It helps in deciding the performance standards, evaluation criteria and individual's output. On this basis, the overall performance of an employee is measured and he or she is appraised accordingly.

Training and development. Job analysis can be used to assess the training and development needs of employees. The difference between the expected and actual output determines the level of training that needs to be imparted to employees. It also helps in deciding the training content, tools and equipment to be used to conduct training and methods of training.

Compensation management. Of course, job analysis plays a vital role in deciding the pay packages, extra perks and benefits, and fixed and variable incentives of employees. After all, the pay package depends on the position, job title, duties and responsibilities involved in a job. The process guides HR managers in deciding the worth of an employee for a particular job opening.

Job designing and redesigning. The main purpose of job analysis is to streamline the human efforts and get the best possible output. It helps in designing, redesigning, enriching, evaluating and cutting back and adding the extra responsibilities in a particular job as well. This is done to enhance the employee's satisfaction while increasing the human output.

Therefore, job analysis is one of the most important functions of an HR manager or department. This helps in fitting the right kind of talent at the right place and at the right time.

2. Approaches to Job Analysis

As stated above, the purpose of job analysis is to combine the task demands of a job with our knowledge of human attributes and produce a theory of behavior for the job in question. There are two ways to approach building that theory, meaning that there are two different approaches to job analysis.

Task-oriented. Task-oriented procedure focuses on the actual activities involved in performing work. This procedure takes into consideration work duties, responsibilities, and functions. The job analyst then develops task statements which clearly state the tasks that are performed with great detail. After creating task statements, job analysts rate the tasks on scales indicating importance, difficulty, frequency, and consequences of error. Based on these ratings, a greater sense of understanding of a job can be attained. Task analyses, such as cognitively oriented task analysis (COTA), are techniques used to describe job expertise. For example, the job analysts may tour the job site and observe workers performing their jobs. During the tour the analyst may collect materials that directly or indirectly indicate required skills (duty statements, instructions, safety manuals, quality charts, etc.). For the job of a snow-cat operator at a ski slope, a work or task-oriented job analysis might include this statement: Operates Bombardier Snow-cat, usually at night, to smooth out snow rutted by skiers and snowboard riders and new snow that has fallen.

Worker-oriented. Worker-oriented procedures aim to examine the human attributes needed to perform the job successfully. These human attributes have been commonly classified into four categories: knowledge, skills, abilities, and other characteristics (KSAO). Knowledge is the information people need in order to perform the job. Skills are the proficiencies needed to perform each task. Abilities are the attributes that are relatively stable over time. Other characteristics are all other attributes, usually personality factors. The KSAO required for a job are inferred from the most frequently-occurring, important tasks. In a worker-oriented job analysis, the skills are inferred from tasks and the skills are rated directly in terms of importance and frequency. For the job of a snow-cat operator at a ski slope, a worker-oriented job analysis might include this statement: Evaluates terrain, snow depth, and snow condition and chooses the correct setting for the depth of the snow cat, as well as the number of passes necessary on a given ski slope.

Job analysis methods have evolved using both task-oriented and worker-oriented approaches. Since the final result of both approaches is a statement of KSAO, neither can be considered the "correct" way to conduct job analysis. Because worker-oriented job analyses tend to provide more generalized human behavior and behavior patterns and are less tied to the technological parts of a job, they produce data more useful for developing training programs and giving feedback to employees in the form of performance appraisal information. Also, the volatility that exists in the typical workplace of today can make specific task statements less valuable in isolation. For these reasons, employers are significantly more likely to use worker-oriented approaches to job analysis today than they were in the past.

3. Six Steps of Doing a Job Analysis

Job analysis is performed as a basis for later improvements, including definition of a job domain, description of a job, development of performance appraisals, personnel selection, selection systems, promotion criteria, training needs assessment, legal defense of selection processes, and compensation plans. Doing a job analysis involves the six steps as follows:

Step 1: Decide how to use the information. How the information will be put into use will determine what data to collect and how to collect it. Some data collection techniques, such as interviewing the employee, asking what the job entails are good for writing job descriptions and selecting employees for the job. Other techniques, like the position analysis questionnaire, do not provide qualitative information for job descriptions but numerical ratings for each job. Thus, they can be used to compare jobs for compensation purposes.

Step 2: Review appropriate background information like organization charts, process charts, and job descriptions. Organization charts show the organization-wide work division, how the job in question relates to other jobs, and where the job fits in the overall organization. The chart should show the title of each position and, through connecting lines, show reports to whom and with whom the job incumbent communicates. A process chart provides a more detailed picture of the work flow. In its simplest and most organic form, a process chart shows the flow of inputs to and outputs from the job being analyzed. Finally, the existing job description (if there is one) usually provides a starting point for building the revised job description.

Step 3: Select representative positions. This is because there may be too many similar jobs to analyze. For example, it is usually unnecessary to analyze jobs of 200 assembly workers when a sample of 10 jobs will be sufficient.

Step 4: Actually analyze the job by collecting data on job activities, necessary employee behaviors and actions, working conditions, and human traits and abilities required to perform the job. For this step, one or more than one methods of job analysis may be needed.

Step 5: Verify the job analysis information with the worker performing the job and with his or her immediate supervisor. This will help confirm that the information is factually correct and complete. This review can also help gain the employee's acceptance of the job analysis data and conclusions by giving that person a chance to review and modify descriptions of the job activities.

Step 6: Develop a job description and job specification. These are two tangible products of the job analysis process. The job description is a written statement that describes the activities and responsibilities of the job as well as its important features such as working conditions and safety hazards. The job specification summarizes the personal qualities, traits, skills, and background required for completing a certain job. These two may be completely separate or in the same document.

Over the years, experts have presented several different systems and methods to accomplish job analysis. Many forms of systems are no longer in use, but those systems that still exist have become increasingly detailed over the decades with a greater concentration on tasks and less concentration on human attributes. That trend, however, has reversed in recent years for the better. Newer methods and systems examine more about the behavioral aspects of work.

New Words

attribute [ˈætribjuːt] n. 属性；标志；象征
analyst [ˈænəlist] n. 分析家
crucial [ˈkruːʃəl] adj. 决定性的，关键的
career [kəˈriə] n. 职业，事业
outcome [ˈautkʌm] n. 结果
influence [ˈinfluəns] n. 影响，势力；有影响的人（或事物） v. 影响；支配；对……起作用

application [ˌæpliˈkeiʃən] n. 应用；申请
implicit [imˈplisit] adj. 含蓄的，暗示的；固有的
assumption [əˈsʌmpʃən] n. 假定；设想
presently [ˈprezəntli] adj. 目前，不久，马上
appraise [əˈpreiz] v. 评价，估价；鉴定
characteristic [ˌkæriktəˈristik] n. 特性，特征，特点

Unit 2

personnel [ˌpəːsəˈnel] n. 职员；人事部门
criteria [kraiˈtiəriə] n. 标准，准则；尺度
accordingly [əˈkɔːdiŋli] adv. 因此；相应地
actual [ˈæktjuəl] adj. 实际的，事实上的
perk [pəːk] n. 额外津贴，特权；利益
variable [ˈveəriəbl] adj. 可变的，易变的 n. 变量；易变的东西
incentive [inˈsentiv] n. 刺激，鼓励；动机 adj. 刺激的，鼓励的
involve [inˈvɔlv] v. 包含；牵涉
streamline [ˈstriːmlain] v. 使……成流线型；使……简化
rate [reit] v. 认为；估价；定等级 n. 比率；速度；价格；等级
scale [skeil] n. 刻度；等级，规模
frequency [ˈfriːkwənsi] n. 频繁，频率
consequence [ˈkɔnsikwəns] n. 结果，后果；重要性
rating [ˈreitiŋ] n. 等级；评定
manual [ˈmænjuəl] adj. 手工的；体力的 n. 指南，手册
rut [rʌt] v. 形成车辙；耕犁
proficiency [prəˈfiʃənsi] n. 熟练，精通
stable [ˈsteibl] adj. 稳定的，安定的；可靠的
terrain [təˈrein] n. 地带，地形
given [ˈgivn] adj. 特定的；假设的
generalize [ˈdʒenərəlaiz] v. 概括，归纳；使一般化
feedback [ˈfiːdbæk] n. 反馈，反馈意见
volatility [ˌvɔləˈtiləti] n. 挥发性；轻快；（性格）反复无常
isolation [ˌaisəˈleiʃən] n. 隔离，孤立

domain [dəuˈmein] n. 领地；领域，范围
entail [inˈteil] v. 使必需；限定继承
questionnaire [ˌkwestʃ(ə)ˈneə] n. 调查表，问卷
qualitative [ˈkwɔlitətiv] adj. 性质上的，质的；定性的
numerical [njuːˈmerikəl] adj. 数字的；用数字表示的
chart [tʃɑːt] n. 图表；规划图 v. 制成图表；绘制地图
incumbent [inˈkʌmbənt] adj. 负有义务的；凭依的 n. 在职者
revise [riˈvaiz] v. 校订，修正
representative [ˌrepriˈzentətiv] n. 代表；众议员；典型 adj. 代表的，典型的
sufficient [səˈfiʃənt] adj. 足够的，充分的
verify [ˈverifai] v. 核实，证明
confirm [kənˈfəːm] v. 证实，确定；批准
modify [ˈmɔdifai] v. 修改，更改；修饰
specification [ˌspesifiˈkeiʃən] n. 规格；详述
tangible [ˈtændʒəbl] adj. 可触摸的，有形的
feature [ˈfiːtʃə] n. 特征，特色；特写 v. 以……为特色
accomplish [əˈkɔmpliʃ] v. 完成，实现
increasingly [inˈkriːsiŋli] adv. 逐渐地；越来越多地
concentration [ˌkɔnsenˈtreiʃən] n. 集中，专心；浓度
reverse [riˈvəːs] v. 逆转；倒退 adj. 相反的，颠倒的
behavioral [biˈheivjərəl] adj. 行为的

a family of 一系列的	be classified into 分（类）为……
in terms of 根据，依据；就……而言	infer from 从……中推导出
point out 指明，指出，提示	be tied to 束缚于，捆绑于；以……为条件
impart to 把……告诉/透露给；把……带/传递给	in the form of 以……的形式
play a vital role (in) 起着至关重要的作用	personnel selection 人员挑选
pay packages 全部报酬；综合工资	be put into use 投入使用
cut back 减少；剪（裁，缩）短	relate to 涉及；同……有……关系；将……与……联系起来
combine... with 与……结合，使……化合	work flow 业务流程，加工流程
take into consideration 考虑到，顾及；着想	a starting point 出发点，起点
based on 以……为依据	immediate supervisor 直接领导，顶头上司
smooth out 弄平；缓和，调解	safety hazard 安全隐患，安全危害

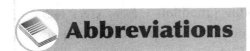

COTA (cognitively oriented task analysis) 认知导向任务分析
KSAO (knowledge, skills, abilities, and other characteristics) 知识、技能、能力和其他特征
（注：KSAO 是人力资源管理中对员工岗位资质的描述模型）

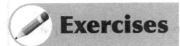

EX. 1 Answer the following questions according to the text.

1. What is job analysis?
2. What is the main purpose of conducting a job analysis process?
3. What role does job analysis play in terms of compensation management? And why?
4. What are the two main approaches to job analysis?
5. What does task-oriented procedure focus on and take into consideration?

Unit 2

6. What are the four categories of human attributes?
7. What do organization charts show according to Text A?
8. With whom should a job analyst verify the job analysis information?
9. What is a job description?
10. What does a job specification summarize?

EX. 2 Translate the following terms or phrases from English into Chinese and vice versa.

1. immediate supervisor
2. pay packages
3. work flow
4. specification
5. proficiency
6. *n.* 职员；人事部门
7. *n.* 额外津贴；特权；利益
8. *n.* 反馈，反馈意见
9. *n.* 职业，事业
10. *v.* 证实，确定；批准

EX. 3 Translate the following text into Chinese.

Job analysis is performed as a basis for later improvements, including definition of a job domain, description of a job, development of performance appraisals, personnel selection, selection systems, promotion criteria, training needs assessment, legal defense of selection processes, and compensation plans. In the fields of human resources (HR) and industrial psychology, job analysis is often used to gather information for use in personnel selection, training, classification, and/or compensation. Industrial psychologists use job analysis to determine the physical requirements of a job, and to determine whether an individual who has suffered some diminished capacity is capable of performing the job with, or without, some accommodation. Professionals developing certification exams use job analysis to determine the elements of the domain which must be sampled in order to create a content valid exam. When a job analysis is conducted for the purpose of valuing the job (i.e. determining the appropriate compensation for incumbents), this is called "job evaluation".

EX. 4 Fill in the blanks with the words given below.

| obtain | conduct | interviews | characteristics | gather |
| viewed | procedure | consuming | observations | analyze |

Methods of Job Analysis

Organizations consist of jobs that have to be staffed. Job analysis is the ___1___ through which you determine the duties of these position and the ___2___ of the people to hire for them.

There are several ways to ___3___ a job analysis, including interviews with incumbents and supervisors. Work methods of analysis can be laborious and time ___4___, and there is always a tendency on the part of management to over ___5___ some jobs and under analyze some others. These traditional job analysis methods include one-on-one interviewing, behavioral event interviews, phone ___6___, surveys, work assessments, developing a curriculum, job analysis worksheets, ___7___ and procedural review. All of these methods can be used to ___8___ information for job analysis. The DACUM process developed in the late 1960s has been ___9___ as the fastest method used, but it can still take two or three days to ___10___ a validated task list.

Text B

Job Design

Job design, which is also referred to as work design or task design, is a core function of human resource management and it is related to the specification of contents, methods and relationship of jobs in order to satisfy technological and organizational requirements as well as the social and personal requirements of the job holder. Its principles are geared towards how the nature of a person's job affects their attitudes and behavior at work, particularly relating to characteristics such as skill variety and autonomy.

The way in which a job is designed has great impact on the attitudes, beliefs and feelings of the employee. This includes organizational commitment, work motivation, performance, job satisfaction, mental health, reduced turnover and sickness absence. A properly designed job guarantees that the worker is able to accomplish what is required in a safe and healthy fashion, and thereby reduces physical and psychological strain. Further, it helps with the organization of work, e.g. in identifying issues such as: work overload, repetitiveness and limited control over work, and thereby improves on occupational safety and health within organizations. A well-designed job could result in more engaged, healthy and productive employees, and these outcomes would benefit both employees and organizations.

1. Job Design Theory

The basis for job design theory is organization theory, which can be classified broadly into three strains of thought: the classical, the behavioral and the situational.

Classical theory was expounded in early writings of Max Weber and Henri Fayol. For the classicist, any organization achieves efficiency through its division of labor. Managers identify the overall purpose of the organization. They then divide this overall purpose into jobs, each rationally related to the whole. Jobs are, in turn, grouped to create work groups, divisions and departments. Finally, each group is assigned to a supervisor, who is responsible for overseeing the work of subordinates and reporting the results to his or her own superior.

Behavioral theory is quite different. Unlike the classicist, the behaviorist is much less interested in allocating specific tasks to specific jobs, making sure that the authority matches the position, and then trying to attain higher efficiency through specialization of labor. Behaviorists prefer simple organizational structure, decentralized decision-making and informal departmentalization. In an organic structure, subordinates feel free to discuss their performance problems with superiors and have a positive view of the organization. They participate in decision-making and communicate with those whose views are needed to solve immediate problems. These characteristics are in stark contrast to conditions in a traditional organization, where subordinates are guarded and negative about the organization, do not feel sufficient trust to communicate openly with those of higher status and are not permitted to participate in decision-making.

Situational theory differs from both classical and behavioral theories. Advocates stress the influence of the external environment on the allocation of responsibilities and tasks within the organization, work groups and jobs. Allocating responsibilities and tasks means creating a structure. Appropriate structures differ according to technology, markets, production, research and information.

2. Job Characteristic Theory

The job characteristic theory proposed by Richard Hackman and Greg Oldham (1976) stated that work should be designed to have five core job characteristics, which engender three critical psychological states in individuals—experiencing meaning, feeling responsible for outcomes and understanding the results of their efforts. In turn, these psychological states were proposed to enhance employees' intrinsic motivation, job satisfaction, quality of work and performance, while reducing turnover. These five core job characteristics can be listed as follows:

Skill variety. This refers to the range of skills and activities necessary to complete the job. The more a person is required to use a wide variety of skills, the more satisfying the job is likely to be.

Task identity. This dimension measures the degree to which the job requires completion of a whole and identifiable piece of work. Employees who are involved in an activity from start to finish are usually more satisfied.

Task significance. This looks at the impact and influence of a job. Jobs are more satisfying if people believe that they make a difference and are adding real value to colleagues, the organization, or the larger community.

Autonomy. This describes the amount of individual choice and discretion involved in a job.

More autonomy leads to more satisfaction. For instance, a job is likely to be more satisfying if people are involved in making decisions, instead of simply being told what to do.

Feedback. This dimension measures the amount of information an employee receives about his or her performance, and the extent to which he or she can see the impact of the work. The more people are told about their performance, the more interested they will be in doing a good job. So, sharing production figures, customer satisfaction scores, etc. can increase the feedback levels.

The five core job dimensions listed above result in three different psychological states:

Experienced meaningfulness of the work. The extent to which people believe that their job is meaningful and that their work is valued and appreciated.

Experienced responsibility for the outcomes of work. The extent to which people feel accountable for the results of their work and for the outcomes they have produced.

Knowledge of the actual results of the work activity. The extent to which people know how well they are doing.

3. Job Design Methods

Job design essentially involves integrating job responsibilities or content and certain qualifications that are required to perform the same. It outlines the job responsibilities very clearly and also helps in attracting the right candidates to the right job. Further, it also makes the job look interesting and specialized. There are various methods in which job design can be carried out. These methods help to analyze the job, to design the contents of the job and to decide how the job must be carried out. These methods can be listed as follows:

Job rotation. Job rotation involves shifting a person from one job to another, so that he is able to understand and learn what each job involves. The company tracks his performance on every job and decides whether he can perform the job in an ideal manner. Based on this he is finally given a particular posting. Job rotation is done to decide the final posting for the employee.

For example, Mr. A is assigned to the marketing department where he learns all the jobs to be performed for marketing at his level in the organization. After this he is shifted to the sales department and to the finance department and so on. He is finally placed in the department in which he shows the best performance. Job rotation gives an idea about the jobs to be performed at every level. Once a person is able to understand this, he is in a better understanding of the working of organization.

Job rotation helps to avoid monopoly of job and enables the employee to learn new things and therefore to enjoy his job. Furthermore, due to job rotation, the person is able to learn different jobs in the organization, which broadens his knowledge. It is also worth noticing that job rotation contributes a lot to avoiding fraudulent practice. Take an organization like bank as an example. In a bank, jobs rotation is undertaken to prevent employees from doing any kind of fraud, i.e. if a person is handling a particular job for a very long time, he will be able to find loopholes in the system and use them for his benefit and indulge (participate) in fraudulent practices. However, job rotation can avoid this.

Job enlargement. Job enlargement is another method of job design. When any organization wishes to adopt proper job design, it can opt for job enlargement. Job enlargement involves combining various activities at the same level in the organization and adding them to the existing job. It increases the scope of the job. It is also called the horizontal expansion of job activities.

Job enlargement can be explained with the help of the following example. If Mr. A is working as an executive within a company and is currently performing three activities on his job, however, through job enlargement, four more activities are added to the existing job, so now Mr. A performs seven activities on the job.

It must be noted that the new activities which have been added should belong to the same hierarchy level in the organization. By job enlargement we provide a greater variety of activities to the individual so that we are in a position to increase the interest of the job and make maximum use of an employee's skill.

Job enlargement helps improve and increase the skills of the employee within organization as well as the individual benefits. Also, by job enlargement, the person learns many new activities, which helps him or her bargain for more salary while applying for jobs to other companies. More importantly, since a single employee handles multiple activities, the company can try and reduce the number of employees, which will greatly reduce the salary bill for the company.

Job enrichment. Job enrichment is a term given by Fedric Herzberg. According to him a few motivators are added to a job to make it more rewarding, challenging and interesting. In other words we can say that job enrichment is a method of adding some motivating factors to an existing job to make it more interesting. The motivating factors can be:
- giving more freedom;
- encouraging participation;
- giving employees the freedom to select the method of working;
- allowing employees to select the place at which they would like to work;
- allowing workers to select the tools that they require on the job;
- allowing workers to decide the layout of plant or office.

Job enrichment gives a lot of freedom to the employee but at the same time increases the responsibility. Some workers are power and responsibility hungry and job enrichment satisfies the needs of the employees. In general, job enrichment increases the employees' autonomy over the planning and execution of their own work. It has the same motivational advantages of job enlargement, however, it has the added benefit of granting workers autonomy.

Job design is a continuous and ever evolving process that is aimed at helping employees make adjustments with the changes in the workplace. By various methods, its ultimate goal is to reduce dissatisfaction, enhance motivation and employee engagement at the workplace.

New Words

gear [giə] v. 使适应
variety [və'raiəti] n. 种类；变化，多样化
belief [bi'li:f] n. 信任；信念；意见
motivation [,məuti'veiʃən] n. 动机；动力；诱因
strain [strein] v. 拉紧，拉伤；用力拉 n. 拉紧；紧张
repetitiveness [ri'petətivnis] n. 重复性
engaged [in'geidʒd] adj. 忙碌的；有人用的；已订婚的
expound [iks'paund] v. 解释，详细讲解
efficiency [i'fiʃənsi] n. 功效；效率，效能；能力
rationally ['ræʃənəli] adv. 讲道理地，理性地
assign [ə'sain] v. 分派，选派，分配
supervisor ['sju:pəvaizə] n. 监督者，管理者
subordinate [sə'bɔ:dinit] adj. 下级的；级别或职位较低的；次要的；附属的 n. 部属；部下，下级
attain [ə'tein] v. 达到；经过努力获得
departmentalization [di:pa:t,mentəlai-'zeiʃən] n. 分部门组织经营法，部门化
positive ['pɔzətiv] adj. 积极的；确实的，肯定的
immediate [i'mi:diət] adj. 立即的；直接的
negative ['negətiv] adj. 消极的；否认的
structure ['strʌktʃə] n. 结构；构造
engender [in'dʒendə] v. 产生；造成；引起
dimension [dai'menʃən] n. 尺寸；面积，范围；度，维

impact ['impækt] n. 影响；碰撞，冲击，撞击
extent [iks'tent] n. 程度；长度；广大地域
appreciate [ə'pri:ʃieit] v. 欣赏；感激；鉴别
essentially [i'senʃəli] adv. 本质上；根本上
integrate ['intigreit] v. 使一体化；使整合；使完整
outline ['autlain] n. 大纲，提纲
track [træk] v. 跟踪，追踪；监看，监测
monopoly [mə'nɔpəli] n. 垄断；专卖；垄断者；专利品
fraudulent ['frɔ:djulənt] adj. 欺骗的，不诚实的
undertake [,ʌndə'teik] v. 承诺，保证；承担
horizontal [,hɔri'zɔntl] adj. 水平的；卧式的；地平线的
executive [ig'zekjutiv] n. 总经理；行政部门 adj. 执行的；管理的；政府部门的
hierarchy ['haiərɑ:ki] n. 等级制度；统治集团；层级
multiple ['mʌltipl] adj. 多重的，多个的；多功能的
rewarding [ri'wɔ:diŋ] adj. 值得的；有报酬的
challenging ['tʃælindʒiŋ] adj. 挑战性的；引起兴趣的；令人深思的
layout ['leiaut] n. 布局，安排；设计
execution [,eksi'kju:ʃən] n. 依法处决；实行，执行

Unit 2

Phrases

job design 工作设计
be referred to as 被称为……
be related to 与……有关，和……有联系
have great impact on 对……有很大的影响
mental health 心理健康
sickness absence 生病缺勤
work overload 超负荷工作；工作负荷
division of labor 劳动分工
be responsible for 为……负责；形成……的原因
participate in 参加，参与
in stark contrast to 与……形成鲜明的对比
psychological state 心理状态；心态
a wide variety of 种种，多种多样
from start to finish 自始至终
feel accountable for 感觉要对……负责的
job rotation 岗位轮换

in an ideal manner 以理想的方式
marketing department 市场部
sales department 销售部
finance department 财务部
due to 由于，因为
broaden one's knowledge 拓宽某人的知识面
it is worth noticing that 值得注意的是
indulge in 沉溺于……
opt for 选择
at the same level 本级；在同一级
belong to 属于；是（某团体）的成员
be in a position to 能够；有做……的机会
make maximum use of 最大限度地利用
apply for 申请
aim at 针对，以……为目标；瞄准
make adjustments 做出调整

Exercises

EX. 5 Answer the following questions according to the text.

1. How many strains of thought can organization theory be classified broadly into? And what are they?
2. How does an organization achieve efficiency according to classical theory?
3. What do advocates of situational theory stress?
4. According to the job characteristic theory, what are the three critical psychological states which five core job characteristics engender in individuals?
5. What are those five core job characteristics on the basis of the job characteristic theory?
6. What does feedback measure?
7. What does job rotation involve?
8. If a person is handling a particular job in a bank for a very long time, what will he probably do?

9. What does job enlargement involve?
10. Which job design method can satisfy those workers who are hungry for power, responsibility and autonomy over their own work?

Supplementary Reading

Text	Notes
Organizational Structure As we know, organizations need to be efficient, flexible, innovative and caring in order to achieve a sustainable[1] competitive advantage. However, to ensure an organization works efficiently, an organizational structure is a real necessity. An organizational structure defines how activities such as task allocation[2], coordination[3] and supervision are directed toward the achievement of organizational aims. It can also be considered as the viewing glass or perspective through which individuals see their organization and its environment. It allows the expressed allocation of responsibilities for different functions and processes to different entities[4] such as the branch, department, workgroup and individual and also affects organizational action in two big ways: • It provides the foundation on which standard operating procedures and routines[5] rest. • It determines which individuals get to participate in which decision-making processes, and thus to what extent their views shape the organization's actions. **1. History of Organizational Structures** Organizational structures developed from the ancient times of hunters and collectors in tribal[6] organizations through highly royal and clerical power structures to industrial structures and today's post-industrial structures. As pointed out by Lawrence B. Mohr, the early theorists of organizational structure, including Taylor, Fayol and Weber, saw the importance of structure for effectiveness and efficiency and assumed without the slightest question that whatever structure was needed, people could fashion accordingly. Organizational	[1] sustainable [sə'steinəbl] *adj.* 可持续的；可以忍受的；可支撑的 [2] allocation [ˌæluˈkeiʃən] *n.* 配给，分配；分配额 [3] coordination [kəuˌɔːdi'neiʃən] *n.* 协调；和谐 [4] entity ['entəti] *n.* 实体；实际存在物；本质 [5] routine [ruːˈtiːn] *n.* 常规；例行程序 [6] tribal ['traibəl] *adj.* 部落的，部族的；种族的

structure was considered a matter of choice. When in the 1930s, there was still not a denial of the idea of structure as an artifact[7], but rather an advocacy[8] of the creation of a different sort of structure, one in which the needs, knowledge, and opinions of employees might be given greater recognition[9]. However, a different view arose in the 1960s, suggesting that the organizational structure is "an externally caused phenomenon, an outcome rather than an artifact".

In the 21st century, organizational theorists such as Lim, Griffiths, and Sambrook (2010) are once again proposing that organizational structure development is very much dependent on the expression of the strategies and behavior of the management and the workers as constrained[10] by the power distribution between them, and influenced by their environment and the outcome.

2. Types of Organizational Structures

The types of organization structure depend on many factors, such as governing style, leadership style, type of organization, work flow, and hierarchy. Wikipedia classifies it into six categories.

Pre-bureaucratic[11] structure type organizations do not have the standard procedures and policies. This type of structure is used by small-scale organization with few employees who handle simple tasks. It has a central command with one decision maker at the top position. The communication is done on a one-on-one basis, and most of the time is informal.

Organizations which use the bureaucratic structure are usually larger and have standard procedures and processes. This type of structure is suitable for very large organizations which involve complex operations and require smooth administration. An example of this type of organization is the food and beverage industry where they have to follow tough rules and regulations.

Post-bureaucratic[12] organizations are fully developed and have various standards and procedures, with a central command consisting of several board members where decision making is done by a democratic[13] procedure. In a post-bureaucratic structure, employees' suggestions are taken into account[14] while making a decision. This encourages employees' participation, trust, personal treatment and responsibility.

---

[7] artifact ['ɑːtifækt] *n.* 人工制品，手工艺品，加工品

[8] advocacy ['ædvəkəsi] *n.* 辩护；支持

[9] recognition [ˌrekəgˈnɪʃən] *n.* 认识，识别；承认，认可

[10] constrain [kənˈstreɪn] *v.* 强迫；限制；强制

[11] pre-bureaucratic [priːˌbjuərəʊˈkrætɪk] *adj.* 前官僚的，前官僚主义的

[12] post-bureaucratic [pəʊstˌbjuərəʊˈkrætɪk] *adj.* 后官僚的，后官僚主义的

[13] democratic [ˌdeməˈkrætɪk] *adj.* 民主的；民主主义的；民主政体的

[14] take into account: 顾及；重视，考虑

Functional[15] organization structure is the most commonly used type of organization structure. In a functional organization structure, the organization is grouped into various departments where people with similar skills are kept together in forms of groups, e.g. sales department, marketing department, finance department, etc. This helps organizations enhance the efficiency of each functional group.

In a divisional[16] structure, an organization is divided into various divisions where people with diverse skills are kept together in the form of groups by a similar product, service or geographic[17] location, and each division itself is capable of[18] doing the task on its own. Each division has its own resources required to function properly. The division can be based on product, service or the geographical area, e.g. Dell USA, Dell India, etc.

Matrix[19] organization structure is a hybrid[20] of the functional organization structure and the projectized organization structure. In a matrix organization structure, you can see two command structures: vertical[21] and horizontal. Here, an employee may be part of a functional group but he may also work on a project. This structure takes the benefits of both worlds.

3. Keys to an Organizational Structure

All sorts of different organizational structures have been proven effective in contributing to business success. Some firms choose highly centralized, rigidly maintained structures, while others—perhaps even in the same industrial sector—develop decentralized, loose arrangements. Both of these organizational types can survive and even thrive[22]. There is no one best way to design an organization or type of structure. Each depends upon the company involved, its needs and goals, and even the personalities of the individuals involved in the case of small businesses. The type of business in which an organization is involved is also a factor in designing an effective organizational structure. Organizations operate in different environments with different products, strategies, constraints and opportunities, each of which may influence the design of an ideal organizational structure.

---

[15] **functional** [ˈfʌŋkʃənl] *adj.* 功能的

[16] **divisional** [dɪˈvɪʒənəl] *adj.* 分割的，分开的

[17] **geographic** [ˌdʒiəˈɡræfɪk] *adj.* 地理学的，地理的

[18] **be capable of**: 能够

[19] **matrix** [ˈmeɪtrɪks] *n.* 矩阵；模型

[20] **hybrid** [ˈhaɪbrɪd] *n.* 混合物

[21] **vertical** [ˈvɜːtɪkəl] *adj.* 垂直的，竖立的

[22] **thrive** [θraɪv] *v.* 茁壮成长；兴盛

But despite the wide variety of organizational structures that can be found in the business world, the successful ones tend to share certain characteristics. Indeed, business experts cite a number of characteristics that separate effective organizational structures from ineffective designs. Recognition of these factors is especially important for entrepreneurs[23] and established small business owners, since these individuals play such a pivotal role in determining the final layout of their enterprises.

[23] entrepreneur [,ɔntrəprə'nəː] n. 企业家；主办人；承包人

As small business owners weigh their various options in this realm[24], they should make sure that the following factors are taken into consideration:

[24] realm [relm] n. 领域，范围

• relative strengths and weaknesses of various organizational forms;
• legal advantages and disadvantages of organizational structure options;
• advantages and drawbacks of departmentalization options;
• likely growth patterns of the company;
• reporting relationships that are currently in place, reporting and authority relationships that you hope will be implemented in the future;
• optimum ratios of supervisors/managers to subordinates;
• suitable level of autonomy/empowerment to be granted to employees at various levels of the organization (while still recognizing individual capacities for independent work);
• structures that will produce the greatest worker satisfaction;
• structures that will produce optimum operational efficiency.

Once all these factors have been objectively examined and blended into an effective organizational structure, the business owner will then be in a position to pursue his/her business goals with a far greater likelihood[25] of success.

[25] likelihood ['laiklihud] n. 可能，可能性

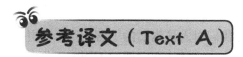

参考译文（Text A）

工 作 分 析

工作分析是用来确定工作内容，如工作所涉及的活动以及执行活动所需的员工品质或

工作要求的一系列程序。工作分析为企业提供信息,以帮助确定就具体工作而言,哪些员工最适合。通过工作分析,分析人员需要了解工作的重要任务是什么、如何执行,以及顺利完成工作所必需的人力资质。

工作分析对于个人发展事业和员工最大限度地施展才能是至关重要的。工作分析的结果对设计学习方式、开发绩效介入措施和改进工序的影响非常关键。运用工作分析技术,人们可隐含地假设目前的工作信息可用于开发项目,以便招聘、选拔、培训和评估将来从事这项工作的员工。

1. 工作分析的目的

工作分析包括收集和记录与工作有关的数据,如工作所需的知识和技能、义务和职责、学历和经验以及能按期完成工作所需要的身体和情感特征。

进行工作分析的主要目的是利用特定的信息在工作和员工之间创建适当的匹配度,评估员工的业绩,确定特定任务的价值,分析对从事具体工作的员工进行培训发展的必要性。

事实上,工作分析在招聘和选拔、工作评价、工作设计、薪酬福利设计、绩效考核、培训和发展需求分析、工作价值评估、人员增加以及组织生产力的提高等方面起着重要的作用。

招聘和甄选。工作分析有助于确定从事某项特定工作的人选。它详细地说明了以理想的方式完成某项工作所需要的学历、经验水平、技术要求、身体状况、情感和个人技能,将合适的员工安置在合适的岗位上。

绩效分析。工作分析是为了核实某项特定工作的目的和目标是否得以实现。它有助于决定绩效标准、评估标准和个人成果,并在此基础上衡量员工的整体绩效,进行相应的评价。

培训和发展。工作分析可用于评估员工的培训发展需求。预期产出和实际产出之差决定了员工需要接受的培训水平。它也有助于决定培训内容、培训所需的工具和设备,以及培训方法。

薪酬管理。当然,工作分析在决定薪酬、额外津贴和福利、固定和可变的员工激励等方面有着至关重要的作用。毕竟,工资的高低取决于职位、职称、职责和责任。这个过程对人力资源经理决定某个特定职位的员工的价值有指导作用。

工作设计和重新设计。工作分析的主要目的是精简人力并获得最好产出。它有助于对工作进行设计、重新设计和充实,对员工进行评估,并对特定的工作增加额外职责。这样做是为了在增加员工产能的同时,提高员工的满意度。

因此,工作分析是人力资源经理或人力资源部最重要的职能之一。这有助于在合适的时间,将合适的人才置于合适的岗位上。

2. 工作分析方法

如前所述,工作分析的目的是将工作的任务要求与我们对人员素质的了解相结合,并创建一种工作的行为理论。有两种方法可以建立这种理论,这意味着有两种不同的工作分析方法。

任务导向。任务导向程序侧重于从事某项工作的实际活动。该程序考虑工作责任、职责和职能。工作分析人员创建任务声明书，清楚地规定完成任务的细节要求。基于声明书，工作分析人员将工作任务评定为各个等级，并注明各等级任务的重要性、难度、频率以及犯错产生的后果。根据等级评定，员工能进一步加强对工作的理解。任务分析，如认知导向任务分析（COTA），是用来描述工作专业知识的方法。例如，工作分析人员可能会去工作现场观察员工的工作情况，其间，分析人员可以收集能直接或间接说明工作所需技能的相关材料（如责任声明、操作指南、安全手册、质量图表等）。就在滑雪场操作雪地车这项工作而言，一份以工作或任务为导向的工作分析可能包括这样的声明：庞巴迪雪地车操作通常在晚上进行，具体任务是将滑雪者和滑雪板骑手碾过的雪以及新降的雪铺平。

员工导向。员工导向程序的目标是考查成功地完成工作所需求的人力属性。人力属性通常分成四类，即知识、技能、能力和其他特点（KSAO）。知识是人们为完成一项工作所需要的信息；技能是完成每项工作任务的能力水平要求；能力是长期相对稳定的属性特征；其他特征指的是所有其他属性，通常指个性因素。基于最频繁、最重要的工作任务，工作分析人员推断出一项工作在知识、技能、能力和其他特征四方面的要求。在员工导向的工作分析中，技能是从工作任务中得出的，并与任务的重要性和频率有直接关系。就在滑雪场操作雪地车这项工作而言，一份以员工为导向的工作分析可能会有这样的声明：操作人员需要估计地形、雪的深度和雪情，选择适合雪地车的最好装置，并预估滑雪场所需的通道数量。

通过任务导向和员工导向这两种分析途径，具体的工作分析方法得到了发展。由于这两种途径的最终结果都是一份关于KSAO的声明，所以两者都不能被视作进行工作分析的"正确"方式。以员工为导向的工作分析往往能提供更普遍的人类行为模式，不大受制于工作中的技术成分，因此它们产生的数据更有利于开发培训计划，并以绩效考核的方式反馈给员工。此外，如今的职场反复无常，这使得具体的任务声明价值不大。基于这些原因，雇主明显比以往更倾向于采用以员工为导向的工作分析方法。

3. 进行工作分析的六个步骤

进行工作分析是为今后的工作改进奠定基础，其分析内容包括：工作域界定、工作描述、绩效考核研发、人员选用、选拔制度、晋升标准、培训需求评估、选用过程的合法辩护以及薪酬设计等。进行工作分析涉及以下六个步骤：

第一步：如何使用信息。如何使用信息将决定收集什么数据以及如何收集这些数据。一些数据收集方法，如采访员工、询问工作内容有助于撰写工作说明书以及甄选员工。其他方法，如职位分析问卷，不提供工作描述的定性信息，但提供每项工作的评级。因此，利用这些方法，人们可以比较不同工作的薪酬情况。

第二步：审查相关的背景信息，如组织结构图、流程图和工作说明。组织结构图显示了整个组织的工作分工、所谈工作和其他工作有着怎样的联系，以及该工作与整个组织的协调。图表应显示每个职位的名称，并且应该通过连线指出员工向谁汇报工作、与谁交流。流程图提供了有关工作流程的更为详细的描述。流程图以最简单、最自然的形式展示工作的输入和输出流。最后，现有的工作描述（如果有的话）通常为日后修订版的工作描述提供起点。

第三步：选择具有代表性的职位分析。这是因为有太多类似的工作要分析。例如，如果抽样分析10份工作就有效的话，那就没有必要去分析200名装配工人的工作。

第四步：通过收集有关工作活动、员工的行为行动、工作条件，以及完成工作所需的人力特性和能力等方面的数据来真实地分析工作。对于这一步，可能需要一种或多种工作分析方法。

第五步：与从事该工作的员工以及他或她的直属上司核实分析信息，这将有助于确认信息的真实性和完整性。通过给当事人复查和修改工作活动描述的机会，该工作分析得出的数据和结论能获得员工的认可。

第六步：制定工作描述和工作说明。这两项是工作分析过程生成的实物产品。工作描述是描述工作活动和职责，以及诸如工作条件和安全隐患等重要的工作属性的书面说明；工作说明概括描述了完成某项工作所需要的个人素质、品性、技能和背景条件。这两项说明可以完全分开制定或写入同一份文档。

多年来，专家们提出了几种不同的系统和方法来完成工作分析。许多形式的系统不再被使用，但是那些仍然存在的系统在过去几十年中变得越来越详细，且更多地关注任务本身，而非人力特征。然而，这种趋势近年来有所好转，有一些较新的方法和系统被更多地应用于研究工作的行为层面。

Unit 3

Text A

Human Resource Planning

In today's business world, every organization requires diverse resources for its growth and development, including human resources (HR), financial resources (FR) and technical resources (TR). Of these three resources, human resources (HR) play the most important role since it will determine the potentialities of an organization in terms of its production, marketing and expansion.

Human resource planning, or HRP, is the ongoing, continuous process of systematic planning to achieve optimum use of an organization's most valuable asset: its human resources. It is based on the concept that people are the most important strategic resources of an organization.

A comprehensive human resources plan covers many important goals and responsibilities for businesses, including recruiting talented staff, management of payroll and benefits, administration over employee policies and employee training programs. An HR plan can address both tactical and strategic needs. HR planning that addresses tactics lays out how day-to-day staffing issues and compliance with government regulations are managed. A strategic HR plan helps a company grow by setting up advanced recruitment and training programs as well as detailed timetables and metrics to evaluate progress. High-quality employees can increase productivity, give companies a competitive advantage and help them meet their goals.

In this context, Quinn Mills (1983) observes that "Human resource planning is a decision-making process that combines three important activities:
- identifying and acquiring the right number of people with the proper skills;
- motivating them to achieve high performance;
- creating interactive links between business objectives and people-planning activities."

1. Benefits of HRP

Human resource planning is an outgoing process of appointing the accurate number of employees bearing the right talent and skills in the right jobs at the right time, while avoiding manpower shortages or surpluses as a means to achieve the goals of the organization. The benefits of having strong HR planning tools in place are as follows:

Recruiting. Human resource departments are usually responsible for recruiting new employees when positions are created or vacant. Recruiting and selecting employees is a time-consuming process that involves advertising for the open position, managing the application process, interviewing prospective candidates and making job offers. Effective HR planning helps the company to prepare ahead of time for these vacancies rather than acting in a reactionary manner when an employee resigns unexpectedly. Another benefit of having a recruiting plan in place is that the recruiters know where to target their job search to find the best candidates. Successful recruiters plan ahead and know what skill sets (hard and soft) are essential for the right candidates, and they know how to interview effectively. Companies that include HR planning are prepared for future open positions that result from business growth and expansion.

Career development. Another benefit of HR planning is having career-development procedures, which consist of identifying future company leaders and helping them grow. This means that when an executive or manager leaves or retires, there is already someone ready to promote into the position. Retention is an important factor in successful companies because it means that promotions come from within the organization and current employees are motivated to work harder to get ahead. Career development also looks at cross-training opportunities and has career-path plans in place.

Training. Successful HR planning includes training models and procedures. This training includes new-hire training to teach new employees about the company culture, internal databases, software and the skill sets necessary for specific positions. The benefit of this type of training is that all employees are taught the same thing in the same manner, which creates consistency and accuracy in daily work. Other training models include information about new company initiatives, new product roll outs and career progression classes. For example, if an employee has been successful in his current role, training may include coaching or management classes that will help him prepare for a future promotion.

Employee management. Effective HR planning incorporates aspects of employee management, such as performance reviews and disciplinary procedures. Companies benefit from having these systems in place because they help managers do their jobs and prevent potential lawsuits. Standardized performance reviews help managers look for key items when reviewing and ranking subordinates and ensure that everyone is reviewed on the same scale. Standardized disciplinary procedures ensure that the rules are followed and they clearly identify their consequences when they are broken.

2. Aims of HRP

The aims of human resource planning in any organization will depend largely on its context, but in general terms, the typical aims can be enumerated as below:
- attracting and retaining the number of people required with the appropriate skills, expertise and competencies;
- anticipating the problems of potential surpluses or deficits of people;
- developing a well trained and flexible workforce for contributing to the organization's ability to adapt to an uncertain and changing environment;
- reducing dependence on external recruitment when key skills are in short supply by evolving retention as well as employee development strategies;
- improving the utilization of people by introducing more flexible systems of work.

3. Types of HRP

There are two types of human resource planning:
- soft human resource planning;
- hard human resource planning.

Soft HRP is described by Marchington and Wilkinson (1996) as being more focused on the human aspect side as it gives more involvement and attention to employees in an organization, shaping the culture of the organization and integrating a clear integration between corporate goals and employee values and beliefs. It also gives a broader importance to communication of the company mission and plans.

Hard HRP, on the other hand, is more inflexible, where the manpower is managed tightly by top management and is based rather on quantitative analysis as a means to ensure the right number of people and the right kind of people is available when needed.

Many experts claim that the soft version is on the same line as the whole subject of human resource management, as the soft version focuses much more on the human aspect than the hard version, and is also flexible to changes which can occur in the business context.

4. Challenges of HRP

Human resource planning is about ensuring that the organization has the employees it will need in the future, in the right jobs and with the right skills. In fact, it may be the most complex kind of planning a company can undertake. The challenges of human resources planning can be listed out as mentioned here below:
- Human resource planning will depend largely on the ability of the company to predict what will happen outside the company, economic trends, upturns, downturns, and what competitors are doing, and a raft of other things the company has no control over. Often HR staff don't have the skills and background to predict these events with any success.
- The pace of change is so quick in the workplace that it's hard to predict what skills and therefore, what employees will be needed in even the near future.
- People make decisions about their own careers, whether to stay or go. And these days,

there's much more movement of employees from company to company. No longer do employees expect to stay at the same company for decades, and often their "moves" occur without warning, and even without two weeks' notice. When people are involved, prediction becomes much harder.

• Company growth (or for that matter, contraction) is difficult to predict in today's world. Successful companies can crash and burn quickly, or lose revenue, resulting in a need to lay off staff in an uncontrolled and unplanned way. The flip side is that as companies succeed and expand, not only do they need more employees, but also the skills they require will change.

• Human resources planning needs to be linked to the overall strategic direction of the company, and HR needs to have a seat at the strategic table to both define that strategic direction and to have information about corporate strategy. Unfortunately, HR is still seen as a nuts and bolts part of the organization rather than a strategic lever to make things happen. Not only is HR left "unheard", but also the skills of HR staff are often not strategic in nature but oriented towards the completion of short term tasks, like getting people hired, or more tactical functions.

New Words

financial [fai'nænʃəl] *adj.* 金融的；财务的，财政的

potentiality [pə,tenʃi'æləti] *n.* （用复数）潜能，潜力

expansion [iks'pænʃən] *n.* 扩张；扩大；膨胀

ongoing ['ɔngəuiŋ] *adj.* 不间断的，进行的；前进的

optimum ['ɔptiməm] *adj.* 最适宜的 *n.* 最佳效果；最适宜条件

valuable ['væljuəbl] *adj.* 有价值的；贵重的，宝贵的

concept ['kɔnsept] *n.* 观念，概念；观点，想法

comprehensive [,kɔmpri'hensiv] *adj.* 综合的；有理解力的，悟性好的

benefit ['benifit] *n.* 益处；利益；津贴费

tactical ['tæktikəl] *adj.* 战术的；策略上的；巧妙设计的

issue ['iʃuː] *n.* 问题；（报刊的）期，号；发行物 *v.* 发行；发布

regulation [regju'leiʃən] *n.* 规则；管理；控制

advanced [əd'vɑːnst] *adj.* 先进的；高等的，高深的；年老的

timetable ['taimteibəl] *n.* 计划；时刻表

metric ['metrik] *n.* 度量标准

acquire [ə'kwaiə] *v.* 学到；获得，取得

proper ['prɔpə] *adj.* 适当的，正当的

interactive [,intər'æktiv] *adj.* 互动的；互相作用的，相互影响的

appoint [ə'pɔint] *v.* 任命，委派；约定；指定

manpower ['mænpauə] *n.* 人力；人力资源；劳动力

surplus ['səːpləs] *n.* 剩余额；公积金；盈余 *adj.* 过剩的，多余的

vacant ['veikənt] *adj.* 空缺的；空虚的

time-consuming ['taim-kən,sjuːmiŋ] *adj.* 费时的；花费大量时间的

Unit 3

prospective [prəs'pektiv] *adj.* 未来的；可能的，有希望的
reactionary [ri'ækʃənəri] *adj.* 反动的；保守的；[化]反应的
resign [ri'zain] *v.* 辞职；放弃；屈从
target ['tɑ:git] *n.* 目标，目的；（服务的）对象；（射击的）靶子 *v.* 瞄准；把……作为攻击目标
retention [ri'tenʃən] *n.* 保留；滞留
database ['deitəbeis] *n.* 数据库；资料库，信息库
consistency [kən'sistənsi] *n.* 连贯，前后一致；符合
initiative [i'niʃiətiv] *n.* 倡议；主动性，主动精神
incorporate [in'kɔ:pəreit] *v.* 包含；使混合；使具体化
disciplinary ['disiplinəri] *adj.* 纪律的；训练的；惩罚的
lawsuit ['lɔ:su:t] *n.* 诉讼；诉讼案件
standardize ['stændədaiz] *v.* 使标准化；用标准校检
context ['kɔntekst] *n.* 语境，上下文；背景；环境
enumerate [i'nju:məreit] *v.* 列举；计算
competency ['kɔmpitənsi] *n.* 资格，能力

deficit ['defisit] *n.* 赤字，亏空；不足额
flexible ['fleksəbl] *adj.* 灵活的，柔韧的；易弯曲的
involvement [in'vɔlvmənt] *n.* 牵涉；参与，加入
mission ['miʃən] *n.* 使命；代表团
quantitative ['kwɔntitətiv] *adj.* 定量的；数量（上）的
claim [kleim] *v.* 声称，断言；索取
occur [ə'kə:] *v.* 发生；出现
complex ['kɔmpleks] *adj.* 复杂的，难懂的
undertake [ˌʌndə'teik] *v.* 承诺，保证；承担，从事
predict [pri'dikt] *v.* 预言，预测；预示
upturn ['ʌptə:n] *n.* 好转；上升趋势
downturn ['dauntə:n] *n.* （价格或活动）开始下降；衰退，低迷时期
prediction [pri'dikʃən] *n.* 预言，预报
contraction [kən'trækʃən] *n.* 收缩，缩减
crash [kræʃ] *n.* 崩溃；碰撞；暴跌 *v.* 碰撞；暴跌；（指商业公司、政府等）破产、垮台
revenue ['revəju:] *n.* 收益；财政收入，税收收入
bolt [bəult] *n.* 螺栓，螺钉；门闩 *v.* 筛选；（把门、窗等）闩上

Phrases

lay out 展示；设计
set up 建立；准备
ahead of time 提前
rather than （要）……而不……，与其……倒不如

have... in place 使……到位
result from 产生于……，由……引起
roll out 铺开；推出
benefit from 受益，通过……获益

on the same scale (as) 与……规模相同；与……等级相同
in general terms 概括地，笼统地
as below 如下
be in short supply （物资）紧缺供应
on the other hand 在另一方面
on the same line (as) 和……在同一直线上

have control over 对……有控制力
lay off 暂时解雇，裁员
the flip side 另一面
be linked to 与……连接；与……有关联
be seen as 被视为；被看作
nuts and bolts 具体细节；基本要点
in nature 实际上；性质上

Abbreviations

FR (Financial Resources) 财政资源
HRP (Human Resource Planning) 人力资源规划

Exercises

EX. 1 Answer the following questions according to the text.

1. What resources does every organization require?
2. What is human resource planning?
3. As Quinn Mills observed, what activities does the process of human resource planning combine?
4. Why is the process of recruiting and selecting employees time-consuming?
5. How do standardized performance reviews help managers?
6. What are the two general aims of HRP?
7. How many types of human resource planning are there? And what are they?
8. Why is soft HRP described as being more focused on the human aspect?
9. What challenge will it pose to HRP staff if the pace of change is so quick in the workplace?
10. What challenge will HRP staff face if successful companies crash and burn quickly?

EX. 2 Translate the following terms or phrases from English into Chinese and vice versa.

1. be linked to _____   1. _____
2. lay off _____   2. _____

Unit 3

3. set up _____   3. _____
4. lay out _____   4. _____
5. appoint _____   5. _____
6. *n.* 资格，能力 _____   6. _____
7. *n.* 连贯，前后一致；符合 ____   7. _____
8. *n.* 牵涉；参与，加入 _____   8. _____
9. *adj.* 定量的；数量（上）的 ___ 9. _____
10. *adj.* 空缺的；空虚的 _____ 10. _____

EX. 3 Translate the following text into Chinese.

In uncertain business settings, the significance of strategic human resources planning can become obvious very quickly. A company that reacts to circumstances by cutting staff as a measure to reduce short-term overhead can create unwanted repercussions. What initially looked like a smart and necessary move to economize in lean times can end up costing the company much more in the long-run. The resources that will be needed to subsequently recruit, hire, and train new employees may well exceed any short-term cost savings.

Forward-looking human resources planning typically anticipates future staffing requirements. It can help organizations avoid cost errors. Strategies are formulated to not only anticipate their needs over time, but also to consider optimal solutions for the long-term and under challenging economic conditions. This approach minimizes the chance of short-sighted and reactive choices being implemented by decision-makers. Organizations with a plan in place and a keen understanding of their long-range objectives may instead decide to weather the economic storm and keep trained, talented, and dedicated staff in place for the inevitable business uptrend.

EX. 4 Fill in the blanks with the words or phrases given below.

revenue	work out	visible	ensure	effective
expectations	staff morale	integral	satisfied	issues

Problems of Human Resource Planning

Problems which arise from human resource planning relate to the changing face of the workplace and the developing needs of employers and employees in the 21st century. The HR specialist is now an ___1___ member of the leadership team in any company and can help business owners avoid future problems relating to staffing by making ___2___ employment decisions from the very start. However, managing an HR department comes not without its own difficulties.

Human resources is not a department designed to bring in ___3___. It's a department which spends money. HR specialists, who are hired to search for top quality employees, train existing employees and offer advice for keeping levels of ___4___ high, will need to be paid, but the fruits of their work might not be ___5___ to company directors for a number of months. It can be difficult to ___6___ how much money to invest in HR planning and development at first and it can be risky for any company, particularly new start-ups, to stick with HR directives which don't seem to be working for too long.

HR planning can also fall short of ___7___ if it doesn't take existing staff needs into account. Existing employees will need training, supports and opportunities for professional development in order to feel ___8___ and happy in their work. Losing effective employees by failing to recognize what these employees need is one of the largest ___9___ faced by HR specialists in the workplace today. All companies must ___10___ that their HR departments are working just as hard for existing employees as they are in the search for new ones.

Text B

The Process of Human Resource Planning

As Michael Armstrong (2008) spells out, the process of human resource planning is not necessarily a linear one, starting with the business strategy and flowing logically through to resourcing, flexibility and retention plans. According to Hendry (1995), the process of HRP may be circular rather than linear, with the process starting anywhere in the cycle. For instance, scenario planning may impact on resourcing strategy, which in turn, may influence the business strategy. Alternatively, the starting point could be demand and supply forecasts which form the basis for the resourcing strategy. The analysis of labor turnover may feed into the supply forecast, but it could also lead directly to the development of retention plans.

There can not be a well articulated business plan as a basis for the HR plans. The business strategy may be evolutionary rather than deliberate. It may be in parts intuitive and incremental. Resourcing decisions may be based on scenarios riddled with assumptions that may or may not be correct and can not be tested. Resourcing strategy may be equally vague or based on unproven beliefs about the future. It may contain statements about, for example, building the skills base, which are little more than rhetoric.

There is a systematic approach to developing, resourcing strategy, scenario planning, demand and supply forecasting and labour turnover analysis. The degree to which HRP can be carried out systematically will depend on the nature of the organization. If the future is fairly predictable, then formal planning might be appropriate. If it is not so, the approach to human resource planning might have to rely on broad scenarios rather than precise forecasts.

1. Resourcing Strategy

According to Keep (1989), the objective of HRM resourcing strategy is to obtain the right basic material in the form of a work force endowed with the appropriate qualities, skills, knowledge and potential for future training. The selection and recruitment of workers best suited to meeting the needs of the organization ought to form a core activity upon which most other HRM policies geared towards development and motivation could be built.

The strategic capability of an organization depends on its resource capability in the form of people. This concept provides the rationale for resourcing strategy. The aim of this strategy is, therefore, to ensure that an organization achieves competitive advantage by employing more capable people than its rivals. These people will have a wider and deeper range of skills and they behave in ways that maximize their contribution. The organization retains them by providing better opportunities and rewards than others. It also develops a positive psychological contract which increases commitment and creates mutual trust. Besides, the organization deploys its people in ways that maximize the added value that they supply.

Michael Armstrong (2008) identified three components of resourcing strategy:

- Resourcing plans find people from within the organization and/or form training programmes to help people learn new skills. If needs are not satisfied from within the organization, resourcing plans prepare longer term by attracting more qualitative candidates as the employer of choice.

- Flexibility plans increase the feasibility in the use of human resource to enable the organization to make the best use of people and adapt swiftly to changing circumstances.

- Relation plans are intended to retain the people the organization needs.

Resourcing strategy provides the basis for these plans within the frame work of business needs. It will be more effective, if it is supported by scenario planning.

2. Scenario Planning

Scenario planning is also called by the name, the formal strategic planning technique. *Oxford Advanced Learner's Dictionary of Current English* defines a scenario as "an imagined sequence of future events". It is a more or less formalized process for establishing a view about any changes that can be seen to the scale and type of activities in the organization and to its structure. It identifies all external environmental changes that are likely to affect it. It aims at obtaining a better understanding of the possible situation that may have to be dealt with in the future.

In this context, Reill (1999) observes that "Scenario planning tries to open minds to a range of possibilities that organizations may have to confront. These possibilities are then ordered to produce a series of internally consistent pictures of alternative futures. It is an intellectual process that seeks to identify issues and examine the possible consequences of events."

The scenario planning involves making broad assessments of likely internal developments. It shows the direction in which the organization is going and the implications this has on people requirements. According to Michael Armstrong (2008), the assessments may have to be made in the absence of any articulated business plan, and thus involve questioning top management and key line managers on how they see the future, and asking them to interpret what this means in terms of their human resource needs. Assessments also have to be made on likely changes in the external environment as it may affect the labor market.

3. Demand/Supply Forecasting

Demand forecasting is a process of human resource planning by which the number of people, their skills and competencies required for an organization are estimated. The ideal basis of the forecast is an annual budget and longer term business plan, translated into activity levels for each function and department or decision on downsizing.

Supply forecasting is a process of human resource planning by which the number of people to be available within and outside the organization is measured. Supply forecasting is based on the following six factors:

- an analysis of existing human resources in terms of numbers in each occupation, skills and potentials;
- forecasting losses to existing resources through attrition;
- forecasting changes to existing resources through internal promotion;
- effecting changing conditions of work and absenteeism;
- sources of supply from within the organization;
- sources of supply from outside the organization in the national and local labor markets.

The analysis of demand and supply forecasts determines whether there are any deficits or surpluses. It provides the basis for recruitment, retention and downsizing. If necessary, computerized planning models can be used for this purpose. The basic forecasting calculations can be carried out with a spread sheet that sets out and calculates the number required for each occupation.

4. Labor Turnover Analysis

In human resources context, turnover is the act of replacing an employee with a new employee. Partings between organizations and employees may consist of termination, retirement, death, interagency transfers, and resignations. An organization's turnover is measured as a percentage rate, which is referred to as its turnover rate. Turnover rate is the percentage of employees in a workforce that leave during a certain period of time. Organizations and industries as a whole measure their turnover rate during a fiscal or calendar year.

The analysis of the number of people leaving the organization which includes labor turnover or wastage provides data for use in supply forecasting so that calculations can be made on the number of people lost who may have to be replaced. The analysis of the number of leavers and the reasons why they leave provides information that will indicate if any action is required to be taken to improve retention rates. It can encourage further investigations underlying causes and identifying remedies.

5. Environmental Analysis

This step of human resource planning process is to understand the context of human resource management. Human resource managers should understand both internal and external environments. Data on external environments includes the following: the general status of the economy, industry, technology and competition, labor market regulations and trends, unemployment rate, skills available, and the age and sex distribution of the labor force. Internal data required include short- and long-term organizational plans and strategies and the current status of the organization's human resources.

6. Action Plan

Human resource plan depends on whether there is deficit or surplus in the organization. Accordingly, the plan may be finalized either for new recruitment, training, interdepartmental transfer in case of deficit of termination, or voluntary retirement schemes and redeployment in case of surplus.

Developing action plans is based on the gathered data, analysis and available alternatives. The key issue is that the plans should be acceptable to both top management and employees. Plans should be prioritized and these plans include employee utilization plan, appraisal plan, training and management development plan, human resource supply plan, retention plan and downsizing plan.

New Words

linear [ˈlɪniə] *adj.* 直线的，线形的；长度的	**unproven** [ʌnˈpruːvən] *adj.* 未被证实的
logically [ˈlɔdʒikəli] *adv.* 逻辑上，符合逻辑地；能推理地	**rhetoric** [ˈretərik] *n.* 修辞学；雄辩术；华丽的文辞
flexibility [ˌfleksəˈbiləti] *n.* 柔韧性；机动性；灵活性	**predictable** [priˈdiktəbəl] *adj.* 可预见的，可预言的；可预报的
circular [ˈsəːkjulə] *adj.* 环行的；迂回的；流通的	**precise** [priˈsais] *adj.* 精密的；精确的
alternatively [ɔːlˈtəːnətivli] *adv.* 或者，二者择一；要不然	**rationale** [ˌræʃəˈnæl] *n.* 基本原理，基础理论；根据
forecast [ˈfɔːkɑːst] *v.* 预报，预测；预示	**rival** [ˈraivəl] *n.* 对手，竞争者 *v.* 与……竞争；比得上某人
deliberate [diˈlibəreit] *adj.* 深思熟虑的；故意的，蓄意的	**deploy** [diˈplɔi] *v.* 部署；配置
intuitive [inˈtjuːitiv] *adj.* 直观的；直觉的，凭直觉获知的	**feasibility** [ˌfiːzəˈbiləti] *n.* 可行性；可能性，现实性
incremental [inkriˈmentəl] *adj.* 增加的	**confront** [kənˈfrʌnt] *v.* 面对；对质
vague [veig] *adj.* 模糊的；（表达或感知）含糊的	**alternative** [ɔːlˈtəːnətiv] *adj.* 替代的；另类的；备选的

implication [ˌimpliˈkeiʃən] n. 含意；含蓄；言外之意
interpret [inˈtə:prit] v. 解释；理解；口译
calculation [ˌkælkjuˈleiʃən] n. 计算，盘算；估计
parting [ˈpɑ:tiŋ] n. 分离；分道扬镳的时刻
termination [ˌtə:miˈneiʃən] n. 结束；终止
interagency [ˌintərˈeidʒənsi] adj. 跨机构的
transfer [trænsˈfə:] v. 转移；调动；转让（权利等）n. 转移；调动
resignation [ˌrezigˈneiʃən] n. 辞职；顺从，听从
fiscal [ˈfiskəl] adj. 财政上的；国库的

calendar [ˈkælində] n. 日历；日程表；一览表
investigation [inˌvestiˈgeiʃən] n. 调查
underlying [ˌʌndəˈlaiiŋ] adj. 潜在的，含蓄的；基础的
remedy [ˈremidi] n. 补救办法；治疗法 v. 补救；治疗；改正，纠正
status [ˈsteitəs] n. 地位；身份；情形，状态
unemployment [ˌʌnimˈplɔimənt] n. 失业；失业人数；失业状况
distribution [ˌdistriˈbju:ʃən] n. 分配，分布
interdepartmental [ˌintədiˌpɑ:tˈmentl] adj. 部际的，各部门间的
voluntary [ˈvɔləntəri] adj. 志愿的；自愿的，自发的

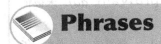

Phrases

spell out 阐明；拼出，读出
not necessarily 不见得；未必，不一定
demand and supply 供与求，供求
labor turnover 劳工移动率
feed into 注入（流入，装进）
in part 部分地
be riddled with 布满，充满
rely on 依靠；信赖
be endowed with 具有；赋有
a wide range of 范围广泛的；大范围的
psychological contract 心理契约
mutual trust 相互信任
added value 净增值，增值价值
adapt to 变得习惯于……，使适应于
scenario planning 远景规划（公司战略的一个阶段）

a series of 一系列；一连串
in the absence of 缺乏……；当……不在时
labor market 劳动市场
annual budget 年度预算
spread sheet 总分析表；棋盘式对照表
percentage rate 百分率
turnover rate 流动率；转换率；更新率
fiscal year 财政年度，会计年度
calendar year 历年
take action 采取行动；提起诉讼
retention rate 保留率，滞留率
underlying cause 潜在的深层次原因，根本原因
unemployment rate 失业率
in case of 防备；假如；如果发生

Unit 3

Exercises

EX. 5 Read the following statements and then decide whether each of them is true or false based on the information in Text B. Write T for True and F for False in the space provided before each statement.

_____ 1. According to Hendry (1995), the process of HRP may be linear rather than circular, with the process starting with the business strategy.

_____ 2. Resourcing strategy is sure to be specific or based on proven assumptions about the future.

_____ 3. Since the strategic capability of an organization depends on its resource capability in the form of people, resourcing strategy is aimed to ensure that an organization achieves competitive advantage over its rivals by employing more competent people.

_____ 4. Scenario planning identifies all the environmental changes within an organization that are likely to affect it.

_____ 5. The scenario planning involves making broad assessments of likely internal developments and likely changes in the external environment.

_____ 6. Supply forecasting is a process of human resource planning which measures the number of people to be available only within the organization.

_____ 7. Labor turnover may result from termination, retirement, death, interagency transfers, and resignations.

_____ 8. By analyzing the number of leavers and the reasons why they leave, human resource staff will get to know whether any action is required to be taken to improve retention rates or not.

_____ 9. Environmental analysis is an important step of human resource planning which analyzes data on external environment far more than on internal environment.

_____ 10. The surplus of work force within an organization is the sole determinant of the human resource plan.

Supplementary Reading

Text	Notes
Factors Affecting Human Resource Planning	
Human resource management helps to maintain sufficient staff levels for current productivity and projected[1] company growth. A human resources department often makes decisions	[1] projected [prə'dʒektid] *adj.* 规划的，设计的；预期的

based on the projected financial return of hiring a candidate. However, the effectiveness of human resource planning is greatly affected by several factors. The more important of them are type and strategy of organization, organizational growth cycles and planning, environmental uncertainties[2], time horizons[3], type and quality of forecasting information, and labor market.

1. Type and Strategy of Organization

The type of organization is an important consideration because it determines the production processes involved, the number and type of staff needed, and the supervisory and managerial personnel required. Manufacturing organizations are more complex in this respect than those that render[4] services.

The strategic plan of the organization defines the organization's HR needs. For example, a strategy of organic growth means that additional employees must be hired. Acquisitions[5] or mergers[6], on the other hand, probably mean that the organization will need to plan for layoffs, since mergers tend to create, duplicate or overlap[7] positions that can be handled more efficiently with fewer employees.

Primarily, the organization decides either to be proactive[8] or reactive[9] in human resource planning. It can either decide to carefully anticipate the needs and systematically plan them to fill them far in advance[10], or it can simply react to needs as they arise. Of course, careful planning to fill HR needs better helps ensure that the organization obtains the right number of HR people with proper skills and competencies when they are needed.

Similarly, the organization must determine the breadth of the plan. Essentially, the organization can choose a narrow focus by planning in only one or two HR areas, such as recruitment or selection, or it can choose a broad focus by planning in all areas including training, remuneration and so on.

The organization must also decide upon the formality[11] of the plan. It can decide to have an informal plan that lies mostly in the minds of the managers and personnel staff. Alternatively, the organization can have a formalized plan which is clearly spell out in writing, backed by documentation and data.

[2] uncertainty [ʌnˈsɜːtənti] n. 无把握，不确定；不可靠
[3] time horizon: 时程
[4] render [ˈrendə] v. 给予；递交
[5] acquisition [ˌækwɪˈzɪʃən] n. 收购；获得
[6] merger [ˈmɜːdʒə] n. （两个公司的）合并；联合体；吸收
[7] overlap [ˌəʊvəˈlæp] v. 重叠；与……部分相同
[8] proactive [ˌprəʊˈæktɪv] adj. 积极主动的；主动出击的，先发制人的
[9] reactive [rɪˈæktɪv] adj. 反应的；反作用的
[10] in advance: 提前
[11] formality [fɔːˈmæləti] n. 礼节；程序；拘谨

Finally, the organization must make a decision on flexibility—the ability of the HR plan to anticipate and deal with contingencies[12]. No organization likes high levels of uncertainty. Organizations seek to reduce uncertainty by planning, which includes forecasting and predicting possible future conditions and events. Human resource planning can contain many contingencies, which reflect different scenarios thereby assuring that the plan is flexible and adaptable[13].

2. Organizational Growth Cycles and Planning

The stage of an organization's growth can have considerable influence on human resource planning. Small organizations in the embryonic[14] stage may not have personnel planning.

Need for planning is felt when the organization enters the growth stage. HR forecasting becomes essential. Internal development of people also begins to receive attention in order to keep up with the growth.

A mature organization experiences less flexibility and variability[15]. Growth slows down. The workforce becomes old as few younger people are hired. Planning becomes more formalized and less flexible and innovative. Issues like retirement and possible retrenchment[16] dominate[17] planning.

Finally, in the declining stage, human resource planning takes a different focus. Planning is done for layoff, retrenchment and retirement. Since decisions are often made after serious financial and sales shocks experienced by the organization, planning is often reactive in nature.

3. Environmental Uncertainties

HR managers rarely have the privilege[18] of operating in a stable and predictable environment. Political, social and economic changes affect all organizations. Personnel planners deal with environmental uncertainties by carefully formulating[19] recruitment, selection, and training and development policies and programs. Balancing mechanisms are built into the HRM programme through succession[20] planning, promotion channels, layoffs, flexitime[21], job sharing, retirement, VRS and other personnel related arrangements.

[12] contingency [kən'tindʒənsi] n. 意外事故，偶发事件；可能性

[13] adaptable [ə'dæptəbl] adj. 可适应的；有适应能力的

[14] embryonic [,embri'ɔnik] adj. 胚芽的，胎儿的；初期的

[15] variability [,vεəriə'biləti] n. 变化性，易变，变化的倾向

[16] retrenchment [ri'trentʃmənt] n. 节省；删除

[17] dominate ['dɔmineit] v. 支配，影响；占有优势

[18] privilege ['privilidʒ] n. 特权

[19] formulate ['fɔ:mjuleit] v. 构想出，规划

[20] succession [sək'seʃən] n. 继承人，继承权；继承顺序

[21] flexitime ['fleksitaim] n. 弹性上班制

4. Time Horizons

Yet another major factor affecting personnel planning is the time horizon. A plan cannot be for too long on a time horizon as the operating environment itself may undergo[22] charges. On one hand, there are short-term plans spanning[23] six months to one year. On the other hand, there are long-term plans—which spread over three to twenty years. The exact time span, however, depends on the degree of uncertainty prevailing[24] in an organization's environment.

Plans for companies operating in an unstable environment, computers for example, must be for a short period. Plans for others where environment is fairly stable, for example a university plan, may be long-term. In general, the greater the uncertainty, the shorter the plan's time horizon and vice-versa.

5. Type and Quality of Information

The information used to forecast personnel needs originates from[25] a multitude of[26] sources. A major issue in personnel planning is the type of information which should be used in making forecasts.

Closely related to the type of information is the quality of data used. The quality and accuracy of information depend upon the clarity[27] with which the organizational decision makers have defined their strategy, organizational structure, budgets, production schedules and so forth. In addition, the HR department must maintain well-developed job-analysis information and HR information systems (HRIS) that provide accurate and timely data. Generally speaking, organizations operating in stable environments are in a better position to obtain comprehensive, timely and accurate information because of longer planning horizons, clearer definition of strategy and objectives, and fewer disruptions[28].

6. Labor Market

Labor market comprises people with skills and abilities that can be tapped as and when the need arises. Thanks to the mushrooming[29] of educational, professional and technical institutions adequately trained human resource is always available on the market. Nevertheless, shortages do occur. For example, the Confederation of Indian Industry (CII) estimates

---

[22] undergo [ˌʌndəˈɡəu] v. 经历，经验；遭受，承受

[23] span [spæn] v. 延续；横跨；贯穿

[24] prevail [priˈveil] v. 流行，盛行；获胜，占优势

[25] originate from: 起源；来自……，源于

[26] a multitude of: 大量的

[27] clarity [ˈklærɪti] n. 清晰度；明确；透明

[28] disruption [disˈrʌpʃən] n. 中断；分裂，瓦解

[29] mushrooming [ˈmʌʃrumiŋ] n. 迅速增长

that by 2017, India will be requiring 35 million additional skilled workers in sectors such as health care, banking and financial services, retail, auto and construction. It is doubtful whether so many skilled workers would be available in the country.

When one talks about labor supply, the following deserve due[30] consideration:
- the size, age, sex and educational composition of the population;
- the demand for goods and services in the country;
- the nature of production technology;
- employability[31] of the people.

[30] due [dju:] *adj.* 适当的；预定的

[31] employability [imˈplɔiəˈbiləti] *n.* 可雇性；可用性

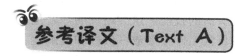

参考译文（Text A）

人力资源规划

在当今商界，为了成长和发展，每个企业都需要不同的资源，包括人力资源、财务资源和技术资源。在这三种资源中，人力资源起着最重要的作用，因为它将决定一个企业在生产、营销和扩展方面的潜力。

人力资源规划（HRP）是一个不断发展的、持续的系统规划过程，旨在优化利用一个组织最有价值的资产，即人力资源。人力资源规划基于一种理念，即人是企业中最重要的战略资源。

综合全面的人力资源规划涵盖了企业许多重要的目标和职责，包括人才招聘、薪资与福利管理、员工管理政策与员工培训计划。人力资源规划可以兼顾战术性和战略性两方面的需求。战术性人力资源规划规定了管理日常人员的配置问题和遵守政府规章的方式；战略性人力资源规划通过建立先进的招聘培训计划、详细的日程表以及公司发展的评估标准来帮助公司发展。高素质员工可以提高生产力，给公司带来竞争优势，帮助公司实现目标。

在这种情况下，Quinn Mills（1983）指出："人力资源规划是一个决策过程，结合了下列三项重要活动：
- 识别和确定具有适当技能的人才数量；
- 激励员工取得高绩效；
- 创建企业目标与人力规划活动之间的互动环节。"

1. 人力资源规划的益处

人力资源规划是一项输出过程。它在适当的时间内，将具有真正才能的员工按精确数量配置在合适的工作岗位上，同时避免人力短缺或过剩，以实现企业目标。配置强有力的人力资源规划能带来以下好处：

招聘。人力资源部通常在有职位空缺时招聘新员工。招聘和甄选员工是一个耗时的过程，包括刊登招聘广告、管理申请程序、面试潜在候选人和提供工作机会。有效的人力资源规划有助于公司提前做好填补职位空缺的准备，不会在一名员工突然离职时，被动地应对。制订招聘计划的另一个好处是招聘人员知道在何处发布工作信息能招到最佳求职者。成功的招聘人员都会事先做好计划。他们知道合适的候选人必须具备的技能（包括硬技能和软技能），也知道如何有效地面试候选人。具有人力资源规划职能的公司能够应对因业务发展与扩张出现的职位空缺问题。

职业发展。人力资源规划的另一个好处是制定职业发展程序，包括确定未来的公司领导并帮助他们发展。这意味着，当某个主管或经理离职或退休时，公司可以随时将某个人晋升到该职位。保留员工是公司成功的重要因素，因为它意味着晋升机会来自公司内部，这种机会能激励在职员工更加努力地工作并取得进步。职业发展还需要考虑交叉培训，并制订职业发展计划。

培训。成功的人力资源规划包括培训模式和培训程序。该培训包括培训新员工，引导新员工了解公司文化、内部数据库、软件以及具体职位所需的技能。这类培训的好处是，所有员工都以同样的方式接受同样的培训内容，从而在日常工作中形成一致性和准确性。其他培训模式包括了解公司的新举措和新产品信息，以及职业发展班。例如，如果一名员工在目前的职位上很成功，那么对他的培训可能包括有助于他将来职位晋升的辅导或管理课程。

员工管理。有效的人力资源规划包括员工管理等方面的工作，如绩效评估和纪律程序。公司受益于这些规划系统，因为它们有助于管理者开展工作，防止潜在的法律诉讼。标准化的绩效评估有助于经理在评估和排名下属时，找到关键性依据，并确保按同样的标准对每个人进行评估。标准化的纪律程序确保员工遵守公司规章制度，并且明确指出员工违反规章制度时应承担的后果。

2. 人力资源规划的目标

任何企业的人力资源规划目标在很大程度上都取决于其具体情况。但总的来说，常见的目标有以下几种：

- 吸引并留住具有合适技能、专业知识和能力的员工；
- 预测可能性的员工过剩或短缺问题；
- 发展一批训练有素、灵活的劳动力，从而促进企业发展，以适应不确定的、瞬息变化的环境；
- 通过实施保留员工和发展员工的战略，减少在重要技能短缺时对外聘员工的依赖程度；
- 引进更灵活的工作制度，提高员工效率。

3. 人力资源规划的类型

人力资源规划有两种类型，即：
- 软人力资源规划；
- 硬人力资源规划。

Marchington 和 Wilkinson（1996）认为，软人力资源规划更注重"人"，因为它更多地涉及和关注企业员工、企业文化，以及企业目标和员工价值观之间的彻底整合。它也更广泛地重视公司使命和计划的上传下达。

硬人力资源规划则不那么灵活。人力由高层管理人员严格管理，并且基于定量分析来确保在需要的时候，有适量的合适员工可供使用。

许多专家认为，软人力资源规划与人力资源管理的整个主旨是一致的，因为软人力资源规划比硬人力资源规划更侧重于人的方面，而且能灵活适应商业领域中的各种变化。

4. 人力资源规划面临的挑战

人力资源规划是为了确保企业在将来需要之时，能够就适当的工作岗位，招聘具有相应技能的员工。事实上，它可能是公司所承担的最复杂的一项规划工作。人力资源规划所面临的挑战如下：

• 人力资源规划在很大程度上取决于公司的预测能力。它要能够预测将要发生之事，如经济发展趋势（上升或下降）、竞争对手正在做的事，以及其他一系列公司无法控制的事。通常，人力资源部的工作人员不具备成功地预测这些事件的技能和背景知识。

• 职场的变化速度很快，因此很难预测在不久的将来企业需要哪些技能和员工。

• 员工就自己的职业生涯做出决定：去或留。而如今，公司员工的流动性越来越大。员工不再期望在同一家公司待上几十年，而且他们的"离职"也常常毫无预兆，甚至没有正式提出辞职申请。当涉及"人"的时候，预测变得尤为困难。

• 在当今世界，人们很难预测公司是否在发展（或是收缩）。一些成功的公司可能很快会破产，或者失去效益，要无节制、无计划地解雇员工。而另一方面，随着公司发展壮大，他们不仅需要更多的员工，而且员工需要掌握的技能也会改变。

• 人力资源规划需要与公司的整体战略方向相关联，因此人力资源需要在"战略桌"上占有一席之地，以便能参与制定并通晓公司的战略方向。不幸的是，人们仍然把人力资源部视为企业中最基础的部门，而不是一个有创造性的战略性工具。不仅人力资源部"鲜有耳闻"，就连人力资源部员工的能力往往在本质上也不具有战略性。相反，他们只着眼于完成短期任务，如聘用员工，或更多的战术职能。

Unit 4

Text A

Recruitment

Recruitment is a core function of human resource management. Recruitment refers to the overall process of attracting, selecting and appointing suitable candidates for jobs (either permanent or temporary) within an organization. Recruitment can also refer to processes involved in choosing individuals for unpaid positions, such as voluntary roles or unpaid trainee roles. Managers, human resource generalists and recruitment specialists may be tasked with carrying out recruitment. But in some cases public-sector employment agencies, commercial recruitment agencies, or specialist search consultancies are used to undertake parts of the process.

1. Recruitment Goals and Objectives

Each company will have unique goals and objectives that should be taken into account when developing recruiting strategies. A successful recruiting strategy allows a company to find the human capital it needs to move forward with business objectives and goals while growing profits. The most profitable innovations often come from a diverse team of individuals with shared goals.

Attract Top Talent

Recruiting is a way to bring in fresh new ideas and overcome company shortcomings. With targeted recruiting efforts, generous pay and benefits and a strong company culture, it is possible to attract the top talent in your given industry. While hiring the best candidate from your applicant pool is a fairly easy task, attracting top talent often takes more networking, outsourcing to a recruiting firm or recruiting from local universities to increase the candidate pool to include the types of skills and experience you desire.

Gain Competitive Advantage

In many industries, gaining a competitive edge is accomplished by hiring and retaining the best and brightest candidates. Often, experts in the industry bring with them a loyal following of customers when they change jobs. Recruiting candidates based on their industry clout is an excellent way to gain ground in competitive markets.

Workplace Diversity

The Americans with Disabilities Act and the Equal Employment Opportunity Commission provide guidelines for workplace diversity. For companies with more than 15 employees, hiring a diverse workforce is a legal requirement. If your company lacks diversity, extending your recruiting strategies to include networking, job fairs and college recruiting will provide a much broader reach that will include diverse candidates.

Company Growth

Recruiting allows for the acquisition of skills and experience that your business may currently lack. Recruiting fuels company growth by bringing new ideas and opportunities for expansion. New hires, ranging from fresh college graduates to industry leaders, will bring with them new ideas and innovative solutions to the challenges your company faces.

2. Recruitment Plan

The process of recruitment has to be completed in a very organized and systematic manner for taking in the right kind of candidates. A well designed recruitment plan, which is a proactive method for helping businesses attract and hire the best candidates for each position, can help you complete the recruitment process in your organization successfully and help you in knowing the steps involved in the recruitment process one after the other. By recruiting the right candidates, the HR managers can create a good work environment which will lay the foundation of fast and future growth of the company. Any confusion in the recruitment process steps can lead to the selection of wrong candidates affecting the efficiency and profitability of the organization. To draft a perfect recruitment plan for your organization, you are required to take the recruiting tips and strategies given below into account.

Number of Workers to Be Recruited

Whether it is the volunteer, college or any corporate recruitment plan, deciding the number of candidates to be recruited for various tasks is of prime importance. This number would be on the basis of actual need in various departments of the company. If candidates recruited are less than the actual requirement, then there will be much work pressure on the existing employees and over recruitment will affect the company financially. So, recruiting the exact number of employees as needed is a must.

Decide the Requirements for the Job

The plan involves the expectations from candidates and the knowledge which they should have for getting the job. The company HR can prepare a list of qualifications and skills set which he will be looking for in the candidates before recruiting them. Naturally, those who fulfill these requirements shall be recruited and the ones who do not will not be considered fit for the job.

Unit 4

Decide the Nature of the Selection Process

It is very important to decide the selection steps beforehand to avoid any last-minute confusion. Ideally, the selection process should consist of a written test, a group discussion round and a personal interview. Organizations in different sectors may have a diverse selection process depending on their needs. Deciding this process is indeed a big challenge for the HR managers of today's competitive times. For judging the candidates, standards must be set and followed by the recruiters. When we think of the selection process, deciding the panel for recruitment also assumes big importance. The recruiter job description will help you know more.

Venue of Recruitment

In the corporate world, company offices, executive hotels and job fairs can be the venues for recruiting. Job fairs can be useful for large-scale recruiting for selecting positions. The recruitment place needs to be well equipped with essential materials for organizing interviews in a professional way.

Recruitment Budget

An ideal recruitment plan should consist of a recruitment budget which will help the company senior management know how much money they will have to spend on the entire recruitment process. With the help of this data, if the amount to be spent on recruitment is too high, then cost cutting methods can be used to bring down the company expenses.

Such an effective recruitment plan can be the best way for growing the business for corporations. Implementing the plan in a good way is even more important to see positive results.

3. Recruitment Process

The recruitment and selection process is important for new and established businesses alike. Human resources department has the support and expertise of employment specialists who assist hiring managers with the procedures to ensure that the company's leaders are making wise hiring decisions. There are several steps to the recruitment and selection process given below:

Step 1: Job analysis. In situations where multiple new jobs are created and recruited for the first time or vacancies are there or the nature of a job has substantially changed, a job analysis might be undertaken to document the knowledge, skills, abilities and other characteristics (KSAOs) required or sought for the job. From these, the relevant information is captured in such documents as job descriptions and job specifications. Often, a company already has job descriptions for existing positions. Where already drawn up, these documents may require review and updating to reflect current requirements. Prior to the recruitment stage, a person specification should be finalized.

Step 2: Sourcing. Sourcing is the use of one or more strategies to attract or identify candidates to fill job vacancies. It may involve internal and/or external recruitment advertising, using appropriate media, such as job portals, local or national newspapers, social media, business media, specialist recruitment media, professional publications, window advertisements, job centers, or in a variety of ways via the Internet.

Alternatively, employers may use recruitment consultancies or agencies to find otherwise scarce candidates, who, in many cases, may be content in their current positions and are not actively looking to move. This initial research for candidates, also called name generation, produces contact information for potential candidates, whom the recruiter can then discreetly contact and screen.

Step 3: Screening and selection. Various psychological tests can assess a variety of KSAOs, including literacy. Assessments are also available to measure physical ability. Recruiters and agencies may use applicant tracking systems to filter candidates, along with software tools for psychometric testing and performance-based assessment. In many countries, employers are legally mandated to ensure their screening and selection processes meet equal opportunity and ethical standards.

Employers are likely to recognize the value of candidates who encompass soft skills such as interpersonal or team leadership. Many companies, including multinational organizations and those that recruit from a range of nationalities, are also often concerned about whether candidate fits the prevailing company culture.

Additionally, as for most companies, money and job stability are two of the contributing factors to the productivity of a disabled employee, which in return equates to the growth and success of a business. Hiring disabled workers produces more advantages than disadvantages. There is no difference in the daily production of a disabled worker. Given their situation, they are more likely to adapt to their environmental surroundings and acquaint themselves with equipment, enabling them to solve problems and overcome adversity as with other employees.

Meanwhile, many major corporations recognize the need for diversity in hiring to compete successfully in a global economy. Other organizations, for example, universities and colleges, have been slow to embrace diversity as an essential value for their success.

Step 4: Recruitment Process Outsourcing (RPO). Recruitment Process Outsourcing, or commonly known as "RPO" is a form of Business Process Outsourcing (BPO) where a company engages a third party provider to manage all or part of its recruitment process.

4. Recruitment and Selection Tests

Recruitment and selection tests aim to provide a potential employer with an insight into how well job applicants work with other people, how well they handle stress, and whether they will be able to cope with the intellectual demands of the job.

Recruitment and selection tests are only part of the selection process and the applicant will still be asked to complete an application form, send in a copy of his resume and attend at least one interview. All of these things will tell the employer something about the applicant and help them to choose the most appropriate candidate for the vacancy. Recruitment and selection tests can be split into personality tests and aptitude/ability tests.

The principle behind personality tests is that it is possible to quantify the applicant's personality characteristics by asking about his or her feelings, thoughts and behavior. Personality has a significant role to play in deciding whether the job applicants have the enthusiasm and motivation that the employer is looking for and whether they are going to fit into the organization, in terms of their personality, attitude and general work style. Personality tests can be applied in a straightforward way at the early stages of selection to screen-out candidates who are likely to be unsuitable for the job.

Aptitude and ability tests are designed to assess the candidate's intellectual performance. These types of test can be broadly classified into the groups shown and the applicant may be asked to sit a test which consists only of "numerical" questions or these may form part of a test which consists of questions of different types.

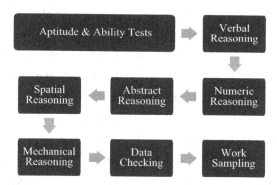

This will depend very much on the job the applicants are applying for. For example, jobs that require a candidate to handle figures on a day to day basis may have a higher proportion of numerical reasoning questions, whereas tests used for information technology jobs tend to have a higher proportion of abstract reasoning questions.

 New Words

permanent ['pəːmənənt] adj. 永久（性）的，永恒的，不变的
temporary ['tempərəri] adj. 短暂的；临时的，暂时的
trainee [trei'niː] n. 受训练的人；新兵；实习生
generalist ['dʒenərəlist] n. 通才，多面手
public-sector ['pʌblik-'sektə] n. 公共部门
consultancy [kən'sʌltənsi] n. 咨询公司；顾问工作，顾问职位
unique [juː'niːk] adj. 唯一的，仅有的，独特的

innovation [ˌinə'veiʃən] n. 改革，创新；新观念；新发明
shortcoming ['ʃɔːtkʌmiŋ] n. 短处，缺点
generous ['dʒenərəs] adj. 丰厚的；慷慨的，大方的
networking ['netwəːkiŋ] n. 人际网，联网
outsourcing ['autˌsɔːsiŋ] n. 外包
loyal ['lɔiəl] adj. 忠诚的，忠心的
clout [klaut] n. （尤指政治上的）影响；敲打
guideline [gaidlain] n. 指导方针，指导原则

extend [iks'tend] v. 延伸；扩大，推广
fuel [fjuəl] v. 激起，促进；给……加燃料
solution [sə'lu:ʃən] n. 解决，解决方案
confusion [kən'fju:ʒən] n. 混乱，混淆，困惑
draft [drɑ:ft] v. 起草，制定
prime [praim] adj. 最好的；首要的，基本的
must [mʌst] n. 必须做的事，必不可少的事物
fulfill [ful'fil] v. 履行（诺言等）；执行（命令等）
beforehand [bi'fɔ:hænd] adv. 提前，事先，预先
panel ['pænl] n. 座谈小组；仪表盘；面板
venue ['venju:] n. 会场，场所
large-scale [lɑ:dʒ-skeil] adj. 大规模的，大范围的
senior ['si:njə] adj. 资深的；（级别、地位等）较高的；年长的
substantially [səb'stænʃəli] adv. 本质上，实质上；相当多地
capture ['kæptʃə] v. 引起（注意等）；俘获；夺取
update [ʌp'deit] v. 更新，使现代化；校正
finalize ['fainəlaiz] v. 完成，使结束；使落实
media ['mi:djə] n. 媒体，介质
portal ['pɔ:təl] n. 门户；入口，大门
publication [,pʌbli'keiʃən] n. 出版，发表；出版物；公布

via ['vaiə, 'vi:ə] prep. 通过，凭借；经过，取道
scarce [skeəs] adj. 缺乏的，罕见的
content [kən'tent] adj. 满足的，满意的；愿意的
discreetly [dis'kri:tli] adv. 谨慎地，小心地
literacy ['litərəsi] n. 识字，有文化，能读能写
filter ['filtə] v. 过滤，渗透
psychometric [saikəu'metrik] adj. 心理测量的
mandate ['mændeit] v. 强制执行；委托办理
ethical ['eθikəl] adj. 道德的，伦理的
prevailing [pri'veiliŋ] adj. 盛行的，普遍的，占优势的
disabled [dis'eibld] adj. 残废的，有缺陷的
equate [i'kweit] v. 等同，使相等
acquaint [ə'kweint] v. 使熟悉，使认识
adversity [əd'və:siti] n. 逆境，不幸，灾难
insight ['insait] n. 顿悟，领悟；洞察力
intellectual [,inti'lektjuəl] adj. 智力的，有才智的 n. 知识分子
quantify ['kwɔntifai] v. 确定……的数量
enthusiasm [in'θju:ziæzəm] n. 热情，热忱
straightforward [streit'fɔ:wəd] adj. 直截了当的；坦率的
spatial ['speiʃəl] adj. 空间的
abstract ['æbstrækt] adj. 抽象的；理论的

Unit 4

Phrases

refer to 涉及；指的是，提及
be involved in 涉及；与……有关联
be tasked with 负责
shared goal 共同目标
bring in 把……拿进来，带进来
applicant pool 求职群体，申请者群
gain a competitive edge 赢得竞争优势
gain ground (in) 前进，取得进展；占优势
job fair 招聘会
take in 接受；让……进入
one after the other 一个接着一个（陆续，相继）
work environment 工作环境
be of prime importance 极其重要
fulfill the requirement 满足要求
a list of 一列，一栏；一份……的单子
set standard 制定标准
be equipped with 装备着

in a professional way 以专业的方式
bring down 降（价）
draw up 拟定，起草
fill job vacancy 填补职位空缺
social media 社会媒体
professional publication 专业刊物
meet ethical standards 符合道德标准
contributing factors 影响因素，促成因素
in return 作为报答；反过来
acquaint oneself with 熟悉（知道，通晓）
cope with 对付，应付，处理
split into 分为，分裂成
personality test 人格测验
fit in to （使）适合；与……融为一体
spatial reasoning 空间推理
abstract reasoning 抽象推理
on a day to day basis 每日
a proportion of 一定比例的

Abbreviations

RPO (Recruitment Process Outsourcing) 招聘流程外包
BPO (Business Process Outsourcing) 业务流程外包

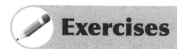

Exercises

EX. 1 Answer the following questions according to the text.

1. What does recruitment refer to within an organization?
2. How can a company possibly attract the top talent in a given industry?
3. What is an excellent way for an organization to gain ground in competitive markets?

4. Among the recruiting tips and strategies mentioned in Text A, which one is of prime importance?
5. Among the venues for recruiting, which one can be useful for a large-scale recruiting for selecting positions?
6. In situations where multiple new jobs are created, why is a job analysis necessary?
7. How do recruiters and agencies filter candidates?
8. What is Recruitment Process Outsourcing, or commonly known as "RPO"?
9. What tests can recruitment and selection tests be divided into?
10. What is the principle behind personality tests?

EX. 2 Translate the following terms or phrases from English into Chinese and vice versa.

1. applicant pool
2. contributing factors
3. fill job vacancy
4. gain a competitive edge
5. in a professional way
6. 招聘会
7. 人格测验
8. *n.* 混乱，混淆，困惑
9. *n.* 咨询公司；顾问职位
10. *n.* 通才，多面手

EX. 3 Translate the following text into Chinese.

Evaluating your organization's strengths, weaknesses, opportunities and threats is referred to as a SWOT analysis. For human resources, a SWOT analysis can be especially helpful in identifying the external factors the company must consider when developing a recruitment and selection process. Carefully weigh your decisions in modifying HR selection methods or strategy based on external factors related to the labor market, economic conditions and industry competitors.

Industry competitors that offer better pay, generous benefits or guaranteed opportunities for professional development can affect the way you recruit and select potential employees. If you're not able to pay more than your competitor or if you can't match tangible rewards and benefits your competitor offers, focus on your company's strengths. A collegial work environment, low turnover, job satisfaction and security, and flexible scheduling often are appealing to job seekers looking for a quality of life instead of the biggest paycheck. Changing the way you hire candidates in the face of industry competition might also include streamlining your selection process so candidates aren't put off by the length of time from application to hire date.

Unit 4

EX. 4 Fill in the blanks with the words given below.

| fill | internally | mission | consistently | proper |
| available | advertised | agencies | approach | utilizing |

Internal and External Recruitment

The recruitment process supplies the organization a pool of potential candidates from which thoughtful selection should be made to fill positions. Successful recruitment begins with __1__ predictive measures. In this phase of the recruitment process, an organization develops plans to __2__ future job openings based on an exploration of future requirements. Steps must be taken to measure available internal and external talent and the present and expected resources __3__ to be expended in order to attract and retain talent.

Recruitment may be conducted __4__ through the promotion of current employees or by way of employee referrals. Internal recruitment is generally the most cost-effective recruitment __5__. Job openings can be __6__ through physical and electronic job postings, in organizational newsletters and office memos. Not only are these methods low-cost, but are also completely controlled by internal recruitment managers who are more in line with the corporate __7__ and goals.

Internal recruitment strategies do not __8__ produce the number or quality of personnel needed. In these cases, the organization needs to recruit from external sources, either by encouraging walk-in applicants, publicizing vacancies in periodicals and internet job boards, and __9__ visual and audio media sources. More direct talent "head hunting" is available in the forms of third-party employment __10__ that orchestrate and maintain through talent searches, corporate job fairs, and college recruitment efforts.

Text B

Recruitment Sources

Every organization has the option of choosing the candidates for its recruitment processes from two kinds of sources: internal and external sources. The sources within the organization itself (like transfer of employees from one department to other, promotions) to fill a position are known as the internal sources of recruitment. Recruitment candidates from all the other sources (like outsourcing agencies, etc.) are known as the external sources of recruitment.

1. Internal Sources

Best employees can be found within the organization. When a vacancy arises in the organization, it may be given to an employee who is already on the pay-roll. Internal sources include promotion, transfer and in certain cases demotion. When a higher post is given to a deserving employee, it motivates all other employees of the organization to work hard. The employees can be informed of such a vacancy by internal advertisement.

1.1 Methods of Internal Sources

Present employees. Promotions and transfers from among the present employees can be a good source of recruitment. Promotion implies upgrading of an employee to a higher position carrying higher status, pay and responsibilities. Promotion from among the present employees is advantageous because the employees promoted are well acquainted with the organizational culture; they get motivated, and it is cheaper also.

Promotion from among present employees also reduces the requirement for job training. However, the disadvantage lies in limiting the choice to a few people and denying hiring of outsiders who may be better qualified and skilled. Furthermore, promotion from among present employees also results in inbreeding which creates frustration among those not promoted.

Transfer refers to shifting an employee from one job to another without any change in the position/post, status and responsibilities. The need for transfer is felt to provide employees a broader and varied base which is considered necessary for promotions. Job rotation involves transfer of employees from one job to another on the lateral basis.

Former employees. Former employees are another source of applicants for vacancies to be filled up in the organization. Retired or retrenched employees may be interested to come back to the company to work on a part-time basis. Similarly, some former employees who left the organization for any reason may again be interested to come back to work. This source has the advantage of hiring people whose performance is already known to the organization.

Employee referrals. This is yet another internal source of recruitment. The existing employees refer their family members, friends and relatives to the company as potential candidates for the vacancies to be filled up in the organization.

This source serves as one of the most effective methods of recruiting people in the organization because employees refer to those potential candidates who meet the company requirements known to them from their own experience. The referred individuals are expected to be similar in type in terms of race and sex, for example, to those who are already working in the organization.

Previous applicants. This is considered as internal source in the sense that applications from the potential candidates are already lying with the organization. Sometimes, the organization contact through mail or messenger these applicants to fill up the vacancies particularly for unskilled or semi-skilled jobs.

1.2 Evaluation of Internal Source

Let us try to evaluate the internal source of recruitment. Obviously, it can be done in terms of its advantages and disadvantages.

The advantages of the internal source of recruitment include the following:

Familiarity with own employees. The organization has more knowledge and familiarity with the strengths and weaknesses of its own employees than of strange and unknown outsiders.

Better use of the talent. The policy of internal recruitment also provides an opportunity to the organization to make a better use of the talents internally available and to develop them further and further.

Economical recruitment. In case of internal recruitment, the organization does not need to spend much money, time and effort to locate and attract the potential candidates. Thus, internal recruitment proves to be economical, or say, inexpensive.

Improving morale. This method makes employees be sure that they would be preferred over the outsiders as and when vacancies will be filled up in their organization.

A motivator. The promotion through internal recruitment serves as a source of motivation for employees to improve their career and income. The employees feel that organization is a place where they can build up their life-long career. Besides, internal recruitment also serves as a means of attracting and retaining competent employees in the organization.

The main drawbacks associated with internal recruitment are as follows:

Limited choice. Internal recruitment limits its choice to the talent available within the organization. Thus, it denies the tapping of talent available in the vast labor market outside the organization. Moreover, internal recruitment serves as a means for "inbreeding", which is never healthy for the future of the organization.

Discouraging competition. In this system, the internal candidates are protected from competition by not giving opportunity to otherwise competent candidates from outside the organization. This, in turn, develops a tendency among the employees to take promotion without showing extra performance.

Stagnation of skills. With the feeling that internal candidates will surely get promoted, their skill in the long run may become stagnant or obsolete. If so, the productivity and efficiency of the organization, in turn, decreases.

Creating conflicts. Conflicts and controversies surface among the internal candidates, whether or not they deserve promotion.

2. External Sources

All organizations have to use external sources for recruitment to higher positions when existing employees are not suitable. More persons are needed when expansions are undertaken.

2.1 Methods of External Sources

Advertisement. It is a method of recruitment frequently used for skilled workers, clerical and higher staff. Advertisement can be given in newspapers and professional journals. These advertisements attract applicants in large number of highly variable quality. The main advantage of this method is that it has a wide reach.

Preparing good advertisement is a specialized task. If a company wants to conceal its name, a "blind advertisement" may be given asking the applicants to apply to postbag or box number or to some advertising agency.

Employment exchanges. Government establishes public employment exchanges throughout the country. These exchanges provide job information to job seekers and help employers in identifying suitable candidates. It is often used as a source of recruitment. In certain cases, it has been made obligatory for the business concerns to notify their vacancies to the employment exchange. In the past, employers used to turn to these agencies only as a last resort. The job-seekers and job-givers are brought into contact by the employment exchanges.

Educational institutes. Various management institutes, engineering colleges, medical colleges are a good source of recruiting well qualified executives, engineers, medical staff, etc. They provide facilities for campus interviews and placements. A close liaison between the company and educational institutions helps in getting suitable candidates. Junior level executives or managerial trainees may be recruited in this way. And this source is also known as campus recruitment.

Placement agencies. Several private consultancy firms perform recruitment functions on behalf of client companies by charging a fee. These agencies are particularly suitable for recruitment of executives and specialists. It is also known as RPO (Recruitment Process Outsourcing).

Labor contractors. Manual workers can be recruited through contractors who maintain close contacts with the sources of such workers. This source is usually used to recruit unskilled and semi-skilled workers for construction jobs. The contractors keep themselves in touch with the labor and bring the workers at the places where they are required. They get commission for the number of persons supplied by them.

Employee referrals/recommendations. Since the present employees know both the company and the candidate being recommended, many organizations have structured system where the current employees of the organization can refer their friends and relatives for some position in their organization. In some organizations these are formal agreements to give priority in recruitment to the candidates recommended by the trade union. In certain cases rewards may also be given if candidates recommended by them are actually selected by the company. However, if recommendation leads to favouritism, it will impair the morale of employees.

Recruitment at factory gate. Unskilled or semi-skilled workers may be recruited at the factory gate. They may be employed whenever a permanent worker is absent. The desirable candidates are typically selected by the first line supervisors. The major disadvantage of this system is that the person selected may not be suitable for the vacancy.

Unsolicited applicants. Many job seekers visit the office of well-known companies on their own. Such callers are considered nuisance to the daily work routine of the enterprise. But it can help in creating the talent pool or the database of the probable candidates for the organization. In the advanced countries, this method of recruitment is very popular.

Labor unions. In certain occupations like construction, hotels, maritime industry, etc. (i.e. industries where there is instability of employment), all recruits usually come from unions. It is advantageous from the management point of view because it saves expenses of recruitment. However, in other industries, unions may be asked to recommend candidates either as a goodwill gesture or as a courtesy towards the union.

Apart from these major sources of external recruitment, there are certain other sources which are exploited by companies from time to time. These include special lectures delivered by recruiter in different institutions, though apparently these lectures do not pertain to recruitment directly. Then there are video films which are sent to various concerns and institutions so as to show the history and development of the company. These films present the story of company to various audiences, thus creating interest in them. Moreover, various firms organize trade shows which attract many prospective employees. Many a time advertisements may be made for a special class of work force (say married ladies) who worked prior to their marriage. These ladies can also prove to be very good source of work force. Similarly there is the labor market consisting of physically handicapped. Visits to other companies also help in finding new sources of recruitment.

2.2 Evaluation of External Sources

Like internal sources of recruitment, external sources are mixed of merits and demerits. The following are the main merits:

Availability of suitable persons. Internal sources, sometimes, may not be able to supply suitable persons from within. External sources do give a wide choice to the management. A large number of applicants may be willing to join the organization. They will also be suitable as per the requirements of skill, training and education.

Bringing new ideas. The selection of persons from outside sources will have the benefit of new ideas. The persons having experience in other concerns will be able to suggest new things and methods. This will keep the organization in a competitive position.

Economical. This method of recruitment can prove to be economical because new employees are already trained and experienced and do not require much training for the jobs.

Providing healthy competition. The external members are supposed to be more trained and efficient. With such a background, they work with positive attitude and greater vigor. This helps create healthy competition and conducive work environment in the organization.

However, the external sources of recruitment suffer from certain demerits too:

Demoralization. When new persons from outside join the organization, present employees feel demoralized because these positions should have gone to them. There can be a heart burning among old employees. Some employees may even leave the enterprise and go for better avenues in other concerns. Worse still, the old staff may not co-operate with the new employees because they feel that their right has been snatched away by them. This problem will be acute especially when persons for higher positions are recruited from outside.

Expensive and time consuming. The process of recruiting from outside is very expensive. It starts with inserting costly advertisements in the media and then arranging written tests and conducting interviews. In spite of all this, there is no guarantee that organization will get good and suitable candidates and if suitable candidates are not available, the whole process will have to be repeated.

Problem of maladjustment. There may be a possibility that the new entrants have not been able to adjust in the new environment. They may not temperamentally adjust with the new persons. In such cases either the persons may leave themselves or management may have to replace them. These things have adverse effect on the working of the organization.

However, in spite of its demerits, external sources of recruitment are desirable for the following reasons:

• The required qualities such as will, skill, talent, knowledge are available from external sources.

• It can help in bringing new ideas, better techniques and improved methods to the organization.

• The selection of candidates will be without pre-conceived notions or reservations.

• The cost of employees will be minimum because candidates selected in this method will be placed in the minimum pay scale.

• The entry of new persons with varied experience and talent will help in human resource mix.

• The existing employees will also broaden their personality.

• The entry of qualitative persons from outside will be in the long-run interest of the organization.

source [sɔ:s] n. 来源，发源地
option ['ɔpʃən] n. 选项，选择权
deserving [di'zə:viŋ] adj. 应得的，值得的
imply [im'plai] v. 暗示，意味，隐含
advantageous [,ædvən'teidʒəs] adj. 有利的
deny [di'nai] v. 拒绝承认，否认知情
inbreeding [in'bri:diŋ] n. 同系繁殖，近亲交配
frustration [frʌs'treiʃən] n. 挫折，失败；令人沮丧的东西
lateral ['lætərəl] adj. 横向的，侧面的
retrench [ri'trentʃ] v. 减少开支，削减花费
referral [ri'fə:rəl] n. 介绍，指引
similar ['similə] adj. 相似的，类似的
familiarity [fə,mili'ærəti] n. 熟悉，通晓，认识
outsider ['aut'saidə] n. 局外人，圈外人

economical [,i:kə'nɔmikəl] adj. 经济的，节约的，合算的
locate [ləu'keit] v. 查找……的地点，确定……的位置
tap [tæp] v. 开发，利用
tendency ['tendənsi] n. 趋势，倾向
stagnant ['stægnənt] adj. 不流动的，停滞的；不景气的
obsolete ['ɔbsəli:t] adj. 已废弃的；过时的
surface ['sə:fis] v. 浮到水面；显露
clerical ['klerikəl] adj. 文书的，办事员的
conceal [kən'si:l] v. 隐藏，隐瞒，遮住
obligatory [ɔ'bligətəri] adj. 强制性的，义务的，必需的
notify ['nəutifai] v. 通知，布告
resort [ri'zɔ:t] n. 求助；诉诸；求助或凭借的对象
institute ['institju:t] n. （教育、专业等）机构

Unit 4

liaison [li(:)'eizɑːn] n. 联络，联络人
junior ['dʒuːnjə] adj. 资历较浅的，下级的；年少的
charge [tʃɑːdʒ] v. 索价
contractor [kən'træktə] n. 订约人，承包人
priority [prai'ɔrəti] n. 优先权；优先
favoritism ['feivəritizəm] n. 偏爱，得宠，偏袒
impair [im'pεə] v. 损害；削弱
unsolicited ['ʌnsə'lisitid] adj. 未经请求的，主动提供的
nuisance ['njuːsns] n. 讨厌的人或东西
routine [ruː'tiːn] n. 例行公事，常规
maritime ['mæritaim] adj. 海事的，海运的
instability [,instə'biləti] n. 不稳定，不稳固
goodwill [gud'wil] n. 善意，友好；信誉
courtesy ['kəːtəsi] n. 礼貌，好意
exploit [iks'plɔit] v. 利用，开发；剥削
apparently [ə'pærəntli] adv. 表面上，似乎，显然

handicapped ['hændikæpt] adj. 残废的，有生理缺陷的
demerit [di'merit] n. 缺点，短处，过失
demoralization [di,mɔrəlai'zeiʃən] n. 士气沮丧；道德颓废，堕落
avenue ['ævinjuː] n. 途径，手段；林荫道；大街
snatch [snætʃ] v. 夺取，抓住
acute [ə'kjuːt] adj. 严重的；急性的；剧烈的
insert [in'səːt] v. 插入，嵌入
maladjustment [,mælə'dʒʌstmənt] n. 不适应环境，失调
entrant ['entrənt] n. 新就业者，新成员
temperamentally [,tempərə'mentli] adv. 喜怒无常地；气质地
pre-conceived [,priː-kən'siːvd] adj. （思想、观点等）事先形成的

Phrases

outsourcing agency 外包机构
be informed of 得知，知悉；接到……的通知
be acquainted with 熟悉
lie in 在于；位于
public employment exchange 公共就业服务
turn to 求助于；转向
educational institute 教育机构
on behalf of 为了……的利益，代表
charge a fee 收取费用

labor contractor 包工头
talent pool 人才库；人才储备
labor union 工会
point of view 观点
pertain to 属于；关于
trade show 销售展
as per 按照，根据
worse still 更糟的是
in spite of 不顾，不管；尽管
have adverse effect on 对……有不利影响

Exercises

EX. 5 Fill in the following blanks with the information from Text B.

1. The sources within the organization itself (like transfer of employees from one department to other, promotions) to fill a position are known as _____ of recruitment.

2. _____ implies upgrading of an employee to a higher position carrying higher status, pay and responsibilities.

3. _____ refers to shifting an employee from one job to another without any change in the position/post, status and responsibilities.

4. _____ may be interested to come back to the company to work on a part-time basis.

5. The promotion through internal recruitment serves as _____ for employees to improve their career and income.

6. _____ are established by the government to provide job information to job seekers and help employers in identifying suitable candidates.

7. Some organizations usually recruit unskilled and semi-skilled workers for construction jobs through _____.

8. Although _____ are seen as nuisance to the daily work routine of the enterprise, yet it can help in creating the talent pool for the organization.

9. With the outsiders joining the organization, present employees tend to feel _____ because they maintain that the outsiders have deprived them of their positions.

10. By external sources of recruitment, the recruiters will select the candidates without _____.

Supplementary Reading

Text	Notes
Job Interview In common parlance[1], the word "interview" refers to a one-on-one conversation with one person acting in the role of the interviewer and the other in the role of the interviewee. The interviewer asks questions, the interviewee responds, with participants taking turns talking. Interviews usually involve a transfer of information from interviewee to interviewer, which is	[1] parlance ['pɑːləns] n. 说法，用语

usually the primary[2] purpose of the interview, although information transfers can happen in both directions simultaneously[3].

Interviews can happen in a wide variety of contexts. Interviews in an employment context are typically called job interviews. A job interview is a one-on-one interview consisting of a conversation between a job applicant and a representative[4] of an employer which is conducted to assess whether the applicant should be hired. Interviews are one of the most popularly used devices for employee selection. Interviews vary in the extent to which the questions are structured, from a totally unstructured and free-wheeling conversation to a structured interview in which an applicant is asked a pre-determined[5] list of questions in a specified order; structured interviews are usually more accurate predictors[6] of which applicants will make good employees, according to research studies.

A job interview typically precedes[7] the hiring decision. The interview is usually preceded by the evaluation of submitted[8] resumes from interested candidates, possibly by examining job applications or reading many resumes. Next, after this screening, a small number of candidates for interviews is selected.

1. Process

One way to think about the interview process is as three separate, albeit[9] related, phases:

- the pre-interview phase which occurs before the interviewer and candidate meet;
- the interview phase where the interview is conducted;
- the post-interview phase where the interviewer forms judgments of candidate qualifications and makes final decisions.

Although separate, these three phases are related. That is, impressions interviewers form early on may affect how they view the person in a later phase.

1.1 The Pre-interview Phase

It encompasses the information available to the interviewer beforehand (e.g. resumes, test scores, social networking site information) and the perceptions[10] interviewers form about applicants from this information prior to the actual face-to-face interaction between two individuals. In this phase,

[2] **primary** ['praɪməri] *adj.* 首要的，主要的

[3] **simultaneously** [ˌsɪməl'teɪniəsli] *adv.* 同时地

[4] **representative** [ˌreprɪ'zentətɪv] *n.* 代表；众议员

[5] **pre-determined** [ˌpriː-dɪ'tɜːmɪnd] *adj.* 预先决定的

[6] **predictor** [prɪ'dɪktə] *n.* 预言者；预报器

[7] **precede** [prɪ'siːd] *v.* 在……之前，先于

[8] **submit** [səb'mɪt] *v.* 提交，递交

[9] **albeit** [ɔːl'biːɪt] *conj.* 虽然（即使）

[10] **perception** [pə'sepʃən] *n.* 观念；洞察力

interviewers are likely to already have ideas about the characteristics that would make a person ideal or qualified for the position. Interviewers also have information about the applicant usually in the form of a resume, test scores, or prior contacts with the applicant. Interviewers then often integrate information that they have on an applicant with their ideas about the ideal employee to form a pre-interview evaluation of the candidate. In this way, interviewers typically have an impression of you even before the actual face-to-face interview interaction. Nowadays with recent technological advancements, we must be aware that interviewers have an even larger amount of information available on some candidates. For example, interviewers can obtain information from search engines (e.g. Google, Bing, Yahoo), blogs, and even social networks (e.g. Linkedin, Facebook, Twitter). While some of this information may be job-related, some of it may not be. In some cases, a review of Facebook may reveal undesirable[11] behaviors such as drunkenness or drug use. Despite the relevance of the information, any information interviewers obtain about the applicant before the interview is likely to influence their pre-interview impression of the candidate. And, why is all this important? It is important because what interviewers think about you before they meet you can have an effect on how they might treat you in the interview and what they remember about you. Furthermore, researchers have found that what interviewers think about the applicant before the interview (pre-interview phase) is related to how they evaluate the candidate after the interview, despite how the candidate may have performed during the interview.

1.2 The Interview Phase

The interview phase entails[12] the actual conduct of the interview, the interaction[13] between the interviewer and the applicant. The interviewer's initial impressions about the applicant before the interview may influence the amount of time an interviewer spends in the interview with the applicant, the interviewer's behavior and questioning of the applicant, and the interviewer's post-interview evaluations. Pre-interview impressions can also affect what the interviewer notices about the interviewee, recalls from the interview, and how an

[11] undesirable [ˌʌndɪˈzaɪərəbl] *adj.* 不受欢迎的

[12] entail [ɪnˈteɪl] *v.* 使必需
[13] interaction [ˌɪntərˈækʃən] *n.* 相互作用，相互影响；互动交流

interviewer interprets what the applicant says and does in the interview.

As interviews are typically conducted face-to-face, over the phone, or through video conferencing[14], they are a social interaction between at least two individuals. Thus, the behavior of the interviewer during the interview likely "leaks" information to the interviewee. That is, you can sometimes tell during the interview whether the interviewer thinks positively or negatively about you. Knowing this information can actually affect how the applicant behaves, resulting in a self-fulfilling prophecy[15] effect. For example, interviewees who feel the interviewer does not think they are qualified may be more anxious and feel they need to prove they are qualified. Such anxiety may hamper[16] how well they actually perform and present themselves during the interview, fulfilling the original thoughts of the interviewer. Alternatively, interviewees who perceive[17] an interviewer believes they are qualified for the job may feel more at ease[18] and comfortable during the exchange, and consequently actually perform better in the interview. It should be noted again, that because of the dynamic[19] nature of the interview, the interaction between the behaviors and thoughts of both parties is a continuous process whereby information is processed and informs subsequent behavior, thoughts, and evaluations.

1.3 The Post-interview Phase

After the interview is conducted, the interviewer must form an evaluation of the interviewee's qualifications for the position. The interviewer most likely takes into consideration all the information, even from the pre-interview phase, and integrates it to form a post-interview evaluation of the applicant. In the final stage of the interview process, the interviewer uses his/her evaluation of the candidate (i.e. in the form of interview ratings or judgment) to make a final decision. Sometimes other selection tools (e.g. work samples, cognitive ability[20] tests, personality tests) are used in combination with the interview to make final hiring decisions; however, interviews remain the most commonly used selection device in North America.

[14] video conferencing: 视频会议

[15] self-fulfilling prophecy: 应验的预言

[16] hamper ['hæmpə] v. 妨碍，阻止

[17] perceive [pə'siːv] v. 认为，理解；注意

[18] at ease: 不拘束，自在

[19] dynamic [dai'næmik] adj. 动力的，动态的；有活力的

[20] cognitive ability: 认知能力

Although the description of the interview process above focuses on the perspective[21] of the interviewer, job applicants also gather information on the job and/or organization and form impressions prior to the interview. The interview is a two-way exchange and applicants are also making decisions about whether the company is a good fit for them. Essentially, the process model illustrates[22] that the interview is not an isolated interaction, but rather a complex process that begins with two parties forming judgments and gathering information, and ends with a final interviewer decision.

2. Constructs

Researchers have attempted to identify which interview strategies or "constructs" can help interviewers choose the best candidate. Research suggests that interviews capture a wide variety of applicant attributes. Constructs can be classified into three categories: job-relevant content, interviewee performance (behavior unrelated to the job but which influences the evaluation), and job-irrelevant interviewer biases[23].

2.1 Job-relevant Interview Content

Interview questions are generally designed to tap applicant attributes that are specifically relevant to the job for which the person is applying. The job-relevant applicant attributes that the questions purportedly assess are thought to be necessary for one to successfully perform on the job. The job-relevant constructs that have been assessed in the interview can be classified into three categories: general traits, experiential factors, and core job elements. The first category refers to relatively stable applicant traits. The second category refers to job knowledge that the applicant has acquired over time. The third category refers to the knowledge, skills, and abilities associated with the job.

2.2 Interviewee Performance

Interviewer evaluations of applicant responses also tend to be colored by how an applicant behaves in the interview. These behaviors may not be directly related to the constructs the interview questions were designed to assess, but can be related to aspects of the job for which they are applying. Applicants without realizing it may engage in a number of behaviors that influence ratings of their performance. The applicant may have

[21] perspective [pə'spektiv] n. 观点，看法

[22] illustrate ['iləstreit] v. （用示例、图画等）说明

[23] bias ['baiəs] n. 偏见，倾向，偏爱

acquired these behaviors during training or from previous interview experience. These interviewee performance constructs can also be classified into three categories: social effectiveness skills, interpersonal presentation[24], and personal/contextual factors.

2.3 Job-irrelevant Interviewer Biases

The following are personal and demographic[25] characteristics that can potentially influence interviewer evaluations of interviewee responses. These factors are typically not relevant to whether the individual can do the job (that is, not related to job performance), thus, their influence on interview ratings should be minimized or excluded. In fact, there are laws in many countries that prohibit consideration of many of these protected classes of people when making selection decisions. Using structured interviews with multiple interviewers coupled with[26] training may help reduce the effect of the following characteristics on interview ratings. The list of job-irrelevant interviewer biases is presented below:

Attractiveness. Applicant physical attractiveness can influence interviewer's evaluation of one's interview performance.

Race. Whites tend to score higher than Blacks and Hispanics[27]; racial[28] similarity between interviewer and applicant, on the other hand, has not been found to influence interview ratings.

Gender. Females tend to receive slightly higher interview scores than their male counterparts[29]; gender similarity does not seem to influence interview ratings.

Similarities in background and attitudes. Interviewers perceived interpersonal attraction was found to influence interview ratings.

Culture. Applicants with an ethnic[30] name and a foreign accent were viewed less favorably than applicants with just an ethnic name and no accent or an applicant with a traditional name with or without an accent.

The extent to which ratings of interviewee performance reflect certain constructs varies widely depending on the level of structure of the interview, the kind of questions asked, the interviewer or applicant biases, applicant professional dress

[24] presentation [ˌprezenˈteiʃən] n. 表现，显示，呈现

[25] demographic [deməˈgræfik] adj. 人口统计学的，人口统计的

[26] couple with: 接在一起

[27] Hispanic [hisˈpænik] n. 讲西班牙语的人；美籍西班牙人

[28] racial [ˈreiʃəl] adj. 种族的，人种的

[29] counterpart [ˈkauntəpɑːt] n. 职务相当的人；对应物

[30] ethnic [ˈeθnik] adj. 种族的，民族的

or non-verbal[31] behavior, and a host of other factors. For example, some research suggests that the applicant's cognitive ability, education, training, and work experiences may be better captured in unstructured interviews, whereas the applicant's job knowledge, organizational fit, interpersonal skills, and applied knowledge may be better captured in a structured interview.

[31] non-verbal [nɒn-'vɜ:bəl] adj. 非言辞语的，不用语言的

参考译文（Text A）

招　聘

招聘是人力资源管理的核心职能。招聘指的是企业吸引、甄选和指定合适的工作人选（无论是永久性的还是临时性的）的整个过程。招聘还可以指为无薪职位甄选工作人员的过程，如志愿者或无报酬的实习生。经理、人力资源专家、招聘专员都可以负责实施招聘工作，但在某些情况下，企业可利用公共部门的就业机构、商业招聘机构，或专业猎头公司来承担部分招聘工作。

1. 招聘的目的和目标

在制定招聘策略时，每个公司都需要考虑其特定的目的和目标。成功的招聘策略允许一家公司在增长利润的同时，找到其所需要的人力来实现业务目标和目的。最有利的创新举措是创建一支拥有共同目标的多样化团队。

吸引顶尖人才

招聘能引入创新想法并解决公司缺点。通过有针对性的招聘工作、优厚的薪酬和福利，以及强大的企业文化，公司有可能吸引到某个特定行业的顶尖人才。虽然从求职者库招聘最佳候选人是一件易事，但吸引顶尖人才往往需要更多的人际网络。通过外包给招聘公司或从当地大学招聘能扩充候选人库，从而覆盖需要的技能和经验。

获得竞争优势

在许多行业，企业通过雇用并留住最有潜质的求职者来获得竞争优势。通常，行业专家在更换工作时，会带走一批忠实的顾客。借助行业影响力招聘求职者是在竞争激烈的市场中取得优势的最好途径。

工作场所多样性

《美国残疾人法案》和平等就业机会委员会为工作场所的多样性提供了指导方针。对于拥有超过15名员工的公司来说，雇佣多样化的劳动力是一项法律要求。如果公司的劳动力缺少多样性，那么你可以将招聘场所延伸至网络、招聘会和大学，以扩大范围，招聘到各种各样的求职者。

公司发展

招聘可以使公司获得目前缺乏的技能和经验。通过注入公司在壮大过程中所需的新思

路和机会，促进公司的发展。新员工，从应届大学毕业生到行业领导，都会给公司带来新的想法和创新的解决方案，以应对公司面临的挑战。

2. 招聘计划

要获得合适候选人，必须有组织、有系统地完成招聘过程。精心设计的招聘计划是一种有助于企业吸引和聘用到每个职位最佳候选人的积极方法。它可以帮助公司成功地完成招聘过程，同时帮助你了解招聘过程涉及的一系列步骤。通过招聘合适的应聘者，人力资源经理能够创造一个良好的工作环境，为公司未来的快速发展奠定基础。招聘过程中的任何混乱都会导致候选人的误选，从而影响公司效率和盈利。为了给公司起草一份完善的招聘计划，你必须考虑以下招聘技巧和策略：

招聘的员工人数

无论是志愿者、学院或任何企业的招聘计划，决定各项工作的求职者数量非常重要。这个数字是根据公司各部门的实际需要而定的。如果招聘的候选人数量低于实际要求，那么现有员工会将有很大的工作压力，而过度招聘又会影响公司的财务状况。因此，必须根据需要确定招聘数量。

决定工作要求

招聘计划涉及公司对求职者的期望以及他们获得这份工作所应具备的知识。公司人力资源部可以在招聘前准备一份求职者具备的资格和技能清单，满足这些要求的人自然应该被招聘进来，而那些不符合要求的人将被认为不适合从事这份工作。

决定甄选类型

事先决定甄选步骤，避免最后一分钟的混乱，这一点非常重要。理想情况下，甄选过程应该包括笔试、小组讨论和面试。不同的部门组织可能有不同的甄选过程，这取决于他们的需要。对处于当今竞争时代的人力资源经理来说，决定这个过程确实是一个很大的挑战。就评定求职者而言，招聘人员必须制定并遵循标准。当我们考虑甄选过程时，决定招聘小组同样很重要。招聘人员的工作描述提供了更多的信息：

招聘场所

在企业，公司办公室、行政酒店和招聘会都可以作为招聘的场所。招聘会对大规模的招聘活动很有用。招聘场所需要备齐专业面试的必要设备。

招聘预算

理想的招聘计划应该包括招聘预算，这将有助于公司高级管理层知道他们在整个招聘过程中的必要花费。基于这些数据，如果招聘的费用太高，那么可以采取一些削减花费的措施来降低公司的开支。

这种有效的招聘计划可能是促进企业业务增长的最佳途径，以良好的方式实施计划对于取得积极的成果则更为重要。

3. 招聘过程

招聘和甄选过程对新老企业都很重要。人力资源部需要获得人才专家的支持和专业知识。他们协助招聘经理制定程序，确保公司领导做出明智的招聘决定。下面是招聘和甄选过程的几个步骤：

步骤1：工作分析

在产生了多个新的工作岗位并首次招募，或出现职位空缺，或工作性质发生了根本性转变的情况下，可进行工作分析来记录工作所要求的知识、技能、能力和其他特性（KSAO）。工作分析中要有诸如工作描述和工作规范的相关信息文档。通常，公司对现有的职位已经有了一些工作描述，而这些文件可能需要审查和更新，以反映当前的要求。在招聘之前，应该完成规范的说明。

步骤2：采购

采购是指利用一个或多个战略来吸引或确定填补职位空缺的候选人。它可能涉及内部或外部的招聘宣传，利用适当的媒体，如门户网站、地方或全国性报纸、社交媒体、商业媒体、专业招聘媒体、专业刊物、橱窗广告、职业介绍所，或以互联网为媒介的各种方式。

另外，雇主可利用招聘咨询公司或机构找一些稀缺候选人。这类候选人对现在的工作通常很满意，对离职不积极。这项对候选人的初步研究——也叫"名单生成"——可以产生潜在候选人的相关联系信息，招聘人员可以谨慎地联系并筛选他们。

步骤3：筛选和甄选

心理测试可以测评候选人的各种知识、技能、能力及其他特质，包括读写能力。评估也可用来测量身体能力。招聘人员和机构可以使用求职者跟踪系统来筛选求职者，用软件对求职者进行心理测试和绩效评估。在许多国家，法律要求雇主必须确保其筛选和甄选过程遵守平等机会原则，符合道德标准。

雇主往往会承认这类候选人的价值，他们具备人际交往或团队领导等常用技能。许多公司，包括跨国公司和那些招聘大量不同国籍员工的公司，还经常关注候选人是否能适应公司的主流文化。

此外，对于大多数公司而言，钱和工作稳定性这两个因素能促进残疾员工的生产力，反过来，也促进了企业的发展和成功。雇用残疾员工利大于弊，他们的日常生产没有差别。考虑到他们自身的情况，这些员工更有可能适应环境，熟悉设备，并能够像其他员工一样解决问题，战胜逆境。

与此同时，许多大公司认识到多样化在全球经济中对成功竞争的必要性。其他组织，如大学和学院，都在慢慢地接受多样性，将其看作他们成功的重要价值观。

步骤4：招聘流程外包（RPO）

招聘流程外包，或俗称"RPO"，是一种业务流程外包（BPO），即公司雇佣第三方机构管理其全部或部分招聘流程。

4．招聘和选拔测试

招聘和选拔测试旨在让雇主深入了解求职者与他人共事的情况、处理压力的能力，以及他们是否达到工作的技能需求。

招聘和甄选测试只是招聘过程的一部分。求职者仍要按照要求填写申请表、递交简历并至少参加一次面试。所有这些都会使雇主了解求职者的一些情况，并帮助他们选拔空缺职位的最佳人选。招聘和选拔测试可分为人格测试和能力测试。

人格测试的理念是，通过询问求职者的感受、想法和行为来量化他或她的人格特征。人格发挥着重大作用，它决定求职者是否具有雇主所期望的工作热情和动机，以及在个性、态度和总的工作风格方面,他们是否能融入该组织。甄选的早期阶段可以采取直截了当的人格测试,筛选出不适合这项工作的候选人。

　　能力测试旨在评估求职者的智力表现。这些类型的测试大致可分为以下几组(见下图),求职者按要求可以参加只包含数字问题的考试,或者参加由数字和其他类型的问题组成的考试。

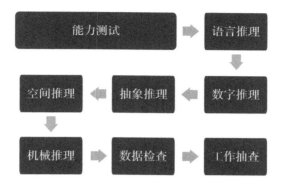

　　这些在很大程度上取决于求职者所申请的工作。例如,要每天与数字打交道的工作,其数字推理题的比例可能较高,而信息技术工作的测试会有更高比例的抽象推理题。

Unit 5

Text A

An Overview of Employee Placement

The ultimate purpose of selection is placement, or fitting a person to the right jobs. Employee placement is a process of allocating employed individuals to certain jobs that match their skills and abilities. By performing this process, a business company attempts to create an effective working environment in which there is a good match between management needs and employee qualifications. Employee placement serves as a great method of avoiding employee overload and layoff. Therefore, more than anything else, placement of human resources should be seen as a matching process. How well an employee is matched to a job affects the amount and quality of the employee's work. This matching also directly affects training and operating costs. Individuals who are unable to produce the expected amount and quality of work can cost an organization a great deal of money and time.

1. Employee Placement Theory

The theory of Person-Environment (P-E) assumes that positive responses occur when individuals tend to fit or match the environment. For example, when a good fit exists in between person and environment, P-E fit theories of vocational choice propose occurrence of high satisfaction, mental and physical well-being. Extensive research supports the proposition that individuals are satisfied with and adjust most easily to jobs that are congruent with their own career-relevant personality types.

P-E fit is conceptualized as a general term, under which fall more specific notions of fit. In the recruitment and selection domain, two common forms of fit identified are Person-Job fit and Person-Organization fit. The former is a match between an individual and requirements of a specific job. Companies often pursue that Person-Job fit so as to match the applicant's knowledge and skills to the requirements of specific job openings and focus on an applicant's ability to perform right away without any training. And the latter is a match between an individual and broader organizational attributes. Companies, while pursuing P-O fit, focus on how well individuals fit with values of their company and culture.

1.1 Person-Job Fit

The concept of Person-Job fit is the traditional foundation for employee selection. The primary concern was limited to finding applicants with the right skills and abilities for an available job in the organization. P-J fit is conceptualized as the match between individual knowledge, skills, and abilities (KSA) and demands of the job or the needs/desires of an individual and what is provided by the job. Based on realistic job previews, accurate and realistic job information enables applicants to assess the degree of congruence between their KSA and the job requirements. Applicants who perceive a fit between their KSA and the job requirements are probable to remain in the selection process and accept a job offer. RJP research has shown that accurate and realistic job information during recruitment and selection is associated with positive work outcomes (e.g. low attrition from recruitment process, high job satisfaction, low voluntary turnover, high work performance).

The operational aspect of P-J fit focuses on need-supplies and demand-abilities perspective. Therefore, P-J fit can be defined as the fit between desires of a person vs. attributes of a job or abilities of a person vs. demands of a job. The need-supplies and demand-abilities fit are extended conceptualizations of complementary fit. In employee selection practices, strategies used to assess P-J fit include tests, reference checks, resumes and a variety of other selection tools.

Considerable evidences show that a high level of P-J fit has positive outcomes. Low stress in job, attendance, retention, performance and job satisfaction are outcomes positively affected by P-J fit. Obviously, without a good fit between the KSA of the person and the demands of the job, the likelihood of lower employee performance, higher turnover and absenteeism, and other HR problems increase. Much of selection is concerned with gathering needed information on the applicants' KSA through application forms, resumes, interviews, tests, and other means.

1.2 Person-Organization Fit

Person-Organization (P-O) fit can be defined as compatibility between people and organizations. With regards to employee selection research, P-O fit can be conceptualized as the match between an applicant and boarder organizational attributes. The key to maintain the flexible and committed work, which is necessary in a competitive and tight labor market, is P-O fit. Typically, four operationalizations of P-O fit are identified:

• measuring the similarity between basic characteristics of people and organizations; the way to measure this is to check the congruence between individual and organizational values;

• determining the goal congruence between individuals and organizational leaders;

• matching between individual preferences or needs and organizational structures and systems;

• matching between individual characteristics of individual personality and organizational climate or organizational personality. Organizational climate is often operationalized in terms of supplies such as rewards systems or communication formats.

Person-Organization fit is important when general factors of job success are as important as specific KSA. For example, if an employer hires at the entry level and promotes from within for most jobs, specific KSA might be less important than general cognitive and problem-solving abilities and work ethic. Ability to learn allows a person to grasp new information and make good decisions based on that job knowledge. Work ethic might include thoroughness, responsibility and an organized approach to the job.

Determining Person-Organization fit may require use of multiple selection means and take considerable time and effort. Multiple in-depth interviews, use of extensive abilities, aptitudes, and psychological tests, and involvement of several levels of managers and supervisors are just some ways of ensuring Person-Organization fit.

High level of P-O fit can be related to positive outcomes. P-O fit can be tied to job satisfaction and organization commitment. This fit could also predict intention of quit and turnover, and is also related to citizenship behaviors, contextual performance and self reported teamwork.

To conclude, as high levels of P-J and P-O fit leads to positive outcomes such as job satisfaction, performance and organizational commitment, both P-J fit and P-O fit elements should be included in the selection process of an employee. Considering P-J fit during the earlier or initial stages of selection and measuring and the P-O fit during the later stages of selection process of an employee would be ideal.

2. Principles of Placement

A few basic principles should be followed at the time of placement of a worker on the job. This is elaborated below:

• Man should be placed on the job according to the requirements of the job. The job should not be adjusted according to the qualifications or requirements of the man. Job first, man next should be the principle of the placement.

• The job should be offered to the person according to his qualification. This should be neither higher nor lower than the qualification.

• The employee should be made conversant with the working conditions prevailing in the organization and all things relating to the job. He should also be made aware of the penalties if he commits the wrong.

• While introducing the job to the new employees, an effort should be made to develop a sense of loyalty and cooperation in him so that he may realize his responsibility towards the job and the organization.

• The placement should be ready before the joining date of the newly selected person.

• The placement in the initial period may be temporary as changes are likely after the completion of training. The employee may be later transferred to the job where he can do better.

Proper placement helps to improve the employees' morale. The capacity of the employees can be utilized fully. The right placement also reduces labor turnover, absenteeism and the accident rate as well. Then the employee can adjust to the required environment of the organization effectively, and the performance of the employee will not be hampered.

3. Problems of the Placement

The main problem of placement arises when the recruiters look at the individuals but not the job. Often, the individual does not work independent of the others. Jobs in this context are classified into the three categories:

- Independent jobs. In the independent jobs the non-overlapping territories are allocated to each employee, e.g. in the sales. In such situations, the activities of the one employee have little bearing on the activities of the other workers. The independent jobs do not pose great problems in placement. Each employee has to be evaluated about his capabilities and the interests and those required on the job. The objective of the placement will be to fill the job with people who have at least the minimum required qualifications. People should be placed on the job that will make the best possible use of their talents, given available jobs or HR constraints.

- Dependent jobs may be sequential or pooled. In sequential jobs, the activities of the one employee are dependent on the activities of the fellow employee, e.g. assembly lines are the best example of such job.

- In pooled jobs, there is a high interdependence among the jobs. The final output is the result of the contribution of all the workers. It is team work that matters. Placement for this is quite difficult.

placement ['pleismənt] *n.* 安置, 放置; 配置
ultimate ['ʌltimit] *adj.* 最后的, 最终的; 极限的
allocate ['æləukeit] *n.* 配给, 分配
match [mætʃ] *v.* 和……相配; 相一致
overload [,əuvə'ləud] *n.* 过多, 过量, 超负荷
layoff ['leiɔ:f] *n.* 临时解雇; 停工, 停止活动
assume [ə'sju:m] *v.* 假定, 认为; 承担
vocational [vəu'keiʃənəl] *adj.* 职业的, 行业的

propose [prə'pəuz] *v.* 提议, 建议; 打算, 计划; 求婚
occurrence [ə'kʌrəns] *n.* 发生; 事件; 出现
extensive [iks'tensiv] *adj.* 广阔的, 广大的; 范围广泛的
proposition [,prɔpə'ziʃən] *n.* 主张, 建议; 命题
congruent ['kɔŋgruənt] *adj.* 一致的, 全等的
conceptualize [kən'septjuəlaiz] *v.* 使概念化
notion ['nəuʃən] *n.* 观念, 概念; 想法, 主张

Unit 5

foundation [faun'deiʃən] n. 基础；地基；基金（会）
congruence ['kɔŋgruəns] n. 一致，全等；适合
perceive [pə'siːv] v. 理解；意识到；察觉
attrition [ə'triʃən] n. 消耗；人员耗损
turnover ['təːnˌəuvə] n. （员工）流动；营业额；成交量
conceptualization [kənˌseptjuəlai'zei-ʃən] n. 化为概念，概念化
complementary [kɔmplə'mentəri] adj. 互补的；补充的，补足的
considerable [kən'sidərəbl] adj. 相当大（或多）的；应考虑的
absenteeism [æbsən'tiːizəm] n. 旷工，旷课
compatibility [kəmˌpæti'biləti] n. 协调；兼容
operationalization [ˌɔpəˈreiʃənəlai'zei-ʃən] n. 操作化
similarity [ˌsimi'lærəti] n. 类似；相像性
cognitive ['kɔgnitiv] adj. 认知的；认识的
ethic ['eθik] n. （复数）行为准则；伦理，伦理观
thoroughness ['θʌrənis] n. 彻底性；完全，十分

commitment [kə'mitmənt] n. 承诺，保证；献身；委任
contextual [kɔn'tekstjuəl] adj. 上下文的；前后有关的
elaborate [i'læbərət] v. 详细地说明；推敲
conversant [kən'vəːsənt] adj. 熟悉的；亲近的
prevail [pri'veil] v. 流行，盛行；获胜，占优势
penalty ['penəlti] n. 刑罚，惩罚
commit [kə'mit] v. 犯罪，做错事；承诺，使……担义务
completion [kəm'pliːʃən] n. 完成，结束；实现
morale [mə'rɑːl] n. 士气，精神面貌
utilize [juː'tilaiz] v. 利用，使用
hamper ['hæmpə] v. 妨碍，限制；使困累
non-overlapping ['nɔn-əuvə'læpiŋ] adj. 无重叠的
constraint [kən'streint] n. 约束，限制；强制
sequential [si'kwenʃəl] adj. 按次序的，相继的
assembly [ə'sembli] n. 装配；集会
interdependence [ˌintədi'pendəns] n. 互相依赖

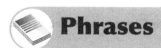

Phrases

attempt to 尝试，企图；试图做某事
employee overload 员工超负荷
be congruent with 与……一致
with regards to 关于，至于
be tied to 以……为条件；束缚于，捆绑于
adjust to 调整，调节

be conversant with 精通，通晓；和……有关
be independent of 独立于……之外的；与……无关的
have bearing on 与……有关
assembly line 装配线，流水线

P-E fit (Person-Environment fit) 人与环境匹配
P-J fit (Person-Job fit) 人与工作匹配
P-O fit (Person-Organization fit) 人与组织匹配
RJP (Realistic Job Preview) 真实工作预览

EX. 1 Answer the following questions according to the text.

1. What is employee placement?
2. What does a business company attempt to do by performing the process of employee placement?
3. What does the theory of person-environment assume?
4. What is Person-Job fit? And what is Person-Organization fit?
5. What problems may increase without a good fit between the KSA of the person and the demands of the job?
6. How can the similarity between basic characteristics of people and organizations be measured?
7. What are some of the ways to ensure Person-Organization fit?
8. What should be the principle of the placement, "job first, man next" or "man first, job next"?
9. When does the main problem of placement arise?
10. Why is placement for pooled jobs quite difficult?

EX. 2 Translate the following terms or phrases from English into Chinese and vice versa.

1. be conversant with   1. _____
2. employee overload   2. _____
3. adjust to   3. _____
4. perspective   4. _____
5. match   5. _____
6. *n.* 协调；兼容   6. _____
7. *n.* 士气，精神面貌   7. _____
8. *adj.* 互补的；补充的，补足的   8. _____

9. *n.* 化为概念，概念化	9. _____
10. *n.* 旷工，旷课	10. _____

EX. 3 Translate the following text into Chinese.

In addition to interviews, many employers use testing to select and place job applicants. Any tests given to candidates must be job related and follow guidelines set forth by the US Equal Employment Opportunity Commission to be legal. For the tests to be effective, they should be developed by reputable psychologists and administered by professionally qualified personnel who have had training in occupational testing in an industrial setting. The rationale behind testing is to give the employer more information before making the selection and placement decision—information vital to assessing how well a candidate is suited to a particular job. Most pre-employment assessment tests measure thinking styles, behavioral traits, and occupational interests. The results are available almost immediately after a candidate completes the roughly hour-long questionnaire. Thinking-styles tests can tell the potential employer how fast someone can learn new things or how well she can verbally communicate. Behavioral-traits assessments measure energy level, assertiveness, sociability, manageability, and attitude. For example, a high sociability score would be a desirable trait for salespeople.

EX. 4 Fill in the blanks with the words given below.

orientation	political	legislation	genuine	entitled
prohibits	unfairly	procedure	criteria	custom

Selection for Redundancy

In selecting a particular employee for redundancy, an employer should apply selection criteria that are reasonable and are applied in a fair manner. You are ___1___ to bring a claim for unfair dismissal if you consider that you were ___2___ selected for redundancy or consider that a ___3___ redundancy situation did not exist. Examples of these situations might include where the ___4___ and practice in your workplace has been last in, first out and your selection did not follow this ___5___. Another example may be where your contract of employment sets out ___6___ for selection which were not subsequently followed.

Under the unfair dismissals ___7___, selection for redundancy based on certain specific grounds is considered unfair. These include redundancy as the result of an employee's trade union activity, pregnancy or religious or ___8___ opinions. The employment equality legislation also ___9___ selection for redundancy that is based on any of the following nine grounds: gender, civil status, family status, age, disability, religious belief, race, sexual ___10___ or membership of the traveller community.

Text B

Employee Selection and Placement

1. Employee Selection

Employee selection is the process of putting right man on right job. It is a procedure of matching organizational requirements with the skills and qualifications of people. Effective selection can be done only when there is effective matching. By selecting the best candidate for the required job, the organization will get quality performance of employees. Moreover, organization will face less of absenteeism and employee turnover problems. By selecting right candidate for the required job, organization will also save time and money. Proper screening of candidates takes place during selection procedure. All the potential candidates who apply for the given job are tested.

But selection must be differentiated from recruitment, though these are two phases of employment process. Recruitment is considered to be a positive process as it motivates more candidates to apply for the job. It creates a pool of applicants. It is just sourcing of data. While selection is a negative process as the inappropriate candidates are rejected here. Recruitment precedes selection in staffing process. Selection involves choosing the best candidate with best abilities, skills and knowledge for the required job.

The employee selection process takes place in following order:

Job analysis. The systematic study of job content in order to determine the major duties and responsibilities of the job. It allows the organization to determine the important dimensions of job performance. The major duties and responsibilities of a job are often detailed in the job description.

The identification of KSA or job requirements. Drawing upon the information obtained through job analysis or from secondary sources, the organization identifies the knowledge, skills, and abilities necessary to perform the job. The job requirements are often detailed in a document called the job specification.

The identification of selection methods to assess KSA. Once the organization knows the KSA needed by job applicants, it must be able to determine the degree to which job applicants possess them. Selection methods include, but are not limited to, reference and background checks, interviews, cognitive testing, personality testing, aptitude testing, drug testing, and assessment centers.

The assessment of the reliability and validity of selection methods. The organization should be sure that the selection methods they use are reliable and valid. In terms of validity, selection methods should actually assess the knowledge, skill, or ability they purport to measure and should distinguish between job applicants who will be successful on the job and those who will not.

The use of selection methods to process job applicants. The organization should use its selection methods to make selection decisions. Typically, the organization will first try to determine which applicants possess the minimum KSA required. Once unqualified applicants are screened, other selection methods are used to make distinctions among the remaining job candidates and to decide which applicants will receive offers.

It is evident that mistakes in selection can have very serious consequences for corporate effectiveness. Such mistakes may very adversely affect colleagues, subordinates and clients. Employee incompetence may lead to costly mistakes, loss and waste of valuable resources, accidents, avoidable expenditure on training, etc.

2. Effective Selection and Placement Strategies

Selection and placement is based on several factors including skill level, work and educational experience, interview results, references, and consultation between the hiring department and the employment services department. For all openings, it is expected that the hiring leader will hire the candidate that best fits the qualifications, skills, behaviors and expectations for the role at the time it is available.

The supervisor of the vacant position, in consultation with the employment services department, will select from the interviewed candidates, the person to be hired. The hiring supervisor, in consultation with employment services, is encouraged to extend the job offer to his prospective new employee. However, letters of employment (initial hire letters) will be issued by the employment services department.

The hiring manager may request to see elements of the internal candidates personnel record, such as past performance reviews or other documentation related to past performance that resides in the personnel file. Access will be limited to the hiring manager and must take place at the employment services office. Additionally, hiring managers are encouraged to speak with previous internal supervisors about the candidates' history and ability to be successful in the open role. Likewise, supervisors are encouraged to be open and honest with internal managerial colleagues when discussing the suitability of the candidate for any given role.

All postings for employment in an organization will be simultaneously posted internally and externally. However, at the discretion of the hiring manager and employment services, a five-day internal priority period may be utilized. Factors that contribute to the posting process are business needs at the time of the opening and/or the nature of the position in question.

To be eligible for consideration with an opening, staff employees must normally have completed one year of service in their current position. Exceptions need to be approved in advance by the director, employment services and the staff members' current supervisor. Internal applicants should follow the same procedure for applying as any other candidate, by submitting an application via the on-line process.

Open positions will be maintained on the employment services website. If an internal applicant for the position meets minimum qualifications for the position as determined by the hiring manager and the employment services department, the internal applicant should normally be granted an interview. However, this is also contingent upon the nature of the position and the performance history of the internal candidate.

In all cases, internal applicants should be notified of any decisions related to their application by either the hiring manager or employment services.

Promotions are defined as being hired into a role that is a higher job grade than the role the individual will be vacating. Unless extenuating circumstances exist, promotions should enable the employee to receive an increase to their pay. Factors that should be considered in determining a new pay rate will include current rate in relation to new job grade, history of experience related to new position, budget, internal equity and proximity to the organization's annual staff salary adjustment date. In all cases, promotional increases will not exceed 10% of an individual's current pay. Exceptions will need approval from the director and employment services.

Lateral moves are defined as being hired into a role that is the same job grade as the role the individual will be vacating. Unless extenuating circumstances exist, lateral movements are not eligible for salary adjustments. Exceptions will need approval from the director and employment services.

Demotions are defined as being hired into a role that is a lower job grade than the role the individual will be vacating. Unless extenuating circumstances exist, demotions will generally result in a downward adjustment to the employee's pay. Factors that should be considered in determining a new pay rate will include current rate in relation to new job grade, history of experience related to new position, budget, internal equity and proximity to the organization's annual staff salary adjustment date. Exceptions will need approval from the director and employment services.

New Words

screen [skri:n] v. 筛，筛选；甄别
differentiate [ˌdifəˈrenʃieit] v. 区分，区别；辨别
source [sɔ:s] v. （从……）获得；向……提供消息；寻求（尤指供货）的来源
inappropriate [ˌinəˈprəuprieit] adj. 不妥的，不宜的，不恰当的
reject [riˈdʒekt] v. 拒绝，排斥；抛弃，扔掉
precede [priˈsi:d] v. 在……之前发生或出现；先于
staffing [ˈstɑ:fiŋ] n. 人员配备；安置职工
detail [ˈdi:teil] v. 详述；详细说明

identification [aiˌdentifiˈkeiʃən] n. 确认，鉴定，识别
obtain [əbˈtein] v. 获得，得到
secondary [ˈsekəndəri] adj. 次要的，从属的
possess [pəˈzes] v. 拥有，持有；支配
reliability [riˌlaiəˈbiləti] n. 可靠性
validity [vəˈlidəti] n. 合法性；有效性
purport [ˈpə:pət] v. 声称；意图；意味着
distinguish [disˈtiŋgwiʃ] v. 区分，辨别，分清
minimum [ˈminiməm] n. 最低限度；最小量

Unit 5

unqualified [ʌnˈkwɔlifaid] adj. 不合格的，无资格的；不胜任的
distinction [disˈtiŋkʃən] n. 区别；荣誉，卓越
adversely [ˈædvə:sli] adv. 不利的，有害地；逆向地
subordinate [səˈbɔ:dinət] n. 属下；附属物
incompetence [inˈkɔmpitəns] n. 无能力；不合格，不能胜任
consultation [ˌkɔnsəlˈteiʃən] n. 咨询，请教
documentation [ˌdɔkjumenˈteiʃən] n. 文件，证明文件；记录
likewise [ˈlaikˌwaiz] adv. 同样地；也，而且
suitability [ˌsju:təˈbiləti] n. 合适，适合

eligible [ˈelidʒəbl] adj. 合适的；（在法律上或道德上）合格的
normally [ˈnɔ:məli] adv. 通常地，一般地；正常地
exception [ikˈsepʃən] n. 例外，除外
contingent [kənˈtindʒənt] adj. 依情况而定的，取决于……的
vacate [vəˈkeit] v. 腾出，空出；辞（职），休假
extenuate [iksˈtenjueit] v. （用偏袒的辩解或借口）减轻；低估，藐视
equity [ˈekwəti] n. 公平，公道；公正裁决
proximity [prɔkˈsiməti] n. 接近，邻近；接近度，距离
approval [əˈpru:vəl] n. 批准，同意，赞成

Phrases

match with （使）与……相配，与……一致
be differentiated from 和……有区别的
staffing process 员工安置
draw upon 利用，使用，采用
be limited to 限于，被限制在……上
make distinctions 区分
hire letter 聘请函
performance review 业绩审查
reside in 存在于；永久地或长久地居住在……

personnel file 人事档案
be open and honest with 对……坦诚
at the discretion of 随……的意见办理；由……斟酌决定
be eligible for 有资格的；符合……的条件
be contingent upon 视……而定（随……而定）
notify sb. of sth. 将某事通知某人
in relation to 关于；和……有关
lateral move 平级调动；横向移动

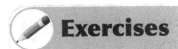

EX. 5 Fill in the following blanks with the information from Text B.

1. _____ is a procedure of matching organizational requirements with the skills and qualifications of people.

2. Selection must be differentiated from recruitment in that the former is _____ as the inappropriate candidates are rejected here.

3. Job analysis is the systematic study of job content in order to determine the major duties and responsibilities of the job, which are often detailed in the _____.

4. The identification of KSA or the _____ are often detailed in a document called the job specification.

5. To actually assess the KSA of job applicants, the organizations should make sure that the selection methods they use are _____.

6. The hiring supervisor is encouraged to extend the job offer to their prospective new employee, whereas _____ will be issued by the employment services department.

7. If an internal applicant for the position meets _____ for the position, he or she should normally be granted an interview.

8. Promotions are defined as being hired into a role that is _____ than the role the individual will be vacating.

9. _____ are defined as being hired into a role that is the same job grade as the role the individual will be vacating.

10. An individual is being hired into a role that is a lower job grade than the role he or she will be vacating, which indicates he or she is being _____.

Supplementary Reading

Text	Notes
Employment Testing Employment testing is the practice of administering written, oral, or other tests as a means of determining the suitability or desirability[1] of a job applicant. The premise[2] is that if scores on a test correlate with[3] job performance, then it is economically useful for the employer to select employees based on scores from that test. Different types of assessments may be used for employment	[1] desirability [di,zaiərə'biləti] *n.* 有利条件；称心如意的人（东西） [2] premise ['premis] *n.* 前提 [3] correlate with: 和……有关联

testing, including personality tests, intelligence tests, work samples, and assessment centers. Some correlate better with job performance than with others; employers often use more than one to maximize predictive power. These tests normally fall into five categories:

- performance assessment tests[4];
- personality tests[5];
- job-knowledge tests[6];
- situational judgment tests[7];
- aptitude tests[8].

1. Performance Assessment Tests

Performance-based assessment testing is a process to find out if applicants can do the job for which they are applying. It is done through tests, which are directly administered and judged by hiring managers who will be supervising the potential hire. Performance assessments can be used as a pre-screening tool to test applied knowledge, skill-job match and commitment of the applicant towards the job position.

The tests are peer-to-peer and reflect real business tasks that candidates have to perform. The tests are open ended, time bound[9], business related questions which applicants need to submit their responses for in order to prove their abilities.

The most important question that performance testing seeks to answer is: How would you solve this problem? Web tools like Hire Vue, Gap Jumpers and Code Eval allow candidate responses to be judged directly by hiring managers of the respective[10] departments to select the ones most suited for the role, thus making the process efficient for the company.

2. Personality Tests

Personality tests may potentially be useful in personnel selection. Of the well-known Big Five personality traits, only conscientiousness[11] correlates substantially with traditional measures of job performance, and that correlation is strong enough to be predictive. However, other factors of personality can correlate substantially with non-traditional aspects of job performance, such as leadership and effectiveness in a team environment. The Myers-Briggs Type Indicator (MBTI) is also used.

---

[4] performance assessment test: 行为表现评估测试

[5] personality test: 人格测试

[6] job-knowledge test: 业务知识测试

[7] situational judgment test: 情景判断测试

[8] aptitude test: 能力测试

[9] bound [baund] *adj.* 受约束的；有义务的；必定的

[10] respective [ris'pektiv] *adj.* 分别的；各自的

[11] conscientiousness [ˌkɔnʃi-'enʃəsnis] *n.* 责任心

The Minnesota Multiphasic Personality Inventory (MMPI) is a highly validated psychopathology[12] test that is generally used in a clinical psychology setting and may reveal potential mental health disorders. However, this can be considered by the Equal Employment Opportunity Commission as the employer having knowledge of a medical condition prior to an offer of employment. This is an illegal basis for a hiring decision in the United States. Employers considering personality tests should focus on tests designed for job purposes and do not provide any information regarding[13] an applicant's mental health or stability.

Notable situations in which the MMPI may be used are in final selection for police officers, fire fighters, and other security and emergency personnel, especially when the employees are required to carry weapons. An assessment of mental stability and fitness can be reasonably related and necessary in the performance of the job.

Employment integrity[14] testing is used to determine an applicant's honesty and integrity.

3. Job-Knowledge Tests

Employers administer job-knowledge tests when applicants must already possess a body of knowledge before being hired. Job-knowledge tests are particularly useful when applicants must have specialized or technical knowledge that can only be acquired through extensive experience or training. Job-knowledge tests are commonly used in fields such as computer programming, law, and financial management.

Licensing exams and certification[15] programs are also types of job-knowledge tests. Passing such exams indicates competence in the exam's subject area. Tests must be representative of[16] the tested field, otherwise litigation[17] can be brought against the test-giver.

4. Situational Judgment Tests

Situational judgment tests are commonly used as employee-selection and employee-screening tools and have been developed to predict employment success. These tests present realistic hypothetical[18] scenarios[19] in a multiple-choice

---

[12] **psychopathology** [ˌsaikəupəˈθɔlədʒi] *n.* 精神病理学

[13] **regarding** [riˈgɑːdiŋ] *prep.* 关于；就……而论

[14] **integrity** [inˈtegriti] *n.* 正直，诚实；完整

[15] **certification** [ˌsəːtifiˈkeiʃən] *n.* 证明，鉴定；证书

[16] **be representative of**: 代表……；是……的典型

[17] **litigation** [ˌlitiˈgeiʃən] *n.* 诉讼

[18] **hypothetical** [ˌhaipəˈθetikəl] *adj.* 假想的，假设的；有前提的

[19] **scenario** [siˈnɑːriəu] *n.* 规划，设想；局面

format. Applicants are asked to state what they would do in a difficult job-related situation.

Situational judgment tests measure the suitability of job applicants by assessing attributes such as problem solving, service orientation, and striving for achievement.

5. Aptitude Tests

Aptitude and ability tests are designed to assess your logical reasoning or thinking performance. They consist of multiple choice questions and are administered under exam conditions. They can be classified as speed tests or power tests. In speed tests the questions are relatively straightforward and the test is concerned with how many questions you can answer correctly in the allotted[20] time. Speed tests tend to be used in selection at the administrative and clerical level. A power test on the other hand will present a smaller number of more complex questions. Power tests tend to be used more at the professional or managerial level.

There are at least 5,000 aptitude and ability tests on the market. Some of them contain only one type of question (for example, verbal ability, numeric reasoning ability, etc.), while others are made up of different types of question, which can be classified as follows:

Verbal ability. Including spelling, grammar, ability to understand analogies and follow detailed written instructions. These questions appear in most general aptitude tests because employers usually want to know how well you can communicate.

Numeric ability. Including basic arithmetic, number sequences and simple mathematics. In management level tests you will often be presented with charts and graphs that need to be interpreted. These questions appear in most general aptitude tests because employers usually want some indication[21] of your ability to use numbers even if this is not a major part of the job.

Abstract reasoning. Measuring your ability to identify the underlying logic of a pattern and then determine the solution. Because abstract reasoning ability is believed to be the best indicator of fluid intelligence and the ability to learn new things quickly, these questions appear in most general aptitude tests.

[20] allot [ə'lɒt] v. 分配，拨给，摊派

[21] indication [ˌɪndɪˈkeɪʃən] n. 指示，表明；标示，象征

Spatial ability. Measuring your ability to manipulate shapes in two dimensions or to visualize[22] three-dimensional objects presented as two-dimensional pictures. These questions not usually found in general aptitude tests unless the job specifically requires good spatial skills.

Mechanical reasoning. Designed to assess your knowledge of physical and mechanical principles. Mechanical reasoning questions are used to select for a wide range of jobs including the military, police forces, fire services, as well as many craft, technical and engineering occupations[23].

Fault diagnosis[24]. These tests are used to select technical personnel who need to be able to find and repair faults in electronic and mechanical systems. As modern equipment of all types becomes more dependent on electronic control systems (and arguably more complex), the ability to approach problems logically in order to find the cause of the fault is increasingly important.

Data checking. Measuring how quickly and accurately errors can be detected in data and used to select candidates for clerical and data input jobs.

Work sample. Involving a sample of the work that you will be expected do. These types of test can be very broad ranging. They may involve exercises using a word processor or spreadsheet if the job is administrative or they may include giving a presentation or in-tray exercises[25] if the job is management or supervisory[26] level.

[22] **visualize** ['vɪʒuəlaɪz] *v.* 设想；形成思维图像

[23] **occupation** [ˌɒkjuˈpeɪʃən] *n.* 职业，工作；占有，占领

[24] **diagnosis** [ˌdaɪəgˈnəʊsɪs] *n.* 诊断；诊断结论；判断，结论

[25] **in-tray exercise:** 实际业务演练

[26] **supervisory** [ˌsjuːpəˈvaɪzəri] *adj.* 监督的；管理的

参考译文（Text A）

员 工 配 置

挑选员工的最终目的是配置员工，或者使其胜任合适的工作。员工配置是指将受雇员工配置到与其技能和能力相匹配的工作岗位上的过程。通过员工配置，企业试图创造一个有效的工作环境，使管理需求和员工资格形成良好的匹配。员工配置是避免员工过度工作和下岗的有效方法。因此，与其他事务相比，人力资源配置最应该被视为一个匹配的过程。员工与工作的匹配程度会影响员工的工作量和质量，并直接影响培训和运营成本。员工不能完成预期的生产量，无法达到预期的工作质量标准，这将使企业损耗大量的金钱和时间。

1. 员工配置理论

人与环境（P-E）匹配理论认为，当个体倾向于适应或匹配环境时，就会产生积极的反应。例如，当人与环境之间存在良好的匹配时，职业选择的 P-E 匹配理论认为会出现员工工作满意度较高而且身心健康的情形。大量的研究表明：个人最容易满足并最易于适应那些职业和人格类型相一致的工作。

P-E 匹配是一个概念化的通用术语，包含多个更具体的匹配概念。在招聘和甄选员工领域，两种常见形式是个人与工作匹配和个人与组织匹配。前者是个人与具体工作要求之间的匹配。为了使求职者的知识和技能与特定职位的要求相匹配，公司通常会寻求个人与工作之间的匹配，并重视求职者在未经培训的情况下即刻完成工作的能力。而后者指的是个人和更广泛的组织属性之间的匹配。在寻求个人与组织匹配时，公司往往重视个人与公司价值观和文化观的契合程度。

1.1 个人与工作匹配

个人与工作（P-J）匹配是选拔员工的常规基础，其主要关注的问题是：如何找到具有相应技能和能力的、适合组织内某项工作的求职者？P-J 匹配概念是个体的知识、技能和能力（KSA）与工作要求之间的匹配，或个人的欲望需求与工作所提供之物之间的匹配。根据真实的工作预览，求职者能掌握准确、真实的工作信息，这样他们就能评估其知识、技能和能力与工作要求之间的一致性程度。如果求职者认为他们的知识、技能和能力与工作要求相匹配，那么他们有可能会继续参与求职过程，并接受这份工作。有关真实工作预览的研究表明，在员工招聘和选拔过程中，向求职者提供准确、真实的工作信息可以产生积极的工作效果（如招聘过程中的低人员耗损率、高工作满意度、低主动离职率、高绩效等）。

在操作方面，P-J 匹配侧重需求与供给之间、要求与能力之间的契合。因此，P-J 匹配可以被定义为个人欲望与工作属性之间的，或者个人能力与工作要求之间的契合。这种需要与供给、要求与能力之间的匹配是互补匹配的延伸概念。在选拔员工时，用于评估个人与工作匹配度的策略包括测试、背景调查、简历以及其他各种甄选工具。

大量证据表明，P-J 匹配程度高会带来积极的效果。它对降低工作压力、提高出勤率、员工保留率、绩效以及工作满意度等方面能产生积极的影响。显然，如果个人的知识、技能和能力与工作要求不相匹配，出现低绩效、高离职率和缺勤率，以及其他人力资源问题的可能性就会增加。甄选员工可以通过审核申请表格、简历、面试、测试以及其他方式来收集有关求职者知识、技能及能力等方面的相关信息。

1.2 个人与组织匹配

个人与组织（P-O）匹配可以定义为人与组织之间的相容性。就甄选员工而言，P-O 匹配可以概括为求职者与更广泛的组织属性之间的契合。在竞争激烈、劳动力短缺的劳动力市场中，设法留住灵活、敬业的员工是必要的，而员工与组织匹配是实现这一目标的关键因素。通常，测评个人与组织匹配程度有以下四种方法：

• 测评人与组织的基本特征之间的相似性，核查个人价值观和组织价值观之间的一致性；

- 确定个人与组织领导之间目标的一致性；
- 测评个人偏好或需求与组织结构和体制之间的匹配程度；
- 测评个人个性特征与组织氛围或组织人格之间的匹配程度。而组织氛围的衡量通常是通过对组织的奖励制度或沟通方式等方面的测评来实现的。

当工作成功的综合性因素与具体的KSA同等重要时,个人与组织匹配就很重要。例如,当一位雇主雇佣低级工作岗位的员工,并提拔内部员工来承担大部分工作时,综合的认知能力、解决问题的能力以及职业道德可能比员工具体的KSA更重要。学习能力可以使员工掌握新的信息,并根据业务知识做出正确的决定；职业道德则包括工作的彻底性、责任感和系统性。

确定个人与组织是否匹配可能需要使用多种甄选方法,并耗费大量的时间和精力。多样化的深度面试、广泛的能力和心理测试、多层管理人员和主管共同参与等只是确保个人与组织匹配的一些方式。

高程度的个人与组织匹配能产生积极的结果。个人与组织匹配可以促进工作满意度和敬业精神。这种匹配还可以预测员工离职倾向,并对员工个人公民行为、周边绩效和自我报告式的团队协作有一定的影响。

总之,由于P-J和P-O匹配程度高可以带来积极的结果,如工作满意度、绩效和敬业精神等,在员工甄选过程中,应该考虑P-J和P-O匹配因素。其理想的做法是：在选择与测评员工的早期或初始阶段考虑P-J匹配因素,在后期阶段考虑P-O匹配因素。

2. 配置原则

在配置员工时,应该遵循一些基本原则,详述如下：
- 根据工作要求配置员工,而不能根据员工的资格条件或要求来调整工作,"工作第一,员工次之"是配置员工的原则；
- 根据员工的资格条件配置工作,其工作岗位不应该高于或低于员工的资格条件；
- 员工应该熟悉组织的工作环境,精通与工作有关的所有事务,并了解犯错后的惩罚措施；
- 在为新员工配置工作时,应努力培养新员工的忠诚和合作意识,使他意识到自己对工作和组织应尽的责任；
- 工作配置应该在新员工加入组织工作之前准备妥当；
- 最初的工作配置可能是暂时的,因为员工培训结束后可能有一些变化,该员工有可能被调任到他更胜任的工作岗位上。

适当的配置有助于提高员工的士气,有助于员工充分发挥他们的能力。适当的配置还可以降低离职率、缺勤率和事故率。这样一来,员工可以有效地适应组织的工作环境,而且他们的工作表现也不会受到影响。

3. 员工配置问题

员工配置过程中的主要问题通常会在招聘人员关注员工个人而不是工作本身的时候出现。通常,如果个人的工作与其他人有关,这种工作可分为三类：
- 独立的工作。在独立的工作中,每个员工会被分配那些非重叠的工作环节。例如,

Unit 5

在销售行业，员工个人的工作与其他员工的工作几乎没有关联，独立工作不会给工作配置带来很大困难。但组织必须结合员工个人的能力兴趣与工作要求对每个员工进行评估。员工配置的目标是：为该工作岗位配置至少具备最低工作资格的员工。考虑到现有的工作或人力资源限制条件，应该为员工配置能充分发挥他们才华的工作。

- 非独立性的工作可以是连续作业或共同作业。在连续作业中，员工个人的工作要取决于同事的工作状况。例如，流水作业就是这类工作的典型例子。
- 在共同作业中，员工之间有很高的相互依赖性，最终成果是全体员工共同努力的结果。在这种情况下，重要的是团队合作。为这类工作配置员工是相当困难的。

Unit 6

Text A

Training Needs Analysis

Training needs analysis (TNA) is the process of identifying the gap between employee training and needs of training. Training needs analysis is the first stage in the training process and involves a procedure to determine whether training will indeed address the problem which has been identified. Training can be described as "the acquisition of skills, concepts or attitudes that result in improved performance within the job environment". Training needs analysis looks at each aspect of an operational domain so that the initial skills, concepts and attitudes of the human elements of a system can be effectively identified, and appropriate training can be specified.

1. Benefits of Training Needs Analysis

Training needs analysis is used to assess an organization's training needs. The root of the TNA is the gap analysis. This is an assessment of the gap between the knowledge, skills and attitudes that the people in the organization currently possess and the knowledge, skills and attitudes that they require to meet the organization's objectives. It provides insights and concrete data to identify the training needs and gaps within an organization. The benefits of training needs analysis can be enumerated as follows:

First, it's through analysis that we are able to answer these questions:
- Is training needed?
- If yes, where it is to be implemented?
- Which sort of training is required?

For the organization, it is one of those strategic initiatives taken to delve deeper into the ways to enrich the competencies, capabilities, and potential of the workforce. With the successful deployment of training needs analysis, the organization will be in a position to evaluate better outcomes with an optimum utilization of its resources. Thus, it streamlines the organizational objectives and goals. It also helps build credibility among its stakeholders.

Also, it takes note of the efficiency guidelines—labor cost, waste minimization, distribution time, and production rates. It's through an in-depth analysis that all the parameters are recorded— the data so obtained reveals the areas that require training.

Meanwhile, the training needs analysis will answer questions such as how relevant training is for employees. If trained, will they make a difference by improving their job performance? Will this improved job performance have anything to do with the organization's goals? Such a volley of questions are answered through a proper analysis at the employees' level. It also gauges the standard that needs to be followed by employees so as to maintain their competency level.

Additionally, it makes a detailed foray into the areas in which employees lag behind. (Is it in terms of knowledge, skills, or attitude?) Through this understanding, it empowers employees to acquire new skills at a faster pace, and thus enjoy their work.

As a whole, we can rightly presume, with a proper analysis and implementation (which go hand-in-hand), that we can make every employee happy and highly productive. Training needs analysis scrutinizes the gap in performance from theory to its current state.

This gap may occur at the organizational level or at the individual level. From this gap analysis, we can assume the resources required and plan the budget accordingly. It further ensures strategic planning or a SWOT analysis of the organization. These strengths can be further bolstered with requisite training, and any weakness may be assessed as an area one needs to ponder over, while opportunities figure out areas that one needs to harness and threats need to be diminished.

2. Steps of Training Needs Analysis

A training needs analysis is an important first step in sound instructional design. It helps you identify who needs training and what kind of training is needed. (By the way, a well-conducted TNA should also consider whether a non-traditional training solution is a better alternative.) The training needs analysis also helps you get a handle on the most cost-effective means of meeting the training requirements. Below are the steps which can help you conduct an effective training needs analysis:

Step 1: Organizational analysis. Work with leadership to articulate the training priorities and ensure that there is clear alignment between the training goals and business objectives. Write down the desired business outcomes. Also, take a look at organizational readiness for training. This involves identifying and removing (or at least minimizing) obstacles that might make the training less effective.

The more leaders indicate that training is important to the organization, the better the outcomes of training. Training works best when measurable outcomes are clearly defined and articulated in advance.

Step 2: Task analysis. A job-task analysis is a systematic breakdown of a job into its component parts. The goal of a job-task analysis is to produce a list of tasks required to perform a particular job, and then for each task, to identify the skills and competencies needed to perform the task. This will provide a solid foundation for the design of your training. Information from this part of the analysis should be used to decide what to include in the training and determine the standards for performance.

A task needs analysis is usually done by collecting information from subject matter experts through interviews, focus groups, or surveys. The final output should include a detailed description of manual activities, mental activities, task duration and frequency, any necessary equipment, and the skills and competencies required to perform a given task.

As part of the job-task analysis, be alert for the difference between things that a person needs-to-know and information that they will need to access. This can have a big impact on your training design: Teaching people how and where to find job-relevant information can be even more effective than requiring that they memorize certain information.

You might also want to consider cognitive task analysis, which is a close cousin to the job-task analysis. It provides a similar framework for jobs that are more knowledge-based than task-based. Conduct a cognitive task analysis if you need to uncover the cognitive requirements for a job, such as decision-making, problem-solving, memory, attention and judgment. This can be a complex and nuanced analysis.

Lastly, an analysis of teamwork requirements can be a helpful part of a training needs analysis. Team-related tasks and competencies may be missing from other forms of task analysis. A team task analysis helps to highlight coordination patterns between jobs. The information revealed in a team task analysis can be used to determine objectives for training and to determine which employees should attend training together. Effective team training includes general teamwork training as well as training on how to accomplish specific tasks together.

Step 3: Person analysis. This analysis identifies who has mastered and who needs to learn the skills and competencies that were determined in the previous task analysis step. This will help you target your training at those areas with the widest gaps between the status quo and the desired outcome.

The person analysis can help you understand the characteristics of those who will be participating in training. For example, you might discover that they are primarily younger workers. In this case, you might intentionally design your training to resonate with the millennial.

Bear in mind that employees typically aren't that good at self-identifying areas where they need training. There is a well-studied phenomenon in which people who do things badly are often supremely confident of their abilities. One reason that the ignorant also tend to be the blissfully self-assured is that the skills required for competence are often the same skills necessary to recognize competence. This is one of the reasons why a systematic training needs analysis is so important.

Training needs analysis is the first and probably the most important step toward making sure if your organizational training resources are used most effectively. Experts strongly recommend conducting a systematic and thorough training needs analysis. This will help you fully understand the organizational context, to get a clear picture of the competencies needed to achieve the desired outcomes, and to identify which employees and teams most need training.

operational [ˌɔpəˈreiʃənl] adj.（用于）操作的，经营的
concrete [ˈkɔnkri:t] adj. 具体的，有形的
enrich [inˈritʃ] v. 使富裕，使富有
credibility [ˌkrediˈbiləti] n. 可靠性，可信性；确实性
stakeholder [ˈsteikhəuldə] n. 股东
minimization [ˌminimaiˈzeiʃən] n. 最小化
in-depth [ˈinˈdepθ] adj. 深入的，彻底的
parameter [pəˈræmitə] n. 参数，参量；决定因素
volley [ˈvɔli] n. 迸发；（箭、子弹等）齐射
gauge [geidʒ] v. 评估，判断；（用仪器）测量
foray [ˈfɔrei] n. 突袭，侵略；冒险
presume [priˈzju:m] v. 推测，假设；以为，认为
scrutinize [ˈskrutinaiz] v. 仔细检查
bolster [ˈbəulstə] v. 支持，支撑；鼓励
requisite [ˈrekwizit] n. 必需品；要素 adj. 需要的，必要的
harness [ˈhɑ:nis] v. 利用；控制
diminish [diˈminiʃ] v.（使）减少，缩小；减弱……的权势
sound [saund] adj. 合理的；全面的；完好的
instructional [inˈstrʌkʃənəl] adj. 指导的，教育的
articulate [ɑːˈtikjuleit] v. 清楚地表达出

alignment [əˈlainmənt] n. 结盟；队列，排成直线
remove [riˈmu:v] v. 消除，免除
obstacle [ˈɔbstəkl] n. 障碍；障碍物
measurable [ˈmeʒərəbl] adj. 可量度的，可测量的
breakdown [ˈbreikdaun] n. 崩溃，倒塌；损坏，故障
component [kəmˈpəunənt] n. 成分；零件
solid [ˈsɔlid] adj. 固体的；结实的，可靠的
duration [djuəˈreiʃən] n. 持续时间，期间
access [ˈækses] v. 使用；接近，进入 n. 接近（的机会）；使用之权
memorize [ˈmeməraiz] v. 记住，熟记
framework [ˈfreimwə:k] n. 框架，构架
uncover [ʌnˈkʌvə] v. 揭露，发现
nuanced [ˈnju:ɔnst] adj. 有细微差别的
highlight [ˈhailait] v. 强调，突出
intentionally [inˈtenʃənəli] adv. 有意地，故意地
resonate [ˈrezəneit] v. 共鸣或共振；回响
millennial [miˈleniəl] adj. 一千年的
phenomenon [fiˈnɔminən] n. 现象，事件
supremely [sju:ˈpri:mli] adv. 极其，极为
ignorant [ˈignərənt] adj. 无知的，愚昧的
blissfully [ˈblisfuli] adv. 幸福地，充满喜悦地
self-assured [self-əˈʃuəd] adj. 有自信的
recommend [rekəˈmend] v. 推荐，建议
thorough [ˈθʌrə] adj. 彻底的，全面的

Unit 6

be described as 被描述成……
result in 引起，导致
as follows 列举如下
delve into 钻研，深入研究
take note of 注意，留意
make a difference 有影响，起（重要）作用
a volley of 一排
make a foray into 突袭
lag behind 落后，落后于
at a fast pace 快节奏地
as a whole 整体来看，普遍说来

go hand-in-hand (with) 与……共同行动，与……相配合；与……一致
ponder over 思考，沉思，深思
get a handle on 控制，掌握，驾驭
focus group 讨论组，焦点小组
be alert for 对……保持警惕
the status quo 现状
resonate with 引起共鸣
bear in mind 牢记，铭记不忘
be confident of 对……有信心，确信……
get a clear picture of 弄清楚

 Abbreviations

TNA (Training Needs Analysis) 培训需求分析
SWOT (Strength, Weakness, Opportunity and Threat) 优势、劣势、机会和威胁

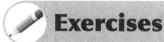

EX. 1 Answer the following questions according to the text.

1. What is training needs analysis?
2. What can training be described as?
3. What is the root of training needs analysis?
4. List at least two benefits of training needs analysis.
5. What are human resource staff generally supposed to do in terms of an organizational analysis?
6. What is the goal of a job-task analysis?
7. What should be included in the final output of a task analysis?

8. What type of analysis should human resource staff conduct if they need to uncover the cognitive requirements for a job?
9. What does a team task analysis help to highlight?
10. Which step of training needs analysis will identify who has mastered and who needs to learn the skills and competencies that are required for a specific job?

EX. 2 Translate the following terms or phrases from English into Chinese and vice versa.

1. focus group
2. ponder over
3. take note of
4. stakeholder
5. phenomenon
6. *vt.* 推荐，建议
7. *n.* 必需品；要素
8. *adv.* 有意地，故意地
9. *vt.* 清楚地表达出
10. *n.* 框架，构架

1.
2.
3.
4.
5.
6.
7.
8.
9.
10.

EX. 3 Translate the following text into Chinese.

Employee training generally refers to programs that provide workers with information, new skills, or professional development opportunities. For example, people might be required to participate in a new employee orientation or on-the-job training when they are hired. Other types of employee training programs include those that encourage staff members to brush up on certain skills, or to stay current with developments in their field. There are also training strategies that deal with specific personnel issues that might arise on the job, such as worker safety or sexual harassment. Depending on the subject matter, training might be conducted by staff members or by outside consultants.

If the training is on a relatively simple topic, like a new software program, the staff members can usually complete training activities themselves. Some organizations employ their own training managers or specialists, whose function is to identify educational needs and organize the activities. If it revolves around a more complex or sensitive topic, however, the employer might hire an outside consultant to conduct the employee training.

EX. 4 Fill in the blanks with the words given below.

| boost | proving | harassment | frequently | claim |
| sharpen | opportunity | positive | foster | specific |

Unit 6

Reasons for Employee Training and Development Programs

There are various other reasons that an employer might offer training and development programs for his or her current employees. For instance, many businesses conduct performance reviews, and use the results to identify areas in which employees need to __1__ their skills. Other goals might be to increase worker productivity, or to __2__ better relations among staff members. The training could also give employees an __3__ to increase their knowledge, leading to more advanced positions. __4__ employee training topics can include technology updates or workplace safety procedures. They might also address potentially difficult issues, such as discrimination or __5__.

Employee training can have both advantages and disadvantages. Though there is little scientific data __6__ that training reduces staff turnover, a number of management experts __7__ that certain training programs can help __8__ staff retention and productivity. Such experts also argue that some specific types of training can promote a more __9__ attitude in the workplace. On the other hand, a __10__ cited disadvantage is that training employees can cause an increase in travel and other expenses. It might also take time away from other job duties.

Text B

Training Organization and Implementation

Helping employees to become effective in their jobs is one of the most fundamentally important tasks that any work organization has to undertake in people management. Employers depend on the quality of their employees' performance to achieve organizational aims and objectives; employees have motivational needs for development, recognition, status and achievement that can and should be met through job satisfaction and performance achievement.

Training is teaching, or developing in oneself or others, any skills and knowledge that relate to specific useful competencies. Training has specific goals of improving one's capability, capacity, productivity and performance. Training in a work organization is essentially a learning process, in which learning opportunities are purposefully structured by the managerial, HR and training staff working in collaboration, or by extend agents acting on their behalf. The aim of the process is to develop the knowledge, skills and attitudes in the organization's employees that have been defined as necessary for the effective performance of their work and hence for the achievement of the organizational aims and objectives by the most effective means available.

1. Training Managers

Since managers are responsible for the effective performance of work to achieve the organizational aims and objectives, they must logically have the responsibility for ensuring that employees are effectively trained for this purpose. Management must take the initiative in setting up, resourcing and monitoring the effectiveness of the training system and its provision in practice. They typically fulfill the following duties:

- assessing employees' needs for training;
- aligning training with the organization's strategic goals;
- creating and managing a training budget, ensuring that operations are within budget;
- developing and implementing training programs that make the best use of available resources;
- updating training programs to ensure that they are up to date;
- overseeing the creation of educational materials, such as online learning modules;
- reviewing training materials from a variety of vendors and selecting materials with appropriate content;
- teaching training methods and skills to instructors and supervisors;
- evaluating the effectiveness of training programs and instructors.

Companies want to promote a more productive and knowledgeable workforce to stay competitive in business. Providing opportunities for development is a selling point for recruiting high-quality employees, and it helps retain employees who can contribute to business growth. Training managers work to align training with an organization's goals.

Training managers oversee training programs, staff, and budgets. They are responsible for organizing training programs, including creating or selecting course content and materials. Training often takes place in classrooms or training facilities. Increasingly, training is in the form of a video, self-guided instructional manual, or online application and delivered through a computer, tablet, or other hand-held electronic device. Training may also be collaborative, with employees informally connecting with experts, mentors, and colleagues, often through social media or other online mediums. Managers must ensure that training methods, content, software, systems, and equipment are appropriate and meaningful.

Training managers typically supervise a staff of training specialists, such as instructional designers, program developers, and instructors. Managers teach training methods to specialists who, in turn, instruct the organization's employees—both new and experienced. Managers direct the daily activities of specialists and evaluate their effectiveness. Although most managers primarily oversee specialists and training program operations, some—particularly those in smaller companies—also may conduct training courses.

To enhance employees' skills and an organization's overall quality of work, training managers often confer with managers of each department to identify its training needs. They may work with top executives and financial officers to identify and match training priorities with overall business goals. They also prepare training budgets and ensure that expenses stay within budget.

While management bears the main responsibility, all staff in the organization are involved in the training task. Effective practice requires the collaboration of managerial, HR and training staff. In addition, employees are expected to take some responsibility for their own learning.

2. Training Design

The design of the training program can be undertaken only when a clear training objective has been produced. The training objective clears what goal has to be achieved by the end of training program, i.e. what the trainees are expected to be able to do at the end of their training. Training objectives assist trainers to design the training program. Before starting a training program, a trainer analyzes his technical, interpersonal, judgmental skills in order to deliver quality content to trainers.

A good training design requires close scrutiny of the trainees and their profiles. Age, experience, needs and expectations of the trainees are some of the important factors that affect training design. There are some primary considerations when designing training:

Learner's readiness. Effective training depends greatly on the learner's readiness. This readiness means they must have the ability to learn, the motivation to learn and self-efficacy. Learners must possess basic skills, such as fundamental reading and math proficiency, and sufficient cognitive abilities. A trainee's desire to learn training content is referred to as motivation to learn and is influenced by numerous factors such as his or her interest in the training contents, the trainer's instruction ability, the training climate, and the training methods used. If a trainee is lack of motivation, little can be accomplished in a training program. For learners to be ready and receptive to the training content, they must also possess self-efficacy, which refers to a person's belief that he/she can successfully learn the training program content. Trainers must help the trainees to appropriately boost their confidence.

Trainees' learning style. The learning style, age, experience, educational background of trainees must be kept in mind in order to get the right pitch to the design of the program. For example, auditory learners are those who learn best by listening to someone else to tell them about the training content. Some are tactile learners who must "get their hands on" and use the training resources. Still there are visual learners who think in pictures and figures and need to see the purpose and process of the training. Trainers who address all of these styles by using multiple training methods can design more effective programs. Additionally, due to cultural, gender and race/ethnic diversities, training many different people from various backgrounds poses a significant challenge in today's workplaces.

Training strategies. Once the training objective has been identified, the trainer translates it into specific training areas and modules. The trainer prepares the priority list of about what must be included and what could be included. The highest possible transfer of training occurs only when trainees actually use what they have learned in training in the job. Effective transfer of training meets two conditions. First, the trainees can take in the material learned in training and apply it to the job context in which they work. Second, employees maintain their use of the learned over time. Therefore, to achieve effective transfer of training, trainers need to adopt a number of methods, such as offering trainees an overview of the training content and process prior to the actual training, ensuring that the training mirrors the job context as much as possible, and etc.

3. Types of Training

There are a number of different types of training we can use to engage an employee. These types are usually used in all steps in a training process (orientation, in-house, mentorship, and external training). The training utilized depends on the amount of resources available for training, the type of company, and the priority the company places on training.

- Technical training addresses software or other programs that employees use while working for the organization.
- Quality training is a type of training that familiarizes all employees with the means to produce a good-quality product. The ISO sets the standard on quality for most production and environmental situations. ISO training can be done in-house or externally.
- Skills training focuses on the skills that the employee actually needs to know to perform their jobs. A mentor can help with this kind of training.
- Soft skills are those that do not relate directly to our jobs but are important. Soft skills training may train someone on how to better communicate and negotiate or provide good customer service.
- Professional training is normally given externally and might be obtaining certification or specific information needed about a profession to perform a job. For example, tax accountants need to be up to date on tax laws. This type of training is often external.
- Team training is a process that empowers teams to improve decision making, problem solving, and team-development skills. Team training can help improve communication and result in more productive businesses.
- Managerial training might be given to get someone ready to take on a management role.
- Safety training is important to make sure an organization is meeting OSHA standards. Safety training can also include disaster planning.

4. Training Methods

Training helps employees enhance their capabilities and acquire new learning, skills and knowledge. Training helps employees come up with unique and innovative ideas, meet targets within the desired time frame and make them efficient resources for the organization. Let us go through various training methods at the workplace:

Induction training. Induction training is often given to new employees to make them feel a part of the organization. How do you think an individual can perform if he/she is not familiar with the policies and rules and regulations of the organization? You can't expect an individual to deliver results on the first day itself. You need to welcome your employees well for them to feel motivated and comfortable. Induction programs need to be designed sensibly. Too much of information on the day of joining will frighten the new employee and he/she will not come from the next day onwards. Induction programs help new employees to get acquainted with the work culture and fellow workers. Induction programs need to be short, crisp but informative.

Refresher training. Refresher training is designed for existing employees to refresh them and also help them acquire new skills and technologies to keep pace with the changing times. Such training programs prepare employees for more responsible positions.

On the job training. On the job training is given to employees at the workplace itself by their superiors and bosses. Managers ought to sit with their team members on a regular basis, train them on new technologies, skill sets to help them cope with the changes. On the job training is given to employees along with their jobs itself and makes them capable to handle bigger responsibilities.

On the job training is imparted by any of the following methods:

Coaching. Coaching is also defined as learning by doing and handling various ongoing projects. In this method of training, team manager assigns certain job responsibilities to team members, monitors their performance, points out their mistakes, provides them feedback and also suggestions for improvement.

Job rotation. In this type of training, employees move from one position to another, thus acquiring new skills and learning. Job rotation acquaints individuals with newer roles and challenges and makes them capable of performing any type of task.

Employees need to be encouraged to go through various online learning sites which would help them in their current job responsibilities. One needs to be aware of the latest developments in his/her domain. Reading helps a lot.

Off the job training. Off the job training is given outside the workplace. It can be provided by any of the following methods:

Seminars/Conferences. Seminars and conferences are effective when training needs to be given to a larger audience. Relevant information, latest developments, new technologies and case studies are discussed on a common platform to acquaint employees with new skill sets.

Simulation exercise. Simulation exercises train the employees in an artificial environment which closely resembles the employee's actual working conditions.

Vestibule training. In vestibule training, employees practice work on the instrument/equipment which they would be using in future when they would be actually working.

New Words

implementation [,implimen'teiʃən] *n.* 贯彻；成就	**capacity** [kə'pæsəti] *n.* 才能；性能；生产力
fundamentally [ˌfʌndə'mentəli] *adv.* 从根本上，根本地；基础地	**purposefully** ['pɜːpəsfuli] *adv.* 有明确目标地
motivational [ˌməuti'veiʃənəl] *adj.* 动机的，动力的	**managerial** [ˌmænə'dʒiəriəl] *adj.* 经理的，管理上的

collaboration [kə,læbə'reiʃən] n. 合作，协作
align [ə'lain] v. 使结盟；使成一线，排整齐
oversee ['əuvə'si:] v. 监督，监视
module ['mɔdju:l] n. 模块，组件
device [di'vais] n. 装置，设备；方法，策略
clear [kliə] v. 清空，清除；澄清
scrutiny ['skru:tini] n. 监督；细看，细阅
profile ['prəufail] n. 简介；形象；轮廓
self-efficacy [self-'efikəsi] n. 自我效能
numerous ['nju:mərəs] adj. 数不清的，许多的
receptive [ri'septiv] adj. 善于接受的，有接受力的
pitch [pitʃ] n. 音调；程度；球场
auditory ['ɔ:ditəri] adj. 听觉的，听觉器官的
tactile ['tæktail] adj. 触觉的；能触知的，有形的
visual ['viʒuəl] adj. 视觉的，看得见的
overview ['əuvəvju:] n. 概观，总的看法；回顾，复习

mentorship ['mentɔ:ʃip] n. 师徒制；良师益友关系
familiarize [fə'miljəraiz] v. 使熟悉
accountant [ə'kauntənt] n. 会计人员，会计师
disaster [di'zɑ:stə] n. 灾难，祸患；不幸
induction [in'dʌkʃən] n. 就职；归纳法
sensibly ['sensəbli] adv. 明智地，理智地
onwards ['ɔnwə:dz] adv. 向前
crisp [krisp] adj. 有力的，有生气的；易碎的
refresher [ri'freʃə] n. 进修；使人清新的事物
impart [im'pɑ:t] v. 传授，告知；赋予
seminar ['seminɑ:] n. 研讨会；(大学的)研究班
platform ['plætfɔ:m] n. 平台；台，站台
simulation [,simju'leiʃən] n. 模仿，模拟
artificial [,ɑ:ti'fiʃəl] adj. 人工的；人造的；人为的
resemble [ri'zembl] v. 与……相像，类似于

Phrases

define as 界定，定义为
a selling point 卖点，优点
confer with 和……商谈
bear responsibility 承担责任
lack of 缺乏

keep in mind 记牢，铭记在心
apply... to 把……应用于；涂，抹
place the priority on 把……放在首位
familiarize sb. with sth. 使某人熟悉或精通某事

Unit 6

tax accountant 税务会计
up to date 最近的；最新的
decision making 决策，判定
problem solving 问题解决
take on 承担；呈现
come up with 提出，想出；赶上
be familiar with 熟悉，通晓，精通
get acquainted with 知道，知悉，了解

induction training 入职培训
refresher training 进修培训
keep pace with 跟上，赶上
on the job training 在职培训
on the regular basis 定期地
be aware of 知道，意识到
off the job training 离职培训
vestibule training 技工训练

Abbreviations

ISO (International Organization for Standardization) 国际标准化组织
OSHA (*Occupational Safety and Health Act*) 《职业安全与卫生条例》

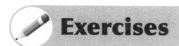

Exercises

EX. 5 Answer the following questions according to the text.

1. On what do employers depend to achieve organizational aims and objectives?
2. What is the aim of the training process?
3. What is a selling point for recruiting high-quality employees?
4. Why do training managers often confer with managers of each department?
5. What does learner's readiness mean?
6. What are those two conditions that effective transfer of training needs to meet?
7. What factors affect the type of the training utilized?
8. Which type of training may train someone on how to better communicate and negotiate?
9. Which training method is often given to new employees to make them feel a part of the organization?
10. What is the aim of refresher training?

Supplementary Reading

Text	Notes

Training Evaluation
 	
    Training evaluation is the systematic analysis of training to demonstrate[1] whether it has met its objectives in an effective and efficient manner. It involves the assessment of the effectiveness of the training programs. This assessment is done by collecting data on whether the participants were satisfied with the deliverables[2] of the training program, whether they learned something from the training and are able to apply those skills at their workplace. There are different measurements[3] for assessment of a training program depending upon the kind of training conducted. For example, if a certain technical training is conducted, the organization will be interested in knowing whether the new skills are being put to use[4] at the workplace or in other words whether the effectiveness of the worker is enhanced. Similarly in case of behavioral training, it will be evaluated on whether there is change in the behavior, attitude and learning ability of the participants[5].
 	
1. Benefits of Training Evaluation
 	
    Evaluation acts as a check to ensure that the training is able to fill the competency gaps within the organization in a cost effective way. This is specially important when the organizations are trying to cut costs and increase globally. Some of the benefits of the training evaluation are as follows:
 	
    Evaluation ensures accountability[6]. Training evaluation ensures that training programs comply with the competency gaps and that the deliverables are not compromised upon[7].
 	
    Check the cost. Evaluation ensures that the training programs are effective in improving the work quality, employee behavior, attitude and development of new skills within the employee within a certain budget. Since global companies are trying to cut their costs without compromising upon the quality, evaluation just aims at achieving the same with training.
	[1] **demonstrate** ['demənstreit]
	　　v. 证明；演示，示范
	
	[2] **deliverable** [di'livərəbl]
	　　n. 应交付的产品
	
	[3] **measurement** ['meʒəmənt]
	　　n. 测量，测量法；尺寸；衡量
	
	[4] **put to use**: 投入使用，利用
	
	[5] **participant** [pɑ:'tisipənt]
	　　n. 参与者
	
	[6] **accountability** [ə,kauntə'biləti]
	　　n. 有责任，有义务
	
	[7] **compromise upon**: 同意

Feedback to the trainer/training. Evaluation also acts as a feedback to the trainer or the facilitator and the entire training process. Since evaluation accesses individuals at the level of their work, it gets easier to understand the loopholes of the training and the changes required in the training methodology[8].

Not many organizations believe in the process of evaluation or at least do not have an evaluation system in place. Many organizations conduct training programs year after year only as a matter of faith and not many have a firm evaluation mechanism[9] in place. Organizations like IBM, Motorala only, it was found out, have a firm evaluation mechanism in place.

2. Levels of Evaluation

There are many methods and tools available for evaluating the effectiveness of training programs. Their usability depends on the kind of training program that is under evaluation. Generally most of the organizations use the Kirkpatrick Model for training evaluations which evaluate training at four levels—reactions, learning, behavior and results. Each of the four levels is explained below:

Level 1: Reaction

Level 1 solicits[10] opinions of the learning experience following a training event or course. Typical questions concern the degree to which the experience was valuable (satisfaction), whether they felt engaged, and whether they felt the training was relevant. Training organizations use that feedback to evaluate the effectiveness of the training, students' perceptions, potential future improvements, and justification[11] for the training expense. A variety of sources estimate that approximately 80 percent of training events include Level 1 evaluation.

Level 2: Learning

Level 2 measures the degree to which participants acquired the intended knowledge, skills and attitudes as a result of the training. This level is used by instructors and training executives to determine if training objectives are being met. Only by determining what trainees are learning, and what they are not, can organizations make necessary improvements. Level 2 can be completed as a pre- and post-event evaluation, or only as a post-evaluation.

[8] methodology [meθə'dɔlədʒi] *n.* 方法学；方法论

[9] mechanism ['mekənizəm] *n.* 机制，原理

[10] solicit [sə'lisit] *v.* 征求，恳求；提起

[11] justification [,dʒʌstifi'keiʃən] *n.* 辩护，正当的理由

Level 3: Behavior

Level 3 measures the degree to which participants' behaviors change as a result of the training—basically whether the knowledge and skills from the training are then applied on the job. This measurement can be, but not necessarily, a reflection[12] of whether participants actually have learned the subject material. For example, the failure of behavioral change can be due to other circumstances[13] such as individual's reluctance[14] to change. Level 3 evaluation involves both pre- and post-event measurement of the learner's behavior.

Level 4: Results

Level 4 seeks to determine the tangible results of the training such as reduced cost, improved quality and efficiency, increased productivity, employee retention, increased sales and higher morale. While such benchmarks[15] are not always easy or inexpensive to quantify, doing so is the only way training organizations can determine the critical return on investment (ROI) of their training expenditures. One typical challenge is to identify whether specific outcomes are truly the result of the training. Level 4 requires both pre- and post-event measurement of the training objectives.

An evaluation at each level answers whether a fundamental[16] requirement of the training program is met. It's not that conducting an evaluation at one level is more important than another. All levels of evaluation are important. In fact, the Kirkpatrick Model explains the usefulness of performing training evaluations at each level. Each level provides a diagnostic[17] checkpoint for problems at the succeeding level. So, if participants did not learn (Level 2), participant reactions gathered at Level 1 (Reaction) will reveal the barriers[18] to learning. Now moving up to the next level, if participants did not use the skills once back in the workplace (Level 3), perhaps they did not learn the required skills in the first place (Level 2).

The difficulty and cost of conducting an evaluation increase as you move up the levels. So, you will need to consider carefully what levels of evaluation you will conduct for programs. You may decide to conduct Level 1 evaluations (Reaction) for all programs, Level 2 evaluations (Learning) for "hard-skills" programs

---

[12] reflection [ri'flekʃən] n. 反射，反映；沉思，考虑

[13] circumstance ['sə:kəmstəns] n. 环境，（复数）境况

[14] reluctance [ri'lʌktəns] n. 不愿意，勉强

[15] benchmark [bentʃma:k] n. 基准，参照

[16] fundamental [,fʌndə'mentl] adj. 基础的，基本的，根本的

[17] diagnostic [,daiəg'nɔstik] adj. 诊断的，判断的

[18] barrier ['bæriə] n. 屏障，障碍；栅栏

only, Level 3 evaluations (Behavior) for strategic programs only and Level 4 evaluations (Results) for programs costing over $50,000. Above all, before starting an evaluation, be crystal[19] clear about your purpose in conducting the evaluation.

3. Using the Kirkpatrick Model

How do you conduct a training evaluation? Here is a quick guide on some appropriate information sources for each level.

Level 1: Reaction
- completed participant feedback questionnaire[20]
- informal comments from participants
- focus group sessions[21] with participants

Level 2: Learning
- pre- and post-test scores
- on-the-job assessments
- supervisor reports

Level 3: Behavior
- completed self-assessment questionnaire
- on-the-job observation
- reports from customers, peers and participant's manager

Level 4: Results
- financial reports
- quality inspections
- interview with sales manager

When considering what sources of data you will use for your evaluation, think about the cost and time involved in collecting the data. Balance this against the accuracy of the source and the accuracy you actually need.

4. Future Applications

In 2011, Atlanta-based Kirkpatrick Partners modified the learning and evaluation model to more easily calculate the return on expectations (ROE) of stakeholders. Kirkpatrick Partners contends[22] that ROE is the "ultimate indicator of value". While ROI and ROE are common methods for evaluating and justifying training, many training organizations still struggle with the four levels, particularly quantifying levels three and four.

---

[19] crystal ['krɪstl] n. 晶体；水晶；结晶 adj. 水晶的，水晶般的，透明的

[20] questionnaire [ˌkwestʃə'neə] n. 调查问卷，调查表

[21] session ['seʃən] n. 开会，会议

[22] contend [kən'tend] v. 声称，主张

As learning content becomes increasingly available through informal channels, learners and training organizations are finding ways to use and incorporate this type of material into personal enrichment or professional training methods. Most of these informal channels, however, do not include pre- and post-evaluations—or any type of measuring tools—to measure effectiveness. To mitigate[23] this issue, advancements like Experience API (or Tin Can API) allow training organizations to effectively track and measure informal learning activities.

[23] mitigate ['mitigeit] v. 使缓和，使减轻

参考译文（Text A）

培训需求分析

培训需求分析（TNA）是确定员工培训与培训需求间差距的过程，是培训过程的第一个阶段，它确定培训是否能真正解决已发现的问题。培训可以是"对工作环境中能提高绩效的技能、观念或态度的获取"。培训需求分析着眼于操作领域的各个方面，以便有效地识别系统中人的基本技能、观念和态度，并明确相应的培训。

1. 培训需求分析的好处

培训需求分析（TNA）可用来评估一个企业的培训需求。它的基础是差距分析，即分析评估该企业员工目前所拥有的知识、技能和态度与为了实现企业目标员工需要掌握的知识、技能和态度之间的差距。培训需求分析提供深层次的见解和具体的数据，以确定组织内的培训需求和差距。培训需求分析有如下好处：

首先，通过分析，我们能够回答以下问题：
- 需要培训吗？
- 如果需要，将在何处实施培训？
- 需要哪一类培训？

对企业而言，培训需求分析是企业的战略举措之一，旨在深入研究如何提高劳动力技能、能力和内在潜力。如果能成功部署培训需求分析，企业将能优化利用资源，更好地对培训结果做出评估。因此，它能使企业的目的、目标趋于合理化，也有助于在股东间建立信誉。

此外，培训需求分析还注意到了效率准则，即人工成本、废物最小化、时间分配和生产速度。通过深入分析，所有的参数都被记录下来，所获得的数据能反映出需要在哪些领域进行培训。

同时，培训需求分析将回答诸如培训与员工的关联性等问题：如果受过培训，他们

会做出改变，并提高工作绩效吗？提高的工作绩效与企业的目标有关联吗等诸如此类的与雇员相关的问题。为了保持员工的能力水平，培训需求分析还要测评他们需要遵循的标准。

此外，培训需求分析还对员工滞后的领域进行了详细调查（如就知识、技能或态度而言，员工有滞后吗？）。通过这种认识，员工能更快地获得新技能，从而享受他们的工作。

总的来说，可以断定，通过正确的培训需求分析及运用（注：两者同时进行），我们能让每个员工快乐、高效地工作。培训需求分析详细审查了理论绩效水平与实际绩效水平之间的差距。

这种差距可能发生在企业层面或个人层面。根据差距分析，我们可以假定所需资源，并相应地计划预算，进一步确保企业的战略规划或 SWOT 分析。员工的优势通过必要的培训得以进一步加强，其任何劣势都可以被评估为需要重点关注的领域，而机会能发现那些需要减少威胁的领域。

2. 培训需求分析步骤

培训需求分析是有效培训设计的首要步骤。它帮助你确定需要培训的人员和培训类型。（顺便说一句，良好的培训需求分析还应该考虑非传统的培训解决方案是否是一个更好的选择。）培训需求分析也有助于掌握能满足培训需求的最有效的方法。下面的步骤能帮助你进行有效的培训需求分析：

步骤1：组织分析

与领导合作，明确培训的优先事项，确保培训目标和业务目标完全一致。记录期望的商业成果，同时，分析企业对培训的准备情况，包括识别和消除（至少是减少）可能使培训效果不佳的障碍。

领导越强调培训对企业的重要性，培训效果就越好。当明确定义并提前说明要测评的培训成果时，培训效果最好。

步骤2：任务分析

工作任务分析是将工作系统地分解成其组成部分的过程。工作任务分析的目标是生成执行特定工作所需要的任务列表，然后针对每个任务，确定执行该任务所需的技能和能力。这将为你的培训设计奠定坚实的基础。工作任务分析报告应该被用来决定培训内容和绩效标准。

分析人员通常通过访谈、小组讨论或调查、收集专家的信息来完成任务分析。最终的分析报告应该详细地描述完成特定任务所需要的体力活动、精神活动、任务持续时间和频率、所有必要设备以及技能和能力。

注意区分员工需要知道的事情和他们需要访问的信息，这也是工作任务分析的一部分。这对你的培训设计有很大的影响：教会员工如何以及在哪里找到与工作相关的信息远比要求他们记住某些信息更有效。

你可能还要考虑与工作任务分析极为相似的认知任务分析，它为知识型而非任务型的工作提供相似的结构框架。如果你需要揭示工作的认知需求，比如决策、解决问题、记忆、注意力和判断等，就实施认知任务分析。这可能是一个复杂而微妙的分析过程。

最后，团队合作需求分析可能是培训需求分析的一个有用部分，其他形式的任务分析可能缺少与团队相关的任务和能力分析。团队任务分析有助于强调工作协调的重要性，分析报告可用来确定培训目标，并决定哪些员工应该一起参加培训。有效的团队培训包括常规团队合作培训以及针对如何完成特定任务的培训。

步骤3：人的分析

这种分析可以确认谁已经掌握了以及谁还需要学习前面的任务分析所确定的技能和能力，并有助于对现状与理想效果之间差距最大的领域进行培训。

人的分析可以帮助你了解培训参与者的特点。例如，你发现他们主要是年轻人。在这种情况下，你可能会有意识地设计培训，使其与"新千年一代"产生共鸣。

记住，通常情况下，员工不擅长识别自身需要培训的领域。一个已被充分研究过的现象是：事情做不好的人往往对自己的能力极度自信。那些无知的人盲目自信的原因是：能力本身所需要的技能往往与认识到能力所需要的技能相似。这就是为什么系统的培训需求分析很重要的原因之一。

培训需求分析是确保企业的培训资源得到最有效利用的第一步，也是最重要的一步。专家强烈建议进行系统全面的培训需求分析。这将有助于你充分了解企业环境，清楚了解实现预期效果所需的能力，并确定哪些员工和团队最需要培训。

Unit 7

Text A

Performance Management

1. Overview

The role of HR in the present scenario has undergone a sea of changes and its focus is on evolving such functional strategies which enable successful implementation of the major corporate strategies. In a way, HR and corporate strategies function in alignment. Today, HR works towards facilitating and improving the performance of the employees by building a conducive work environment and providing maximum opportunities to the employees for participating in organizational planning and decision making process.

Performance management is the current buzzword and is the need in the current times of cut throat competition and the organizational battle for leadership. Performance management is a much broader and a complicated function of HR, as it encompasses activities such as joint goal setting, continuous progress review and frequent communication, feedback and coaching for improved performance, implementation of employee development programmes and rewarding achievements.

Performance management can be regarded as a systematic process by which the overall performance of an organization can be improved by improving the performance of individuals within a team framework. It is a means for promoting superior performance by communicating expectations, defining roles within a required competence framework and establishing achievable benchmarks.

The term performance management gained its popularity in early 1980's when total quality management programs received the utmost importance for achievement of superior standards and quality performance. Tools such as job design, leadership development, training and reward system received an equal impetus along with the traditional performance appraisal process in the new comprehensive and a much wider framework. Performance management is an ongoing communication process which is carried between the supervisors and the employees throughout the year. The process is very much cyclical and continuous in nature. A performance management system includes the following actions:

- developing clear job descriptions and employee performance plans which include the key result areas (KRA) and performance indicators;
- selecting the right set of people by implementing an appropriate selection process;
- negotiating requirements and performance standards for measuring the outcome and overall productivity against the predefined benchmarks;
- providing continuous coaching and feedback during the period of delivery of performance;
- identifying the training and development needs by measuring the outcomes achieved against the set standards and implementing effective development programs for improvement;
- holding quarterly performance development discussions and evaluating employee performance on the basis of performance plans;
- designing effective compensation and reward systems for recognizing those employees who excel in their jobs by achieving the set standards in accordance with the performance plans or rather exceed the performance benchmarks;
- providing promotional/career development support and guidance to the employees;
- performing exit interviews for understanding the cause of employee discontentment and thereafter exit from an organization.

A performance management process sets the platform for rewarding excellence by aligning individual employee accomplishments with the organization's mission and objectives and making the employee and the organization understand the importance of a specific job in realizing outcomes. By establishing clear performance expectations which include results, actions and behaviors, it helps the employees in understanding what exactly is expected out of their jobs and setting of standards help in eliminating those jobs which are of no use any longer. Through regular feedback and coaching, it provides an advantage of diagnosing the problems at an early stage and taking corrective actions.

2. Objectives of Performance Management

According to Lockett (1992), performance management aims at developing individuals with the required commitment and competencies for working towards the shared meaningful objectives within an organizational framework.

The main goal of performance management is to ensure that the organization as a system and its subsystems work together in an integrated fashion for accomplishing optimum results or outcomes. The major objectives of performance management are listed below:

- to enable the employees towards achievement of superior standards of work performance;
- to help the employees in identifying the knowledge and skills required for performing the job efficiently as this would drive their focus towards performing the right task in the right way;
- to boost the performance of the employees by encouraging employee empowerment

motivation and implementation of an effective reward mechanism;

• to promote a two-way system of communication between the supervisors and the employees for clarifying expectations about the roles and accountabilities, communicating the functional and organizational goals, and providing a regular and a transparent feedback for improving employee performance and continuous coaching;

• to identify the barriers to effective performance and resolve those barriers through constant monitoring, coaching and development interventions;

• to create a basis for several administrative decisions: strategic planning, succession planning, promotions and performance based payment;

• to promote personal growth and advancement in the career of the employees by helping them in acquiring the desired knowledge and skills.

The performance management approach has become an indispensable tool in the hands of the corporates as it ensures that the people uphold the corporate values and tread in the path of accomplishment of the ultimate corporate vision and mission. It is a forward looking process as it involves both the supervisor and also the employee in a process of joint planning and goal setting in the beginning of the year.

3. Components of Performance Management System

Any effective performance management system includes the following components:

Performance planning. Performance planning is the first crucial component of any performance management process which forms the basis of performance appraisals. Performance planning is jointly done by the appraiser and also the reviewee in the beginning of a performance session. During this period, the employers decide upon the targets and the key performance areas which can be performed over a year within the performance budget, which is finalized after a mutual agreement between the reporting officer and the employee.

Performance appraisal and reviewing. The appraisals are normally performed twice in a year in an organization in the form of mid reviews and annual reviews which is held in the end of the financial year. In this process, the appraisee first offers the self filled up ratings in the self appraisal form and also describes his/her achievements over a period of time in quantifiable terms. After the self appraisal, the final ratings are provided by the appraiser for the quantifiable and measurable achievements of the employee being appraised. The entire process of review seeks an active participation of both the employee and the appraiser for analyzing the causes of loopholes in the performance and how it can be overcome.

Feedback on the performance followed by personal counseling and performance facilitation. Feedback and counseling is given a lot of importance in the performance management process. This is the stage in which the employee acquires awareness from the appraiser about the areas of improvement and also information on whether the employee is contributing the expected levels of performance or not. The employee receives an open and a very transparent feedback and along with this the training and development needs of the employee is also identified. The appraiser adopts all the possible steps to ensure that the employee meets the expected outcomes for an organization through effective personal counseling and guidance, mentoring and representing the employee in training programmes which develop the competencies and improve the overall productivity.

Rewarding good performance. This is a very vital component as it will determine the work motivation of an employee. During this stage, an employee is publicly recognized for good performance and is rewarded. This stage is very sensitive for an employee as this may have a direct influence on the self esteem and achievement orientation. Any contribution duly recognized by an organization helps an employee in coping up with the failures successfully and satisfying the need for affection.

Performance improvement plans. In this stage, fresh set of goals are established for an employee and a new deadline is provided for accomplishing those objectives. The employee is clearly communicated about the areas in which the employee is expected to improve and a stipulated deadline is also assigned within which the employee must show this improvement. This plan is jointly developed by the appraisee and the appraiser and is mutually approved.

Potential appraisal. Potential appraisal forms a basis for both lateral and vertical movement of employees. By implementing competency mapping and various assessment techniques, potential appraisal is performed. Potential appraisal provides crucial inputs for succession planning and job rotation.

4. Characteristics of Performance Management

Performance management is a planned process of which the primary elements are agreement, measurement, feedback, positive reinforcement and dialogue. It is concerned with measuring outputs in the shape of delivered performance compared with expectations expressed as objectives. In this respect, it focuses on targets, standards and performance measures or indicators. It is based on the agreement of role requirements, objectives and performance improvement and personal development plans. It provides the setting for ongoing dialogues about performance, which involves the joint and continuing review of achievements against objectives, requirements and plans.

But it is also concerned with inputs and values. The inputs are the knowledge, skills and behaviors required to produce the expected results. Developmental needs are identified by defining these requirements and assessing the extent to which the expected levels of performance have been achieved through the effective use of knowledge and skills and through appropriate behavior that upholds core values.

Performance management is a continuous and flexible process that involves managers and those whom they manage acting as partners within a framework that sets out how they can best work together to achieve the required results. It is based on the principle of management by contract and agreement rather than management by command. It relies on consensus and cooperation rather than control or coercion.

Performance management focuses on future performance planning and improvement rather than on retrospective performance appraisal. It functions as a continuous and evolutionary process, in which performance improves over time, and provides the basis for regular and frequent dialogues between managers and individuals about performance and development needs. It is mainly concerned with individual performance but it can also be applied to teams. The focus is on development, although performance management is an important part of the reward system through the provision of feedback and recognition and the identification of opportunities for growth. It may be associated with performance—or contribution-related pay but its developmental aspects are much more important.

New Words

corporate ['kɔ:pərit] adj. 法人的；公司的
conducive [kən'dju:siv] adj. 有助于……的，有益的
buzzword ['bʌzwə:d] n. （报刊等的）时髦术语，流行行话
complicated [kɔmplikeitid] adj. 复杂难懂的，结构复杂的
means [mi:nz] n. 方法，手段
achievable [ə'tʃi:vəbl] adj. 做得成的，可完成的，可有成就的
popularity [,pɔpju'lærəti] n. 普及，流行；通俗性
utmost ['ʌtməust] adj. 极度的，最大的
impetus ['impitəs] n. 动力，势头，声势
cyclical ['siklikəl] adj. 周期的，循环的
indicator ['indikeitə] n. 指示器；[统计学]指标
productivity [,prɔdʌk'tivəti] n. 生产率，生产力
predefined [pridifaind] adj. 预定义的；预先确定的
delivery [di'livəri] n. 传递，运送；交付；陈述；分娩
exceed [ik'si:d] v. 超过，超出
promotional [prə'məuʃənl] adj. 晋升的；推销的；增进的
discontentment [,diskən'tentmənt] n. 不满，不平

accomplishment [ə'kɔmpliʃmənt] n. 成就；完成
diagnose ['daiəgnəuz] v. 判断；诊断（疾病）
commitment [kə'mitmənt] n. 承诺，许诺；委任；献身
subsystem ['sʌb,sistəm] n. 子系统，分系统；
drive [draiv] v. 驱动，迫使
clarify ['klærifai] v. 使清楚，澄清；说明
accountability [ə,kauntə'biləti] n. 有责任，有义务
transparent [træns'peərənt] adj. 易识破的，显而易见的；透明的
resolve [ri'zɔlv] v. 解决；决定，表决
constant ['kɔnstənt] adj. 不变的，经常的
intervention [,intə(:)'venʃən] n. 介入，干预；调停
administrative [əd'ministrətiv] adj. 行政的，管理的
indispensable [,indis'pensəbl] adj. 不可缺少的
uphold [ʌp'həuld] v. 支持，维护，维持
tread [tred] n. 踏步，步行；步法
vision ['viʒən] n. 眼光；洞察力；想象力
appraisee [ə'preizi:] n. 受评人，接受评核人员

quantifiable ['kwɔntəfaiəbl] adj. 可以计量的
participation [pɑ:,tisi'peiʃən] n. 参加，参与；分享
loophole ['lu:phəul] n. 漏洞
facilitation [fə,sili'teiʃən] n. 促进；使人方便的东西
mentor ['mentɔr] v. 做……的良师，指导
self-esteem [,selfis'ti:m] n. 自尊
affection [ə'fekʃən] n. 喜爱，慈爱；情感或感情
deadline ['dedlain] n. 最后期限，截止期限

stipulate ['stipjuleit] v. 规定，明确要求
vertical ['və:tikəl] adj. 垂直的，竖立的
input ['input] n. 输入，投入
reinforcement [,ri:in'fɔ:smənt] n. 加强
coercion [kəu'ə:ʃən] n. 强制，强迫
consensus [kən'sensəs] n. 一致同意，合意
retrospective [,retrəu'spektiv] adj. 回顾的，怀旧的
evolutionary [,i:və'lu:ʃənəri] adj. 进化的，发展的
provision [prə'viʒən] n. 供应；条项，条款

Phrases

cut throat competition 残酷竞争
be regarded as 被视作，被认为
compensation and reward system 薪酬制度
excel in 在……方面十分出众
in accordance with 与……一致，依照
exit interview 离职谈话，辞退面谈
align with 与……结盟，联合
be of no use 无用，无效
take corrective action 采取纠正措施
work performance 工作绩效
succession planning 继任计划
performance-based payment 绩效薪酬
in the hands of 在……掌握中；由……处理，由……负责
performance planning 绩效计划

mutual agreement 双方一致同意
self appraisal 自我考核，自我评估
meet the expected outcome 达到预期效果
have a direct influence on 对……有直接的影响
achievement orientation 成就取向
cope up with 应付
in the shape of 以……形状；通过……方式
compared with 与……比较
in this respect 在这方面
core values 核心价值观
set out 开始；打算
function as 起……的作用
be associated with 和……联系在一起，与……有关

Unit 7

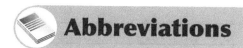

KRA (Key Result Areas) 关键绩效区

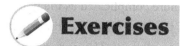

EX. 1 Answer the following questions according to the text.

1. As a means, how can performance management promote superior performance of employees?
2. List at least three actions which a performance management system includes.
3. How does a performance management process help the employees understand what exactly is expected out of their jobs?
4. What does performance management aim at according to Lockett (1992)?
5. Is it one of the major objectives of performance management to promote advancement in the career of the employees?
6. Why is the performance management approach regarded as an indispensable tool in the hands of the corporates?
7. In which stage of performance management process can the employee acquire information on whether he/she is contributing the expected levels of performance or not?
8. During which stage of performance management process is an employee publicly recognized for good performance?
9. Which component of performance management system provides crucial inputs for succession planning and job rotation?
10. What principle is performance management based on in terms of its characteristics?

EX. 2 Translate the following terms or phrases from English into Chinese and vice versa.

1. core values
2. achievement orientation
3. compensation and reward system
4. exit interview
5. performance planning
6. 绩效薪酬
7. 继任计划
8. 工作绩效

1. _____
2. _____
3. _____
4. _____
5. _____
6. _____
7. _____
8. _____

9. *adj.* 晋升的；推销的；增进的   9. _____
10. *n.* 有责任，有义务   10. _____

EX. 3 Translate the following text into Chinese.

In the present scenario, the organizations have shifted their focus from performance appraisals to performance management as a result of internationalization of human resources and globalization of business. The functions of HRM have become far more complicated as today the major focus of strategic HRM practices is on the management of talent by implementing such development programmes which enhance the competencies of the employees. The performance management approach focuses more on observed behaviors and concrete results based on the previously established SMART objectives. By adopting techniques like management by objectives (MBO), SMART objectives are established in terms of either facts and figures and in the entire process the superior plays the role of a coach or a facilitator. The objectives are mutually decided at the beginning of the performance season and serve as a standard of performance for evaluation. In this method, the employees can offer a feedback on their contributions by filling up a self appraisal form. Performance management is a much broader term in comparison with performance appraisal as it deals with a gamut of activities which performance appraisals never deal with. This system is a strategic and an integrated approach which aims at building successful organizations by developing high performance teams and individuals and improving the performance of people.

EX. 4 Fill in the blanks with the words given below.

consistent	assessment	evaluates	advise	specified
comprehensive	basic	outlined	initial	officially

A Performance Management Cycle

A performance management cycle (PMC) is a technique used by company managers and executives to encourage employee growth and job satisfaction. Within a PMC, the employer __1__ an employee's skills and job performance. The employer typically will set goals, as well, help careers develop in a manner __2__ with company goals for the employee. If an employee is not able to meet the goals and expectations __3__ by the company, a performance management cycle usually offers a built-in system for improvement, typically beginning with direct counseling for problem areas. Though __4__ goals may be set by the company when an employee is hired, the performance management cycle usually will not __5__ begin until the first performance review—typically after the first year of employment, but sooner in some cases.

While each company usually develops its own plan for performance management cycles, the __6__ cycle typically includes three phases: planning and goal setting, progress reporting, and review ___7___. When it is time for the first performance review, the employer will assess the employee's work as executed during the ___8___ time frame. After providing the employee with a ___9___ evaluation of his job performance, the employer usually will ___10___ him of the company goals for him over the next review period.

Text B

Performance Appraisal

A performance appraisal (PA), also referred to as a performance review, a performance evaluation (career), a development discussion, or an employee appraisal, is a method by which the job performance of an employee is documented and evaluated. Performance appraisals are a part of career development and consist of regular reviews of employee performance within organizations.

1. Application of Results

A central reason for the utilization of performance appraisals (PAs) is performance improvement (initially at the level of the individual employee, and ultimately at the level of the organization). Other fundamental reasons include as a basis for employment decisions (e.g. promotions, terminations, transfers), as criteria in research (e.g. test validation), to aid with communication (e.g. allowing employees to know how they are doing and organizational expectations), to establish personal objectives for training programs, for transmission of objective feedback for personal development, as a means of documentation to aid in keeping track of decisions and legal requirements and in wage and salary administration. Additionally, PAs can aid in the formulation of job criteria and selection of individuals who are best suited to perform the required organizational tasks. They can be part of guiding and monitoring employee career development and be used to aid in work motivation through the use of reward systems as well.

2. Benefits of Performance Appraisals

There are a number of potential benefits of organizational performance management conducting formal PAs. There has been a general consensus in the belief that PAs lead to positive implications of organizations. Furthermore, PAs can benefit an organization's effectiveness. One way is PAs can often lead to giving individual workers feedback about their job performance. From this may spawn several potential benefits such as the individual workers becoming more productive. Other potential benefits include:

Facilitation of communication. Communication in organizations is considered an essential function of worker motivation. It has been proposed that feedback from PAs aid in minimizing employees' perceptions of uncertainty. Fundamentally, feedback and management-employee communication can serve as a guide in job performance.

Enhancement of employee focus through promoting trust. Behaviors, thoughts, and/or issues may distract employees from their work, and trust issues may be among these distracting factors. Such factors that consume psychological energy can lower job performance and cause workers to lose sight of organizational goals. Properly constructed and utilized PAs have the ability to lower distracting factors and encourage trust within the organization.

Goal setting and desired performance reinforcement. Organizations find it's efficient to match individual worker's goals and performance with organizational goals. PAs provide room for discussion in the collaboration of these individual and organizational goals. Collaboration can also be advantageous by resulting in employee acceptance and satisfaction of appraisal results.

Performance improvement. Well constructed PAs can be valuable tools for communication with employees as pertaining to how their job performance stands with organizational expectations. At the organizational level, numerous studies have reported positive relationships between human resource management (HRM) practices and performance improvement at both the individual and organizational levels.

Determination of training needs. Employee training and development are crucial components in helping an organization achieve strategic initiatives. It has been argued that for PAs to truly be effective, post-appraisal opportunities for training and development in problem areas, as determined by the appraisal, must be offered. PAs can especially be instrumental for identifying training needs of new employees. Finally, PAs can help in the establishment and supervision of employees' career goals.

3. Methods of Performance Appraisals

The main methods used in performance appraisal are:

Graphic rating scale. Graphic rating scales are the most commonly used system in PAs. On several different factors, subordinates are judged on "how much" of that factor or trait they possess. Typically, the raters use a 5- or 7-point scale, however, there are as many as 20-point scales.

Employee-comparison methods. Rather than subordinates being judged against pre-established criteria, they are compared with one another. This method eliminates central tendency and leniency errors but still allows for halo effect errors to occur. The rank-order method has raters ranking subordinates from "best" to "worst", but how truly good or bad one is on a performance dimension would be unknown. The paired-comparison method requires the rater to select the two "best" subordinates out of a group on each dimension, then rank individuals according to the number of times each subordinate was selected as one of the "best". The forced-distribution method is good for large groups of ratees. The raters evaluate each subordinate on one or more dimensions and then place (or "force-fit", if you will) each subordinate in a 5- to 7-category normal distribution. The method of top-grading can be applied to the forced distribution method. This method identifies the 10% lowest performing subordinates, as according to the forced distribution, and dismisses them leaving the 90% higher performing subordinates.

Behavioral checklists and scales. Behaviors are more definite than traits. The critical incidents method (or critical incident technique) concerns specific behaviors indicative of good or bad job performance. Supervisors record behaviors of what they judge to be job performance relevant, and they keep a running tally of good and bad behaviors. A discussion on performance may then follow. The behaviorally anchored rating scale (BARS) combines the critical incidents method with rating scale methods by rating performance on a scale but with the scale points being anchored by behavioral incidents. In the behavioral observation scale (BOS) approach to performance appraisal, employees are also evaluated in the terms of critical incidents. In that respect, it is similar to BARS. However, the BOS appraisal rate subordinates on the frequency of the critical incidents as they are observed to occur over a given period. The ratings are assigned on a 5-point scale. The behavioral incidents for the rating scale are developed in the same way as for BARS through identification by supervisors or other subject matter experts.

Self-assessments. For self-assessments, individuals assess and evaluate their own behavior and job performance.

Peer assessments. Members of a group evaluate and appraise the performance of their fellow group members. There it is common for a graphic rating scale to be used for self-assessments. Positive leniency tends to be a problem with self-assessments. Peer assessments from multiple members of a group are often called crowd-based performance reviews, and solve many problems with peer assessments from only one member.

360-degree feedback. 360-degree feedback is multiple evaluations of employees which often include assessments from superior(s), peers, and one's self.

Negotiated performance appraisal. The negotiated performance appraisal (NPA) is an emerging approach for improving communication between supervisors and subordinates and for increasing employee productivity, and may also be adapted to an alternate mediation model for supervisor-subordinate conflicts. A facilitator meets separately with the supervisor and with the subordinate to prepare three lists: what employees do well, where the employee has improved in recently, and areas where the employee still needs to improve. Because the subordinate will present his or her lists first during the joint session, this reduces defensive behaviors. Furthermore, the subordinate comes to the joint session not only prepares to share areas of needed improvement, but also brings concrete ideas as to how these improvements can be made. The NPA also focuses very strongly on what employees are doing well, and involves a minimum of twenty minutes of praise when discussing what the employee does well. The role of the facilitator is that of a coach in the caucuses, and in the joint sessions the supervisor and subordinate mostly speak to each other with little facilitator interference.

In general, optimal PA process involves a combination of multiple assessment methods. One common recommendation is that assessment flows from self-assessment to peer-assessment, to management assessment—in that order. Starting with self-assessment facilitates avoidance of conflict. Peer feedback ensures peer accountability, which may yield better results than accountability to management. Management assessment comes last for need of recognition by authority and avoidance of conflict in case of disagreements. It is generally recommended that PA is done in shorter cycles to avoid high-stakes discussions, as is usually the case in long-cycle appraisals.

4. Performance Appraisal Biases

Managers commit mistakes while evaluating employees and their performance. Biases and judgment errors of various kinds may spoil the performance appraisal process. Bias here refers to inaccurate distortion of a measurement. These are:

First impression (primacy effect). Raters form an overall impression about the ratee on the basis of some particular characteristics of the ratee identified by them. The identified qualities and features may not provide an adequate base for appraisal.

Halo effect. The individual's performance is completely appraised on the basis of a perceived positive quality, feature or trait. In other words this is the tendency to rate a man uniformly high or low in other traits if he is extra-ordinarily high or low in one particular trait. If a worker has few absences, his supervisor might give him a high rating in all other areas of work.

Horn effect. The individual's performance is completely appraised on the basis of a negative quality or feature perceived. This results in an overall lower rating than may be warranted. "He is not formally dressed up in the office. He may be casual at work too!"

Excessive stiffness or lenience. Depending upon the raters own standards, values and physical and mental makeup at the time of appraisal, ratees may be rated very strictly or leniently. Some of the managers are likely to take the line of least resistance and rate people high, whereas others, by nature, believe in the tyranny of exact assessment, considering more particularly the drawbacks of the individual and thus making the assessment excessively severe. The leniency error can render a system ineffective. If everyone is to be rated high, the system has not done anything to differentiate among the employees.

Central tendency. Appraisers rate all employees as average performers. That is, it is an attitude to rate people as neither high nor low and follow the middle path. For example, a professor, with a view to play it safe, might give a class grade near the equal to B, regardless of the differences in individual performances.

Personal biases. The way a supervisor feels about each of the individuals working under him, whether he likes or dislikes them, as a tremendous effect on the rating of their performances. Personal bias can stem from various sources as a result of information obtained from colleagues, considerations of faith and thinking, social and family background and so on.

Spillover effect. The present performance is evaluated much on the basis of past performance. The person who was a good performer in distant past is assured to be okay at present also.

Recency effect. Rating is influenced by the most recent behavior ignoring the commonly demonstrated behaviors during the entire appraisal period.

Unit 7

New Words

initially [i'niʃəli] adv. 最初；开始；
validation [,væli'deiʃən] n. 验证，确认；批准
transmission [trænz'miʃən] n. 传输，传播，播送
formulation [,fɔ:mju'leiʃən] n. 规划，构想
spawn [spɔ:n] v. 大量产生
consume [kən'sju:m] v. 消耗，消费；耗尽
psychological [,saikə'lɔdʒikəl] adj. 心理的，精神上的
determination [di,tə:mi'neiʃən] n. 确定；决心，决定
argue ['ɑ:gju:] v. 坚决主张；提出理由证明；表明
instrumental [,instru'mentl] adj. 有帮助的；可作为手段的
supervision [,sju:pə'viʒən] n. 监督；管理
graphic ['græfik] adj. 图表的
eliminate [i'limineit] v. 排除，消除
rater ['reitə] n. 定等级者
forced-distribution [fɔ:st-,distri'bju:ʃən] n. 强制正态分布
ratee [rə'ti:] n. 受评者
checklist [tʃeklist] n. (核对用的)一览表
definite ['definit] adj. 明确的；一定的，有把握的
concern [kən'sə:n] v. 涉及，影响；关心
tally ['tæli] n. 账；记分
anchor ['æŋkə] v. 使固定，使稳固；使稳定 n. 锚
self-assessment [self-ə'sesmənt] n. 自我评估

emerging [i'mə:dʒiŋ] adj. 新兴的
defensive [di'fensiv] adj. 防御用的，防守的；辩护的
caucus ['kɔ:kəs] n. 核心成员；干部会议
interference [,intə'fiərəns] n. 干扰；妨碍
optimal ['ɔptiməl] adj. 最理想的，最佳的
recommendation [,rekəmen'deiʃən] n. 推荐；建议
avoidance [ə'vɔidəns] n. 避免；逃避，回避
yield [ji:ld] v. 生产；获利
disagreement [disə'gri:mənt] n. 不合，争议
high-stake [hai-steik] adj. 高风险的，高利害的
inaccurate [in'ækjurət] adj. 不准确，不正确的；不精密的
distortion [dis'tɔ:ʃən] n. 扭曲，变形
primacy ['praiməsi] n. 首位，第一位
uniformly ['ju:nifɔ:mli] adv. 一致地，相同地
extraordinarily [ik'strɔ:dinərəli] adv. 十分，特别，极其
warrant ['wɔrənt] v. 保证，担保；授权，批准
stiffness ['stifnis] n. 僵硬，生硬
lenience ['li:njəns] n. 宽大，仁慈
makeup ['meikʌp] n. 构造；化妆
tyranny ['tirəni] n. 专横，暴虐，暴行
severe [si'viə] adj. 严峻的，严厉的，苛刻的
render ['rendə] v. 使成为；给予；递交
tremendous [tri'mendəs] adj. 极大的，巨大的；惊人的，极好的
ignore [ig'nɔ:] v. 忽视，不顾

人力资源管理 英语

Phrases

test validation 实验验证	peer assessment 同行评议，同行评价
aid in 在……方面帮助	a joint session 联合会议
keep track of 记录；与……保持联系	as to 关于
perception of uncertainty 不确定感	commit mistake 犯错
distract from 分散，转移，使分心	primacy effect 首因效应
distracting factor 分散注意力的因素	form an overall impression 形成整体印象
lose sight of 忽视，忘记；看不见	horn effect 尖角效应
graphic rating scale 图表测度法	dress up 打扮
central tendency 居中趋势	by nature 生性，本性上
halo effect 连锁反应	with a view to play it safe 为了谨慎行事
indicative of 指示，预示	stem from 来自，起源于
keep a running tally of 流水账	recency effect 近因效应
over a given period 在一定时期内	

Abbreviations

PA (Performance Appraisal) 绩效考核
BARS (Behaviorally Anchored Rating Scale) 行为锚定等级评价法
BOS (Behavioral Observation Scale) 行为观察评价法
NPA (Negotiated Performance Appraisal) 协商绩效评估法

Exercises

EX. 5 Read the following statements and then decide whether each of them is true or false based on the information in Text B. Write T for True and F for False in the space provided before each statement.

_____ 1. Performance improvement at the level of the individual employee is the sole reason for the utilization of performance appraisals.

_____ 2. PAs can assist in setting job criteria and selecting individuals best suitable for the required tasks.

_____ 3. Trust issues may bring down the employees' motivation and cause them to ignore

136

organizational goals.

_____ 4. Graphic rating scales eliminates central tendency and leniency errors.

_____ 5. The behavioral observation scale (BOS) approach is similar to the forced-distribution method in that employees are all evaluated in the terms of critical incidents by these two methods.

_____ 6. Peer assessments from multiple members of a group can avoid the problem of positive leniency with self-assessments.

_____ 7. 360-degree feedback is multiple evaluations of employees which often include assessments more from superior(s) than from peers and one's self.

_____ 8. Raters tend to rate a man uniformly high or low in other traits if he is extraordinarily high or low in one particular trait, which is called primacy effect.

_____ 9. With central tendency, the raters tend to appraise a man's performance based on a negative quality and give an overall lower rating.

_____ 10. Spillover effect means that a man's present performance is greatly judged on his past performance while recency effect implies that rating is influenced by the most recent behavior.

Supplementary Reading

Text	Notes
Motivational Theories Employee motivation is an intrinsic[1] and internal drive to put forth[2] the necessary effort and action towards work-related activities. It has been broadly[3] defined as the psychological forces that determine the direction of a person's behavior in an organization, a person's level of effort and a person's level of persistence[4]. Motivation can also be thought of as the willingness to expend energy to achieve a goal or a reward. Motivation at work has been defined as the sum of the processes that influence the arousal[5], direction, and maintenance of behaviors relevant to[6] work settings. **1. Expectancy[7] Theory of Motivation** The expectancy theory was proposed by Victor Vroom of Yale School of Management in 1964. Vroom stresses and focuses on outcomes, not on needs like Maslow and Herzberg. The theory states that the intensity[8] of a tendency to perform	[1] intrinsic [in'trinsik] *adj.* 固有的, 内在的, 本质的 [2] put forth: 提出 [3] broadly [brɔ:dli] *adv.* 大体上; 完全地 [4] persistence [pə'sistəns] *n.* 持续, 坚持不懈 [5] arousal [ə'rauzəl] *n.* 觉醒; 激励 [6] relevant to: 有关的 [7] expectancy [ik'spektənsi] *n.* 期待, 期望; 期望的东西 [8] intensity [in'tensəti] *n.* 强度, 烈度; 强烈

in a particular manner is dependent on the intensity of an expectation that the performance will be followed by a definite outcome and on the appeal[9] of the outcome to the individual.

The expectancy theory states that employee's motivation is an outcome of how much an individual wants a reward (valence[10]), the assessment that the likelihood that the effort will lead to expected performance (expectancy) and the belief that the performance will lead to reward (instrumentality[11]). In short, valence is the significance associated by an individual about the expected outcome. It is an expected but not the actual satisfaction that an employee expects to receive after achieving the goals. Expectancy is the faith that better efforts will result in better performance. Expectancy is influenced by factors such as possession[12] of appropriate[13] skills for performing the job, availability[14] of right resources, availability of crucial information and getting the required support for completing the job.

Instrumentality is the faith that if you perform well, then a valid outcome will be there. Instrumentality is affected by factors such as believing in the people who decide who receives what outcome, the simplicity[15] of the process deciding who gets what outcome, and clarity of relationship between performance and outcomes. Thus, the expectancy theory concentrates on the following three relationships:

Effort-performance relationship. What is the likelihood that the individual's effort be recognized in his performance appraisal?

Performance-reward relationship. It talks about the extent to which the employee believes that getting a good performance appraisal leads to organizational rewards.

Reward-personal goals relationship. It is all about the attractiveness or appeal of the potential reward to the individual.

Considerable attention has been given to the expectancy model of motivations. This model currently offers one of the best explanations of what conditions of the amount of effort an individual will exert[16] on his or her job. A vital component of this model is performance, specifically the effort performance and performance reward linkage[17]. Do people see effort leading to performance and performance to the rewards that they value?

[9] appeal [ə'piːl] n. 吸引力；恳求，呼吁

[10] valence ['veiləns] n. （心理）效价

[11] instrumentality [ˌinstrumen'tæləti] n. 手段，媒介

[12] possession [pə'zeʃən] n. 所有，拥有；财产

[13] appropriate [ə'prəupriət] adj. 适当的，合适的，恰当的

[14] availability [əˌveilə'biləti] n. 有效，可利用性

[15] simplicity [sim'plisəti] n. 简单，朴素

[16] exert [ig'zəːt] v. 发挥；运用

[17] linkage ['liŋkidʒ] n. 联系，联动，连接

Clearly, they have to know what is expected of them. They need to know how their performance will be measured. Further, they must feel confident that if they exert an effort within their capabilities, it will result in a satisfactory[18] performance as defined by the criteria by which they are being measured. Finally, they must feel confident that if they perform as they are being asked, they will achieve the rewards they value.

2. Maslow's Hierarchy of Needs

Abraham Maslow viewed motivation as being based off[19] a hierarchy of needs, of which a person cannot move to the next level of needs without satisfying the previous level. Maslow's hierarchy starts at the lowest level of needs, basic physiological[20] needs. Basic physiological needs include air, water, and food. Employers who pay at least a minimal living wage will meet these basic employee needs. The next level of needs is referred to as safety and security needs. This level includes needs such as having a place to live and knowing one is safe. Employers can meet these needs by ensuring employees are safe from physical, verbal or emotional hazards[21] and have a sense of job security. The third level of needs is social affiliation[22] and belonging. This is the need to be social, have friends, and feel like one belongs and is loved. Implementing employee participation programs can help fulfill the need to belong. Rewards such as acknowledging[23] an employee's contributions can also satisfy these social and love needs. The fourth level on the hierarchy is esteem[24] needs. This level is described as feeling good about one's self and knowing that their life is meaningful, valuable, and has a purpose. Employers should use the job design technique to create jobs that are important to and cherished[25] by the employee. These first four needs, Maslow called D-needs (deficient) and called self-actualization the B-need (being).

The last level Maslow described is called self actualization. This level refers to people reaching their potential states of well-being. An employer who ensures that an employee is in the right job and has all other needs met will help the employee realize this highest need. Maslow further expanded self-actualization into four needs, namely, cognitive, aesthetic,[26] self-actualization, and self-transcendence[27].

[18] satisfactory [ˌsætisˈfæktəri] *adj.* 令人满意的，符合要求的

[19] be based off: 基于

[20] physiological [ˌfiziəˈlɔdʒikəl] *adj.* 生理的，生理学的

[21] hazard [ˈhæzəd] *n.* 危险，冒险的事

[22] social affiliation: 社会归属

[23] acknowledge [əkˈnɔlidʒ] *v.* 承认

[24] esteem [isˈtiːm] *n.* 尊敬，尊重

[25] cherish [ˈtʃeriʃ] *v.* 珍爱，爱护

[26] aesthetic [iːsˈθetik] *adj.* 审美的；美学的

[27] self-transcendence [self-trænˈsendəns] *n.* 自我超越

3. Herzberg's Two-Factor Theory

Frederick Herzberg developed the two-factor theory of motivation based on satisfiers and dissatisfiers. Satisfiers are motivators associated with job satisfaction while dissatisfiers are motivators associated with hygiene[28] or maintenance. Satisfiers include achievement, responsibility, advancement, and recognition. Satisfiers are all intrinsic motivators that are directly related to rewards attainable from work performance and even the nature of the work itself. Dissatisfiers are extrinsic[29] motivators based on the work environment, and include a company's policies and administration such as supervision, peers, working conditions, and salary. Herzberg believed providing for hygiene and maintenance needs could prevent dissatisfaction but not contribute to satisfaction. Herzberg also believed that satisfiers hold the greatest potential for increased work performance. Work-life programs are a form of satisfier that recognizes the employee's life outside of work which, in turn, helps motivate the employee.

4. Locke's Goal Theory

Edwin A. Locke's goal theory describes setting more specific goals to elicit[30] higher performance and setting more difficult goals to increase effort. He also believed that, through employee participation in goal setting the employees would be more likely to accept the goals and have a greater job satisfaction. The goal theory's underlying assumption[31] is that employees who participate in goal setting will set more difficult goals for themselves and yield superior performance. The theory is logical because employees are going to set more difficult goals but the goals will be attainable with increased efforts. Sometimes organizations set goals that their employees will rarely, if ever, be able to meet. If the goals are always unattainable, there is no motivation to try accomplishing them.

---

[28] **hygiene** ['haidʒi:n] *n.* 卫生，卫生学；保健

[29] **extrinsic** [eks'trinsik] *adj.* 外在的，外部的

[30] **elicit** [i'lisit] *v.* 引出，探出；诱出（回答等）

[31] **underlying assumption:** 基本假设

Unit 7

参考译文（Text A）

绩 效 管 理

1. 概述

如今，人力资源所发挥的作用经历了一系列变化，主要是制定一些策略，从而确保公司的主要战略政策能得以顺利实施。在某种程度上，人力资源和企业的战略功能是一致的。目前，人力资源部致力于为员工提供有利的工作环境，让他们有尽可能多的机会参与组织规划和决策过程，以促进和提高绩效。

绩效管理是当前的流行语，是目前残酷竞争时代下组织争夺领导权的需要。绩效管理是一个更广泛、更复杂的人力资源功能。它包括诸多活动，如共同目标的设定、进度的反复审查、频繁的沟通、为提高绩效的反馈与辅导、员工发展计划的实施以及对业绩的奖励等。

绩效管理可以被看作一个系统的过程。基于这一系统过程，组织可以通过提高团队框架内个人的绩效来提高整体绩效。它是一种通过传达期望，在要求的能力框架内定义工作角色，建立可实现的基准来促进实现高绩效的方式。

"绩效管理"这个术语在20世纪80年代初开始流行。当时，为了实现高标准和高质量性能，全面质量管理计划受到了高度重视。工作设计、领导力发展、培训和奖励制度等方式在全面的、更为广泛的新框架内与传统的绩效考核过程一起发挥了同样的推动作用。绩效管理是一个持续的沟通过程，它全年贯穿于管理人员与员工之间。这个过程实质上具有很强的周期性和持续性。绩效管理体系包括以下活动：

- 制定明确的工作描述和员工绩效计划，包括关键结果领域（KRA）和业绩指标；
- 通过实施适当的甄选过程选择合适员工；
- 根据预先设定的基准，商定工作要求以及衡量成果和总体生产力的绩效标准；
- 在绩效考核期间提供持续的培训和反馈；
- 衡量最终业绩是否达到规定的标准，从而确定培训和发展的需要，并实施有效的改进发展方案；
- 举行业绩发展季度讨论会，并根据绩效规划评估员工业绩；
- 设计有效的薪酬和奖励制度，表彰那些达到规定标准或者超过绩效基准的、在工作中表现出色的员工；
- 在职位晋升或职业发展方面对员工提供支持和指导；
- 进行离职面谈，了解员工不满并离职的原因。

绩效管理过程将员工的个人成就与组织的使命和目标结合起来，并使员工和组织都能意识到一份特定的工作在成果实现中的重要性，从而建立起奖励平台。通过建立明确的绩效预期，包括结果、行动和行为，绩效管理有助于员工了解组织对他们的工作期望，并淘汰那些不再有用的工作。通过定期反馈和指导，绩效管理过程能确定早期问题，并采取行动予以纠正。

2. 绩效管理目标

根据 Lockett（1992）理论，绩效管理旨在培养并发展个人，使其具备所需的敬业精神和能力，从而在组织框架内朝着共同的、有意义的目标努力奋斗。

绩效管理的主要目标是确保组织系统及其子系统以一种集成的方式协同作用，以实现最佳结果或成果。绩效管理的主要目标如下：

- 使员工实现高标准的工作业绩；
- 帮助员工确定有效完成工作所需的知识和技能，使他们集中精力以正确的方式执行适当的任务；
- 通过提倡员工赋权、员工激励和实施有效的奖励机制提高员工的业绩；
- 促进发展主管和员工之间的双向沟通体系，以明确工作义务和责任，传达职务和组织目标，提供定期的透明的反馈，提高员工绩效并改进培训工作；
- 通过不断的监测、指导和发展等活动，确认有效业绩的障碍，并清除这些障碍；
- 为若干行政决策奠定基础，如战略规划、继任计划、员工晋升以及基于绩效的薪金支付；
- 通过帮助员工获得所需的知识和技能，促进其个人发展和职业进步。

绩效管理方式已成为企业不可或缺的工具，它确保人们秉持企业价值观，为实现企业的最终梦想和使命而奋斗。这是一个前瞻性的过程，因为它使主管和员工都参与到年初的共同规划和目标制定过程中。

3. 绩效管理系统的构成要素

任何有效的绩效管理系统都包括以下构成要素：

绩效规划。绩效规划是绩效管理过程的首要构成部分，是绩效评估的基础。绩效规划由评估人和受评估人在绩效评估会议初期共同制定完成。在此期间，雇主要决定在绩效预算内，员工一年要完成的目标和关键绩效领域，而这两者最终由评核人员和员工双方协议后确定下来。

绩效评估和评审。通常，企业在一年内进行两次绩效评估：中期审查和年底的财政年度评审。在此过程中，受评估人首先以自我评价的形式填写一份自我考核表，并以可量化的方式细数自己在一年内取得的成就。自我评估后，评估人员提供最终的评级，量化并衡量受评人的业绩。员工和评估人员都要积极参与整个评审过程，分析业绩不足的原因，以及如何克服这一现象。

接下来是个人咨询和绩效促进的绩效反馈。反馈和咨询在绩效管理过程中极为重要。在这个阶段，员工从评估人员那里获悉自身需要改进的领域，也了解到自己的工作是否达到企业期望的业绩水平。员工接受公开的、极为透明的反馈，并以此来确定培训和发展需求。评估人员采取所有可能的措施来确保员工能实现组织的预期成果，如对员工个人提供有效的咨询和引导、在培训方案中指导员工、维护他们的利益，从而培养员工的能力，提高整体生产力。

奖励好业绩。这是非常重要的构成部分，它将决定员工的工作动机。在这个阶段，员工因业绩好受到公开表彰并得到奖励。员工对该阶段非常敏感，因为这可能直接影响到他们的自尊和成就取向。企业适时地表彰员工的贡献有助于员工成功地应对失败，满足情感需求。

绩效改进方案。企业在这个阶段为员工建立一套新的目标，并为员工完成这些目标设定新的期限。企业对员工明确指出期望其改进的领域，并且规定改进成效的工作期限。这个计划是由受评估人和评估人共同制定并相互认可的。

潜力评估。潜力评估是员工调任和职位升降的基础。潜力评估通过能力映射和各种评估技术得以实施。潜力评估为继任计划和岗位轮换提供至关重要的信息数据。

4. 绩效管理的特点

绩效管理是一个有计划的过程，其主要内容是协议、测评、反馈、积极强化和对话。它涉及测评与预期目标相比较的实际业绩。在这方面，绩效管理重点关注绩效目标、标准、业绩测评或指标。它基于角色需求、目标和绩效改进，以及个人发展计划等方面的一致性，为正在进行的有关绩效的对话提供场景，包括对照绩效目标、要求和计划，对员工的业绩进行连续的审查。

但它也涉及输入值。输入的是产生预期成效所需的知识、技能和行为。通过定义这些需求，通过评定知识和技能的有效利用对实现预期绩效水平的影响程度，并通过秉持核心价值的适当行为，确定员工的发展需求。

绩效管理是一个连续、灵活的过程，涉及管理者和员工。他们在同一个组织内合作，所在的组织规定他们如何才能最好地共事，以达到所需结果。绩效管理是基于合同和协议的管理，而不是基于命令的管理。它依靠共识和合作，而不是控制或强制。

绩效管理着眼于未来的绩效规划和改进，而不是回顾性的绩效评估。它是一个连续、渐进的过程。在这个过程中，绩效随着时间的推移而提高，并且为管理人员和员工个人之间定期和频繁地讨论绩效和发展需求提供了基础。绩效管理主要关注个人业绩，但也适用于团队。虽然绩效管理提供反馈、认可以及确定员工的发展机会，是奖励制度的重要组成部分，但是它关注的焦点是发展。它可能与绩效薪酬有关，但发展更为重要。

Unit 8

Text A

Compensation Management

According to Milkovitch and Newman in *Compensation*, compensation is "all forms of financial returns and tangible services and benefits employees receive as part of an employment relationship". The phrase "financial returns" refers to an individual's base salary, as well as short- and long-term incentives. "Tangible services and benefits" are such things as insurance, paid vacation and sick days, pension plans, and employee discounts.

Compensation plays a critical role in aligning employee behavior with business objectives. It is definitely critical for an organization to attract and retain employees. Compensation management deals with processes, policies and strategies which are required to guarantee that the contribution of employees to the business is recognized by all means. Objective of compensation management is to reward employees fairly, equitably and consistently in correlation to the value of these individuals to the organization. Reward system exists in order to motivate employees to work towards achieving strategic goals which are set by entities. Compensation management is not only concerned with pay and employee benefits. It is equally concerned with non-financial rewards such as recognition, training, development and increased job responsibility.

1. Types of Compensation

Rewards serve many purposes in organizations. They serve to build a better employment deal, to hold on to good employees and to reduce employee turnover. The principal goal is to increase people's willingness to work in one's company to enhance their productivity. Rewards can be both intrinsic and extrinsic.

An intrinsic reward is an intangible award of recognition, a sense of achievement, or a conscious satisfaction. For example, it is the knowledge that you did something right, or you helped someone and made their day better. Because intrinsic rewards are intangible, they usually arise from within the person who is doing the activity or behavior. So "intrinsic" in this case means the reward is intrinsic to the person doing the activity or behavior.

An extrinsic reward is an award that is tangible or physically given to you for accomplishing something. It is a tangible recognition of one's endeavor. Because extrinsic rewards are tangible, they are usually given to the person doing the activity; as such, they are typically not from within the person. Extrinsic rewards take both monetary and non-monetary forms. One tangible component of compensation program is direct compensation, whereby the employer provides monetary rewards for work done and performance results achieved. Base pay and variable pay are the most common forms of direct compensation. The most common indirect compensation is employee benefits.

1.1 Base Pay

Base pay, or base wages, is the amount of money that an employee earns for performing duties which excludes any bonuses, raises, or other allowances. Base wages typically depend on the job and the employer. Some companies offer a salaried base pay, while others pay an hourly one. Salaried employees are often given a base amount each year. Hourly employees' wages can fluctuate depending on how many hours are worked within a pay period.

1.2 Variable Pay Programs

Variable pay programs are also sometimes referred to as "pay-for-performance" or "at-risk" pay plans, providing some or all of a work force's compensation based on employee performance or on the performance of a team. Variable pay proponents contend that providing tangible rewards for superior performance—a true merit system—encourages hard work and efficiency and serves as an effective deterrent to mediocre or otherwise uninspired work performance. Variable pay programs can take a range of forms, including annual incentives or bonus payments, individual incentive plans, lump-sum payments, technical achievement awards, cash profit-sharing plans, small group incentives, gain sharing, and payments for skill and knowledge.

1.3 Benefits

Many organizations provide numerous extrinsic rewards in an indirect manner. A benefit is an indirect reward. There is a wide variety of benefits offered to employees such as paid time-off (PTO), various types of insurance (such as life, medical, dental, and disability), pension, or access to a company car, among others. Benefit plans are typically not provided in cash but form the basis of an employees' pay package along with base salary and bonus. It is usually given to an employee or a group of employees as a part of organizational membership, regardless of performance.

2. Performance-Based Compensation

Performance-based compensation is a type of compensation or payment made to employees within a company based on their performance and the achievement of specific goals. This type of compensation can be utilized for employees at any level, from newly hired staff to established management, and can be more reliable than other systems of compensation for inspiring hard work in employees. By rewarding results and efforts, rather than simply assigning payment based on seniority or time, employees are encouraged to produce results and benefit a company. Performance-based compensation can be used at just about any type of business, from retail stores to law firms, and has proven successful in numerous environments.

The basic idea behind performance-based compensation is that employees working for a company receive rewards based on their actual performance and the achievement of goals. Some businesses use a model that rewards employees merely for loyalty to the company, providing compensation in the form of annual salary raises. While this can certainly help ensure employee loyalty, it can also deter an employee from going beyond the call of duty, since doing so nets no real reward. This type of compensation can also create a work environment where someone who has worked at a company for a relatively long time is making far more than someone else doing the same job who has simply not worked at a company as long.

A performance-based compensation strategy gives financial rewards to those who meet sales goals or otherwise accomplish real goals for a business. The value of employees in this type of business is established through work and accomplishment, rather than merely through seniority. By using performance-based compensation, employees are encouraged to try hard and meet goals in order to receive not only praise but real compensation.

3. Compensation Equity

Employees compare their efforts and rewards with those of others in similar work situations. Individuals, who work for rewards from the organization, are motivated by a desire to be equitably treated at work. If rewards are allocated incorrectly on non-performance factors such as seniority, status and job title, employee motivation and effort could be reduced. Managers need to recognize that the perceived value of the direct and indirect compensation depends on employees own perspective on equity.

3.1 Internal Equity

Employers need to establish a pay structure that meets employees' equity expectancies. One way is through internal equity, whereby the system aims to achieve a fair pay differential among all the employees aligned to each position within the organization. Managing and implementing an internally equitable pay structure can be delicate and difficult to achieve. Research has proved that seventy eight percent of employees would be most angered if they found themselves paid less than others doing the same job in their own organization (Nash, 1972). As it is often easy for an employee to know their colleagues' salaries, fairness is essential when a system is chosen. Good communication needs to be present in the organization and employers have to make sure that their employees fully understand the paying decisions in order to keep good morale and low turnover of staff. To have a successfully established compensation system and to correctly evaluate the different jobs within an organization, four techniques are available: job ranking, job classification, point system and factor comparison.

3.2 External Equity

A simple definition of external equity is employee's perception of the conditions and rewards of their employment, compared with employees from other firms. External equity is the term used to describe fair and competitive compensation with respect to the market value of a job. Considering external equity involves researching alignment to what competing employers pay to attract and retain employees who have similar skills and responsibilities as the prospective new hire. Compensation is a tool used by management for a variety of purposes to further the existence of the company. Compensation may be adjusted according to business needs, goals and available resources. External equity is the situation that exists when an organization's pay rates are at least equal to market rates. It is also known as matching strategy. An employer's goal should be to pay what is necessary to attract, retain and motivate a sufficient number of qualified employees. This requires a base pay program that pays competitively. Data as turnover rates and exit interviews can be helpful in determining the competitiveness and fairness of pay rates.

4. Job Evaluation

Job evaluation is closely related to compensation management. It is important to understand and identify a job's order of importance. Job evaluation is the process in which jobs are systematically assessed to one another within an organization in order to define the worth and value of the job, to ensure the principle of equal pay for equal work. In the United Kingdom, it is now illegal to discriminate workers' pay levels and benefits, employment terms and conditions and promotion opportunities. Job evaluation is one method that can be adopted by companies in order to make sure that discrimination is eliminated and that the work performed is rewarded with fair pay scales. This system carries crucial importance for managers to decide which rewards should be handed out by what amount and to whom. Job evaluation provides the basis for grading, pay structure, grading jobs in the structure and managing job and pay relativities. It has been said that fairness and objectivity are the core principles using an assessment of the nature and size of the job each is employed to carry out.

There are primarily three methods of job evaluation: (1) ranking, (2) classification, (3) factor comparison method or point method. While many variations of these methods exist in practice, the three basic approaches are described here.

4.1 Ranking Method

Perhaps the simplest method of job evaluation is the ranking method. According to this method, jobs are arranged from highest to lowest, in order of their value or merit to the organization. Jobs can also be arranged according to the relative difficulty in performing them. The jobs are examined as a whole rather than on the basis of important factors in the job; the job at the top of the list has the highest value and obviously the job at the bottom of the list will have the lowest value. Jobs are usually ranked in each department and then the department rankings are combined to develop an organizational ranking. The variation in payment of salaries depends on the variation of the nature of the job performed by the employees. The ranking method is simple to understand and practice and it is best suited for a small organization. Its simplicity, however, works to its disadvantage in big organizations because rankings are difficult to develop in a large, complex organization. Moreover, this kind of ranking is highly subjective in nature and may offend many employees.

4.2 Grading Method

According to this method, a pre-determined number of job groups or job classes are established and jobs are assigned to these classifications. This method places groups of jobs into job classes or job grades. Separate classes may include office, clerical, managerial, personnel, etc. Following is a brief description of such a classification in an office.

Class I—Executives. Further classification under this category may be office manager, deputy office manager, office superintendent, departmental supervisor, etc.

Class II—Skilled workers. Under this category may come the purchasing assistant, cashier, receipts clerk, etc.

Class III—Semiskilled workers. Under this category may come stenotypist, machine-operator, switchboard operator, etc.

Class IV—Unskilled workers. This category may comprise peon, messenger, housekeeping staff, file clerk, office boy, etc.

The job grading method is less subjective when compared to the earlier ranking method. The system is very easy to understand and acceptable to almost all employees without hesitation. One strong point in favour of the method is that it takes into account all the factors that a job comprises. This system can be effectively used for a variety of jobs.

4.3 Factor Comparison Method or Point Method

This method is widely used and is considered to be one of the reliable and systematic approach for job evaluation in mid and large size organizations. Here, jobs are expressed in terms of key factors. Points are assigned to each factor after prioritizing each factor in order of importance. The points are summed up to determine the wage rate for the job. Jobs with similar point totals are placed in similar pay grades. The procedure involved may be explained thus:

• Select key jobs. Identify the factors common to all the identified jobs such as skill, effort, responsibility, etc.

• Divide each major factor into a number of sub-factors. Each sub-factor is defined and expressed clearly in the order of importance, preferably along a scale.

The most frequent factors employed in point systems are (1) Skill (key factor): education and training required, breadth/depth of experience required, social skills required, problem-solving skills, degree of discretion/use of judgment, creative thinking; (2) Responsibility/Accountability: breadth of responsibility, specialized responsibility, complexity of the work, degree of freedom to act, number and nature of subordinate staff, extent of accountability for equipment/plant, extent of accountability for product/materials; (3) Effort: mental demands of a job, physical demands of a job, degree of potential stress.

Find the maximum number of points assigned to each job (after adding up the point values of all sub-factors of such a job).This would help in finding the relative worth of a job. For instance, the maximum points assigned to an officer's job in a bank come to 540. The manager's job, after adding up key factors and sub-factors points, may be getting a point value of say 650 from the job evaluation committee. This job is now priced at a higher level.

Once the worth of a job in terms of total points is expressed, the points are converted into money values keeping in view the hourly/daily wage rates. A wage survey is usually undertaken to collect wage rates of certain key jobs in the organization.

insurance [in'ʃuərəns] *n.* 保险，保险业；保险费
pension ['penʃən] *n.* 退休金，养老金
retain [ri'tein] *v.* 保留，保持；记住
guarantee [ˌgærən'tiː] *v.* 保证，担保
equitably ['ekwitəbli] *adv.* 公正地，合理地
entity ['entəti] *n.* 实体；实际存在物；本质
principal ['prinsəpəl] *adj.* 主要的，最重要的
willingness ['wiliŋnəs] *n.* 自愿，乐意
conscious ['kɔnʃəs] *adj.* 有意识的；自觉的，有意的
endeavor [in'devə] *n.* 努力，尽力
non-monetary [nɔn-'mʌnitəri] *adj.* 非货币的
exclude [iks'kluːd] *v.* 排斥，排除，不包括
allowance [ə'lauəns] *n.* 津贴，补贴
fluctuate ['flʌktʃueit] *v.* 波动，涨落
proponent [prə'pəunənt] *n.* 提倡者，支持者，拥护者；
merit ['merit] *n.* 价值，优点；功绩
deterrent [di'teːrənt] *n.* 制止物，威慑物 *adj.* 制止的，遏制的
mediocre [ˌmiːdi'əukə] *adj.* 普通的，中等的

uninspired [ˌʌnin'spaiəd] *adj.* 无想象力的，无灵感的；枯燥的
seniority [siːni'ɔrəti] *n.* 资历；年长；职位高
loyalty ['lɔiəlti] *n.* 忠心，忠诚，忠实
deter [di'təː] *v.* 阻止，制止
net [net] *v.* 净赚；捕获
differential [ˌdifə'renʃəl] *n.* 工资级差；差额
implement ['implimənt] *v.* 实施，执行；使生效，实现
adjust [ə'dʒʌst] *v.* （改变……以）适应，调整，校正
systematically [sistə'mætikəli] *adv.* 有系统地；有组织地，有条不紊地；
principle ['prinsəpl] *n.* 原则，原理；准则
illegal [i'liːgəl] *adj.* 不合法的，违法的
objectivity [ˌɔbdʒek'tivəti] *n.* 客观性，客观现实
core [kɔː] *n.* 中心，核心，精髓
subjective [səb'dʒektiv] *adj.* 主观的
offend [ə'fend] *v.* 得罪，冒犯；触怒
deputy ['depjuti] *adj.* 副的；代理的
superintendant [ˌsjuːpərin'tendənt] *n.* 监管人；车间主任

Unit 8

semiskilled [ˌsemiˈskɪld] *adj.* 半熟练的
stenotypist [stenəʊˈtaɪpɪst] *n.* 速记打字员
switchboard [ˈswɪtʃbɔːd] *n.* 电话总机
comprise [kəmˈpraɪz] *v.* 包含，包括；由……组成，由……构成

peon [ˈpiːən] *n.* 日工，雇农，苦工
prioritize [praɪˈɒrɪtaɪz] *v.* 按重要性排列，划分优先顺序
discretion [dɪsˈkreʃən] *n.* 灵活性；谨慎；自行决定

Phrases

compensation management 薪酬管理
financial return 经济报酬；财务收益，财务回报
paid vacation 带薪休假
pension plan 退休金计划，养老金计划
play a critical role in 起关键作用
in correlation to 与……有关联
a sense of achievement 成就感
arise from 产生于，起因于
variable pay 可变薪酬；浮动工资
refer to as 把……称作
at-risk pay plan 风险工资计划
lump-sum payment 一次性支付
regardless of 不管，不顾
performance-based compensation 绩效薪酬
be aligned to 与……结合起来
internal equity 内部公平
pay differential 工资差额

external equity 外部公平
with respect to 关于，至于，谈到
matching strategy 匹配策略
equal pay for equal work 同工同酬
pay scale 薪工标准
hand out 分发；给予
pay relativity 薪酬对比关系
ranking method 排列法
factor comparison method 因素比较法
point method 评分法
to one's disadvantage 对（某人）不利
take into account 考虑，注意；顾及
in favor of 赞成，支持
sum up 总结，概括
sub-factor 次级因素
add up 加起来；总计
be converted into 被转换成
keep in view 留意；把某人或某物放在心里

Abbreviations

PTO (Paid Time-Off) 带薪休假

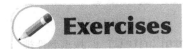

EX. 1 Answer the following questions according to the text.

1. According to Milkovitch and Newman, what is compensation?
2. What is the objective of compensation management?
3. What is the definition of an intrinsic reward?
4. What are the most common forms of direct compensation? And what is the most common indirect compensation?
5. What is the basic idea behind performance-based compensation?
6. What's the major difference between internal equity system and external equity system?
7. What is job evaluation?
8. What are primarily three methods of job evaluation? And which is the simplest method?
9. By grading method, in which job class can stenotypists be placed into?
10. By factor comparison method or point method, how is the wage rate for the job determined?

EX. 2 Translate the following terms or phrases from English into Chinese and vice versa.

1. at-risk pay plan   1. _____
2. compensation management   2. _____
3. equal pay for equal work   3. _____
4. factor comparison method   4. _____
5. lump-sum payment   5. _____
6. 薪酬对比关系   6. _____
7. 薪工标准   7. _____
8. 退休金计划，养老金计划   8. _____
9. 绩效薪酬   9. _____
10. *n.* 刺激，鼓励；动机，诱因   10. _____

EX. 3 Translate the following text into Chinese.

Other factors a compensation manager often considers when setting up compensation plans are rates of retention and other benefits, such as profit sharing or company pension plans. If a job classification has a reputation for high turnover, she may choose to increase the base salary or increase the benefits to make it more attractive to those seeking job stability. She may also promote opportunities for advancement to attract applicants seeking career growth.

In addition to creating salary and benefits packages, a compensation manager frequently writes job descriptions and confers with other managers on classifications. Deciding if a position should be exempt or non-exempt is a determination commonly debated by her and other human resources employees. This difference between paying an employee a salary or an hourly rate and the related overtime factor for non-exempt jobs can be significant. Understanding what local and regional laws govern these classifications is important to a compensation manager's success.

EX. 4 Fill in the blanks with the words given below.

| competitiveness | specialists | appropriate | contribute | evolve |
| advancements | relates | revenue | expertise | sense |

Compensation Philosophy

All companies with employees must determine how and what to pay their workers, and when to offer things like raises, bonuses and other incentives. Businesses of all types tend not to do this haphazardly. Rather, they __1__ what is called a compensation philosophy. This is an actual plan for how employees are to be paid, when payments will rise, and when bonuses are __2__. Such a plan is often made available to employees, so they have a __3__ of the organization's philosophy and can thus determine their treatment by the organization, as it __4__ to compensation, not just at present but also in the future.

Some of the things that influence compensation philosophy include present __5__ of the company and expected profits in the future, market value of the jobs for which the company is hiring, and degree of __6__ in the types of jobs a company offers. The way an organization views its employees and its responsibility for those employees affects the development of a compensation philosophy too. Essentially, many different elements may __7__ to the way an employer determines rate of pay, raises and bonuses.

It may be easy to create a compensation philosophy in some fields. For instance, those that require rising levels of __8__ and education usually have set rates, and they may have a salary range that matches market value prices and that gives employees something to aim for. Hospitals, for example, can hire employees of numerous types, and clearly compensation will be different for nurses, doctors and janitors. Doctors are paid more if they are __9__, and janitors don't have a salary that approaches nurses or doctors. Businesses like hospitals might have to consider any jobs that are union jobs, since this may influence rates of pay or tables for __10__ and raises.

Text B

Compensation Structure Design

A compensation structure is the configuration and scale that determines how people get paid in an organization. Effective compensation structures offer employees a framework for progression and can help to encourage appropriate behaviors and high performance. As part of a reward strategy, a successful pay structure will be transparent, fair and flexible, and most effectual when it aligns with the organization's strategy and its values.

Every company, business, or organization that pays workers has some form of compensation structure. These documents, usually produced and maintained by human resource (HR) departments, establish salary ranges for each paid position. The configuration and scale of pay are dependent on the specific duties to be performed as part of each position. The pay scale for workers at every level includes minimum and maximum amounts that are outlined in the structure, and pay variations on the scale often take skill level and experience into account.

1. Development of Compensation Structures

Done right, compensation structures aren't intended to constrain pay, but to ensure the best fit of resources to organizational objectives. Given the changing nature of work, the workforce, and the competitive landscape, it's no wonder that compensation structures have adapted.

Broadbands, the structure of yesteryear. Broadbands, pay bands that can span as much as 100–300 percent from minimum to maximum, made a lot of sense at a time when people stayed with their company for life. Sometimes, they even stayed within the same role for their full career. An office manager was an office manager and an engineer was an engineer. At a time when the workforce was motivated by pensions, retirement, and forming work families, broadbands fit.

Step structures. Where pay moves up from fixed point to fixed point based on a pre-arranged schedule, which are also a great example of structures that worked better yesterday than today. They are often based on tenure. While some positions still lend themselves well to step structures, especially in industries where rewarding performance doesn't make sense, they fall short for most strategic compensation. Step structures are often too rigid for the flexible needs of today's companies, depending on industry and position.

Grades and ranges. Grades are a set of ranges that are mathematically aligned to one another. Similar jobs are grouped together within grades based on their market rate, level of responsibility, and value to the organization. Ranges are narrower than broadbands, typically around 30–60 percent from minimum to maximum. At a time when employees seek advancement, recognition, and mobility, grades and ranges can help align various levels of positions relative to one another.

2. Major Types of Compensation Structures

Base pay program. A standard base pay program offers fixed salary ranges for each position type for employees performing the standard duties of their jobs. Set up minimum and maximum levels within those pay ranges to account for variations in experience and skill levels. When setting the base pay structure, determine where the company falls within the whole industry as well as competing industries that may also offer job opportunities for their employees. It is vital to set up pay levels to be competitive and use the Internet to find industry-standard salary levels for specific jobs in specific geographical areas.

Merit pay program. Once your base pay structure is in place, most companies then set up a merit pay program that will take the employee through the salary range for their position at a performance-driven speed. This comes into play when the employee's managers do annual employee performance reviews. The downside of this is that employees may begin to see it as a given that they will get a salary increase after each evaluation, and it ceases to be a motivation to perform better in their jobs. For this reason, more companies are moving toward more of a reward-based compensation style, also called incentive compensation.

Incentive pay program. Incentive-based compensation is becoming much more common because of the increased emphasis on performance and competition for talent. This type of compensation structure significantly helps motivate employees to perform well. Hiring bonuses are also frequently used now, even for new college graduates. However, you might want to tie in a specific time period prior to the employee collecting this bonus—for example, one-half after six months and the remainder after one year of employment. Otherwise, you could run the risk of the employee departing after that first check, which would defeat your purpose. So does that mean incentive compensation is the way to go? Maybe so, if your business is in an industry where you really have to compete to get good employees.

Setting up an incentive-based compensation program requires the same research into your industry as the base pay program. You'll still establish base pay levels, but it may be slightly lower and you will build into that base the annual or quarterly (or any other interval) bonuses, commissions, or other types of shared cash compensation.

3. Setting Up Compensation Structures

Well-designed salary structures have compensation levels that are internally equitable, externally competitive, and cost-effective and deliver a positive business impact on the organization in several ways. They also help human resources personnel to fairly administer any given pay philosophy. For example, a company might want to pay everyone at market, or pay some people at market and some above it. Opportunities for incentives are also dealt with in the pay structure. For example, people with strategic roles will likely have opportunities for higher incentives. Here are some suggestions on how to set up competitive compensation structures.

3.1 Outsource if Necessary

Many firms have one or more in-house compensation consultants who can set up a pay structure consistent with the company's pay philosophy. Small organizations and other companies without the resources to hire a compensation consultant can either train someone in how to set up a pay philosophy, or outsource this service.

3.2 Start with a Payroll Budget

When setting up a pay structure, most companies start with a payroll budget. Senior management usually sets payroll budgets during the annual planning. The budget for merit increases is generally kept separate from the overall budget to allow for market adjustments. Companies research what merit increases and salary movements historically have been (approximately 3.5 percent on average in recent years) and then project the budgets for market adjustments and merit increases. If turnover is high, a company may have to move people's salaries more quickly than if turnover is low and there is more time to implement the pay structure.

3.3 Benchmark the Value of Each Job

Once it is known how many jobs are to be priced and the total amount allocated to spend, a company should benchmark as many jobs as possible. Benchmarking means matching an internal job to an external job of similar content. Make sure to benchmark jobs to job content, rather than job title. For example, a bookkeeper and an accountant may seem similar, but a comparison of the job descriptions should reveal the job to which is really being matched.

When benchmarking, the market value goes to the job, not to the person filling it. Price "spaces, not faces". In order to make the best use of an organization's resources, it is important for a company to acquire survey data for similar companies. Salary Wizard Professional (for small businesses) and CompAnalyst (for large businesses) are a great place to get data that represents organizations of similar size, industry, and location.

In small companies people are often called upon to fill hybrid jobs, for example, a person might be asked to be both HR manager and office manager. It is important to review the data for each of the components of the hybrid job, and develop a market price accordingly.

The following are some tips for benchmarking jobs:

• Select surveys that are appropriate for the positions being surveyed: right job, right geographic area, right company size, etc.

• Stay general. Job descriptors such as those found in compensation surveys and in Salary. com products are not intended to be all-inclusive job descriptions. They are generic descriptions that best describe the essential functions of a job rather than the application of that job in a specific company.

• Select job descriptors based on content, rather than job title.

• Match closely. A job descriptor should be at least 70 percent of an incumbent's current job responsibilities.

• Make as many matches as possible.

• Match the job function, not the person.

• Combine judiciously. Job descriptors can be blended, but no more than two descriptors per survey should be combined to represent an incumbent's job.

• Review the level guide. Surveys have a variety of ways for describing and representing different levels for different jobs.

• Involve employees as many as possible in benchmarking jobs.

3.4 Use Internal Equity Method to Create Salary Ranges by Pay Grade

The internal equity method of structuring pay involves creating a series of grades or bands, with wide ranges at the top of the pay structure and narrower ranges at the bottom. Each grade represents a different level within the company.

A company must determine how many grades are required, choosing a reasonable number based on how many employees work in the organization today and the variety of jobs at the organization. The number of grades can always be expanded later. A company of 30 people might start with 10 grades, although small companies normally do not benefit from pay grades as much as larger companies because of the frequent instance of hybrid positions in small companies.

A company should also give each grade a spread, so that people can move within their grade as they progress in their jobs. Additionally, creating a minimum and a maximum for the whole company is recommended. The midpoint of the lowest grade should reflect the lowest value of the lowest job in a benchmarking study. The midpoint of the highest grade should reflect the highest value of the highest job.

From one grade to the next, there should be a 15-percent midpoint progression, meaning the midpoint of one grade should be about 15 percent higher than the midpoint of the grade below it. This is to ensure that promotions are accompanied by meaningful pay increases.

Benchmarked jobs are then slotted into the pay grades. Some positions are often forced into a grade, and some grades won't be fully aligned. Ideally companies look for a narrow margin of approximately 5 to 10 percent between the market median and the midpoint of the grade.

Market data may not be available for all jobs. Such jobs are often slotted into comparable grades for the company according to the scope of the job, the responsibilities, the size of the budget the position handles, etc. For example, if a suitable benchmark for a financial manager cannot be found, the job is slotted into the rough equivalent of the HR manager if they are equally valued at your organization.

Broadbanding is the pay practice of creating large ranges and control points within a grade to give people wide latitude to move within their job without outgrowing the payscale. However, studies have shown that after five to seven years of doing the same job, people no longer improve dramatically in that job. A pay philosophy might take this principle into account by stipulating that no one will be paid more than 120 to 130 percent of market, regardless of how well he or she performs.

3.5 Use Market Pricing to Relate Jobs to External Forces

An alternative to the traditional grid-based pay structure is the market pricing approach, which is rapidly becoming the prevalent method of pricing jobs. With the market pricing approach, people are compensated in relation to the market value of their job, regardless of their level in the organization. The market may suggest, for example, that certain information technology workers should be paid more than chief technology officers.

The pertinent value in the market pricing method is not the midpoint of a grade, but the midpoint of that job in the market, along with the employee's compa-ratio, or salary divided by the market rate. Over time, the employee's pay should move closer to market as performance moves closer to expectations for that job. Under the market pricing method, the salary for a job may still be capped at 120 to 130 percent of market.

Labor unions also typically do market studies in collaboration with the human resources department or with a third party. A company striving to compete with the possibility of a unionized workforce might pay more than the union's market study recommends.

New Words

configuration [kənˌfigju'reiʃən] n. 布局，构造；配置
progression [prə'greʃən] n. 前进，进展；连续
effectual [i'fektʃuəl] adj. 有效果的，有实效的；有法律效力的
variation [ˌveəri'eiʃən] n. 变化，变动；变异，演变；变量
yesteryear ['jestəjiə] n. 过去；去年
broadband ['brɔ:dbænd] n. 宽带
rigid ['ridʒid] adj. 严格的；（规则、方法等）死板的
geographical [ˌdʒiə'græfikəl] adj. 地理学的，地理的
downside ['daunsaid] n. 负面，消极面；下降趋势
given ['givn] n. 不争的事实
cease [si:s] v. 终止，停止
incentive [in'sentiv] n. 刺激，鼓励；动机，诱因
equitable ['ekwitəbl] adj. 合理的；公正的，公平的
outsource ['autsɔ:s] v. 外包；外购
payroll ['peirəul] n. 工资单；工薪总额
approximately [ə'prɔksimətli] adv. 近似地，大约
project ['prɔdʒekt] v. 预计；设计；放映，投射

descriptor [dis'kriptə] n. 描述符，描述信息
all-inclusive ['ɔ:-lin'klu:siv] adj. 包括一切的，无所不包的
generic [dʒi'nerik] adj. 一般的；类的，属性的
judiciously [dʒu'diʃəsli] adv. 明断地，明智而审慎地
midpoint ['midpɔint] n. 中点，正中央
accompany [ə'kʌmpəni] v. 陪伴，陪同；附加，补充
slot [slɔt] v. 插入，放置
margin ['mɑ:dʒin] n. 边缘，范围；利润
median ['mi:djən] n. 中位数；中线；[数] 中值
rough [rʌf] adj. 粗略的，大概的
equivalent [i'kwivələnt] n. 相等物
latitude ['lætitju:d] n. 范围；自由；纬度
dramatically [drə'mætikəli] adv. 戏剧地，引人注目地
grid-based [grid-beist] adj. 基于网格的
prevalent ['prevələnt] adj. 流行的；普遍的
pertinent ['pə:tinənt] adj. 有关的，相干的；中肯的
comparatio [kɔm'pɑ:-eiʃiəu] n. 薪资均衡指标（也称薪酬比较比率）
cap [kæp] v. 超过；加盖于，覆盖

Unit 8

compensation strategy 薪酬策略
reward strategy 奖酬策略
pay band 薪资群；薪酬级别；薪带
make sense 有意义；讲得通；是明智的
fall short 缺乏，不足；达不到（目标）
base pay 基本工资
account for 说明（原因等）；（在数量方面）占
merit pay 绩效工资
in place 在工作；准备就绪
salary range 薪水范围
annual employee performance review 年度员工绩效考核

incentive compensation 奖金
incentive pay 奖励津贴
run the risk of 冒……的危险
pay philosophy 薪酬理念
payroll budget 工资预算
annual planning 年度计划
overall budget 总体预算
make the best use of 充分利用
market median 市场中位数
in collaboration with 与……合作

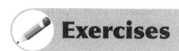

EX. 5 Answer the following questions according to the text.

1. What is a compensation structure?
2. What are broadbands? When did they make a lot of sense?
3. What deficiencies do step structures have in accordance with Text B?
4. What are grades and ranges structures on the basis of Text B?
5. What is the downside of merit pay program?
6. Why is incentive-based compensation becoming much more common?
7. How do most companies set payroll budgets?
8. While benchmarking jobs, are the job descriptors in compensation surveys intended to be all-inclusive job descriptions?
9. What does the internal equity method of structuring pay involve?
10. What is the market pricing approach?

Supplementary Reading

Text	Notes
Compensation Surveys Organizations have to bridge the gap between the industry standards and their salary packages[1]. They cannot provide compensation packages that are either less than the industry standards or are very higher than the market rates. For the purpose they undertake the salary survey. The salary survey is the research done to analyze the industry standards to set up the compensation strategy for the organization. **1. Objectives of Salary Survey** Organizations can either conduct the survey themselves or they can purchase the survey reports from a reputed[2] research organization. These reports constitute[3] the last 2–5 years or more compensation figures for the various positions held by the organizations. The analysis is done on the basis of certain factors defined in the objectives of the research: • to gather information regarding the industry standards; • to know more about the market rate, i.e. compensation offered by the competitors; • to design a fair compensation system; • to design and implement most competitive reward strategies; • to benchmark the compensation strategies. **2. Types of Compensation Surveys** Surveys are conducted on a semiannual[4], annual, or biennial[5] basis. Surveys normally fall into one of two types: standard and custom[6]. Standard surveys are undertaken by organizations on a regular basis. These surveys are conducted annually based on the organizational objectives. These surveys attempt to cover the same companies every year and provide the same time of analysis. The reports are published annually by the research organizations. The organizations willing to formulate[7] their compensations strategies based on the surveys purchase the	[1] salary package: 薪酬 [2] reputed [ri'pju:tid] *adj.* 名誉好的，有名气的 [3] constitute ['kɔnstitju:t] *v.* 构成，组成 [4] semiannual ['semi'ænjuəl] *adj.* 每半年的，半年的 [5] biennial [bai'eniəl] *adj.* 两年一次的 [6] custom ['kʌstəm] *adj.* 定做的，定制的 [7] formulate ['fɔ:mjuleit] *v.* 规划；系统地阐述

reports from the research organization.

At times, a few organizations need to know some specific information. The surveys which cater[8] this need are known as custom surveys. The organizations either hire research organizations to conduct theses surveys for them or they themselves conduct the survey by sampling few of the competitors on their own. These surveys do not have any time interval[9]. They are undertaken as the need arises. They focus on important issues usually one or two.

3. How to Conduct a Compensation Survey

The process of collecting data and producing a salary survey takes careful planning and execution that requires economic investment, people resources, and time. Some companies conduct surveys in-house using their own staff and compensation experts. However, most companies contract a third party to collect the data and do the number crunching[10]. The third-party approach provides a level of independence that most participants want. Some salary surveys are co-sponsored[11] to attract more participants and to add credibility[12] to the numbers. An experienced data provider in survey methods and statistical analysis is expected to put out high-quality, reliable, accurate data.

3.1 Time

Conducting a salary survey is a time-consuming task. A traditional survey of 15 companies encompassing 20 positions can take between 6 and 12 weeks from the initial planning to the time the survey is distributed to participants. For a survey that includes more participants and more positions, it could take as long as four to six months. Survey respondents[13] then have 2 to 6 weeks to complete the questionnaire. The length of time depends on the number of positions surveyed and the amount of information requested for each incumbent[14] (person in a given job). After the data has been collected, it can take two to three months to analyze the data and make the findings available to the survey participants and others. Therefore the time from initiating a survey to providing results can be up to seven months or more.

---

[8] cater ['keitə] v. 投合，迎合；满足需要

[9] interval ['intəvəl] n. 间隔

[10] number crunching: 数字运算

[11] co-sponsor [,kəu-'spɔnsə] v. 共同提案；共同赞助

[12] credibility [,kredi'biləti] n. 可靠性，可信性；确实性

[13] respondent [ris'pɔndənt] n. 应答者；被告

[14] incumbent [in'kʌmbənt] n. 在职者；现任者

3.2 Questionnaire

Traditionally, survey questionnaires are mailed out in paper form or on a diskette[15] to participants, namely company managers or executives and human resources professionals, who will then complete and return the survey before a predetermined closing date. When assessing the methodology of a survey, it is important to look for the number of surveys mailed out, the number of participants, and the number of employees in the report summary. These numbers determine whether the survey is representative of the jobs and the industry.

3.3 Number of Participants

Make sure the participants are a good sample of the recruiting market. Generally, 8 to 10 participating companies is a good sample for positions below the management level. The sample size should increase the more senior the positions being surveyed, both to get a good representation and to allow for more job matches, since each company is organized differently. There could be limited pay data in some industries, or the available data might not be representative of the industry because of a low participation rate in the survey.

3.4 Participant Profiles

The usefulness and relevance of a salary survey depends largely on the survey participants. For a small company, a salary survey of large corporations in the United States will be less helpful in determining what to pay employees than a survey of smaller organizations. Of course, a small company in a "company town" may find itself in a position to[16] pay the same wages as the predominant employer in that town.

Survey participants can be quite different, depending on the goal of the survey. If the survey covers pay in large companies in different geographical locations, the surveying company has to make sure that companies participating in the survey are of similar size but from different locations.

3.5 Job Descriptions

Just as it is important to find surveys that compare companies of a similar stature[17], it's also important that the jobs being surveyed are comparable to the job being benchmarked. When consulting a compensation survey, match the job descriptions

---

[15] diskette [disˈket] n. 磁盘，磁碟

[16] in a position to: 处在可以……的位置；能够

[17] stature [ˈstætʃə] n. 声望；（特指人的）身长，身材

rather than the job titles, even if the survey uses generic or widely used job titles.

A survey job description should list the primary job function in one or two sentences, followed by key responsibilities. While the descriptions should be generic and not specific to any one company, they should contain enough information for participants to match appropriately to ensure the data is accurate. It is also important to match the organizational level of the positions surveyed. A position that is at the group level at one company may be at the sub-group or the sector level at another.

3.6 Compensation Data

There are many things to consider when analyzing the compensation components of a salary survey. Because companies have different pay structures, compensation data is collected in ranges as well as actual pay. Salary surveys can provide employers more information on the marketplace and how to set competitive pay without overpaying or underpaying employees. Surveys should ask for the minimum, midpoint, and maximum for the surveyed positions, in addition to the actual base salary paid.

Usually, the prevailing practice for any one job is to pay a range of incomes. As a result, although the median pay for a job is likely to be a definable number, the range is just as important. Companies pay employees differently for various reasons. It could be the company's pay philosophy. or it could be the geographic location or the industry practice. or it could be the incumbent's length of service or proficiency in the job. Whatever the reason, it is unlikely that two companies will pay an employee doing the same job exactly the same amount.

Base pay figures. When reading the base pay figures, it's important to check how the numbers are calculated. The surveying parties can dictate[18] to the participants how the numbers should be reported. Salaries can be on an annual, monthly, or hourly basis. For example, if the incumbent is a contract employee, hourly salaries are more relevant than an annual figure. The survey may request pay data for individual incumbents or averages for all incumbents matching a specific job description, depending on the types of surveys and their objectives.

[18] dictate [dik'teit] v. 命令，指示；口述

Incentives/Bonuses. Look at both the actual annualized payments and the target level expressed as a percentage of base pay when evaluating incentives or bonuses. This allows for adjustments for atypical[19] incentives and bonuses. Be sure to understand what is included in this figure and how it's collected. Although there is not a right or wrong definition of what is included in this category, it is important to understand how your numbers compare with those reported. In that sense, you need to know what it represents.

Other payments. As compensation changes, salary surveys are changing to include other forms of compensation such as profit sharing and stock grants[20]. For more senior-level positions, long-term incentives are just as important as base salary. For example, an executive's compensation package at a startup company can be made up of mostly stock options rather than cash compensation. For a survey to represent the total compensation, it needs to take into account the cash valuation of stock options[21].

3.7 Effective Date

For those surveys conducted on a regular basis, such as annual surveys, the effective date will be until the next survey is released in the following year. Otherwise, knowing the effective date of the survey can prevent companies from using outdated salary figures and causing error in pay budget forecasts.

If the survey is not current, the person using it should age the salaries to the current date. If a survey was conducted in September, the salaries are likely to be as of September or even August. If you are using the survey in December to benchmark for a new position in the company, you will have to age the number. A simple way to do this is to take the annual rate at which salaries are moving for this job and prorate[22] it, salary increases overall this year are around 3.5% but this may vary by job title.

A similar approach is used in setting pay levels across a company. Sometimes these figures are set at the beginning, middle, or end of the company's payroll year by aging the appropriate compensation data to those dates.

3.8 Survey Reports

The survey reports consist of the analysis and conclusion

---

[19] atypical [ei'tipikəl] *adj.* 非典型的

[20] stock grant: 股票赠予

[21] stock option: 认股权

[22] prorate [prəu'reit] *v.* 比例分配, 分派

drawn from the evaluative[23] data based on the objectives of the study. The reports also include the data, facts and figures to support the analysis and conclusion. The supportive data and annexure[24] provided in the report form the basis for the unbiased[25] conclusion and validation of the analysis.

4. Compensation Survey Checklist

Here are some considerations to weigh for a company who is deciding whether to purchase a compensation survey.

• The background of the survey research firm and cosponsors, if any. Look for reputable firms that follow proven[26] methods to gather and analyze compensation data.

• The scope of the survey. Look for studies that cover industries, jobs, and regions that are most applicable to[27] your purposes, and that provide data on enough jobs to be cost-effective.

• The survey methodology. Review the summary of the methodology to make sure it's consistent with standards set forth[28] by reputable industry associations such as WorldatWork. Be especially sure the research organization is surveying human resource professionals or other people knowledgeable about compensation information within a company, rather than individuals.

• The number of participants in the survey. A good survey should cover a representative number of companies for its target population. A survey doesn't have to cover the entire industry or region to be robust[29]; even a few dozen responding employers in some industries can provide enough data for a valid survey.

• The names of participants. Look for your competitors and peers. For many jobs, you may be competing for candidates with companies in different industries but the same geographic area.

• The number of incumbents covered by the survey, and the sample size for each salary. A sample size of 30 or more is more statistically significant than a sample size of 10, provided[30] the sample is representative of the statistical population.

• The relevance of the job descriptions to the positions being benchmarked. Look for a good match between the survey and your company. Be sure to compare job descriptions, not just job titles.

[23] evaluative [ɪˈvæljueɪtɪv] adj. 可估价的

[24] annexure [əˈnekʃə] n. 附加物，附录

[25] unbiased [ʌnˈbaɪəst] adj. 公正的，无偏见的

[26] proven [ˈpruːvən] adj. 经过验证或证实的

[27] be applicable to: (适) 用于

[28] set forth: 陈述；阐明

[29] robust [rəʊˈbʌst] adj. 坚固的；信心十足的；强健的

[30] provided [prəˈvaɪdɪd] conj. 假如；若是

• The effective date of the survey data. The date a survey is published is always later than the effective date of the data within the survey. If necessary, age the data from the effective date to the current month.

参考译文（Text A）

薪酬管理

根据 Milkovitch 和 Newman 在《薪酬》一书中的定义，薪酬是指"员工因为被雇用而获得的各种形式的经济报酬、有形服务和福利"。经济报酬是指个人的基本工资，以及短期与长期激励性薪水；有形服务和福利包括保险、带薪休假、病假、养老金和员工优惠等。

在确保员工行为符合企业目标方面，薪酬起着关键作用。它对于企业吸引并留住员工无疑是至关重要的。薪酬管理主要应对的是保证员工对企业的贡献能以各种方式得到认可的那些必要的过程、政策和战略。薪酬管理的目标是始终根据个人对企业的价值大小，公正、公平地给予员工报酬。构建薪酬机制是为了激励员工努力实现企业制定的战略目标。薪酬管理不仅涉及工资和员工福利，而且关注非经济报酬，如认可、培训、发展和增加工作职责等。

1. 薪酬的类型

奖励在组织中有多种用途。它能有助于建立更好的就业协议，留住好员工，并减少员工流失。其主要目标是增强员工在公司工作的意愿，提高他们的工作效率。奖励既可以是内在的，也可以是外在的。

内在报酬是无形的认可、成就感或意识上的满足感。例如，你知道自己做对了事，或者你帮助了别人，使别人的日子更美好。由于内在报酬是无形的，并通常来自从事某项活动或行为的人的自身体会。因此，"内在的"这个词在这种情况下是指：对于从事该活动或行为的人来说，奖励是内在的。

外在报酬是实际的补偿或在完成某件事后获得的物质报酬，这是对员工努力的实际认可。因为外在报酬是物质的，通常给予从事某项活动的人，因此，这类报酬一般不是来自人自身。外在报酬采取货币和非货币两种形式。薪酬方案中的一个具体组成部分是直接报酬，即雇主为完成的工作和业绩提供货币酬金。基本薪酬和可变薪酬是最常见的直接报酬形式；最常见的间接薪酬是员工福利。

1.1 基本薪酬

基本薪酬是指雇员履行职责而挣的钱，不包括奖金、加薪或其他津贴。基本薪酬的多少通常取决于工作和雇主。有些公司提供薪水，而有的公司支付计时基本工资。领薪员工每年都有底薪，而计时工资金额可能会随着工作时间的长短有所波动。

1.2 可变薪酬

可变薪酬有时也称为"绩效工资"或"风险薪酬"。该薪酬方案基于员工个人或团队的业绩向员工支付部分或全额劳动报酬。支持可变薪酬方案的人认为,利用物质报酬奖励高业绩才是真正的绩效考核制度。它能鼓励员工努力工作,提高效率,并能有效地遏制员工庸庸碌碌、低绩效的现象。可变薪酬可以采取多种形式,包括年度奖励或奖金、员工个人激励奖、一次性报酬、技术成就奖、现金分红、小团队激励奖、收益分配、技能知识报酬等。

1.3 福利

许多企业以间接的方式提供大量的额外报酬,其中之一便是福利。雇主给员工提供的福利形式多种多样,如带薪休假、各类保险(如人寿险、医保、牙科保险和残疾保险)、养老金,或公司车辆使用权,等等。福利通常不以现金形式提供,但是它们与基本工资和奖金一起构成了员工薪酬的基本组成部分。作为企业成员,员工个人和团体通常都能享受企业福利,无论他或他们的业绩如何。

2. 绩效薪酬

绩效薪酬是公司基于员工的业绩和在特定目标中所取得的成绩而给予员工的一种报酬。这种薪酬适用于任何级别的雇员,新员工到管理人员等都包括在内。比起其他激励员工努力工作的薪酬制度,这种制度更可靠。根据成果和努力奖励员工,而不是简单地根据资历或时间分配报酬,绩效薪酬制度能激励员工出成果,并使公司受益。绩效薪酬可用于任何类型的企业,从零售商店到律师事务所,并在许多环境中被证明是有成效的。

绩效薪酬的基本理念是公司员工根据自身的实际业绩和目标的实现情况获得报酬。有些企业以每年加薪的形式给员工支付薪酬,奖励他们对公司的忠诚。虽然这种模式确实有助于确保员工的忠诚度,但也可能影响员工承担额外的工作,因为额外的工作并不能给他们带来实际的报酬。这类薪酬制度还会创造出这样的工作环境,即在公司工作时间较长的员工远远比在公司工作时间较短的员工挣得多,虽然他们承担的工作一样。

绩效薪酬策略是对那些达到销售目标或以其他方式实现企业目标的员工给予经济报酬。在这类企业中,雇员的价值是通过工作表现和成就,而不是仅仅通过资历来体现的。绩效薪酬能够激励员工努力工作,实现目标,以获得表扬和实际报酬。

3. 薪酬公平

员工会将他们的努力和报酬与类似工作环境下的其他员工进行比较。为了报酬而工作的人渴望能在工作中受到公平地对待。如果报酬分配不当,如根据资历、地位和职称等非绩效因素进行分配,员工的工作动力和努力都可能会下降。管理者需要认识到,员工感受到的直接和间接报酬价值取决于他们自己对公平的看法。

3.1 内部公平

雇主需要建立一个能满足员工公平预期值的薪酬结构。其中一个方法就是内部公平,即该薪酬系统的目标是在企业内所有职位上的全体雇员之间实现公平的薪酬差额。管理和实施内部公平的薪酬结构是棘手的,难以实现。有研究证明,如果发现自己的工资比组织中从事同样工作的其他员工要少,那么78%的员工会非常生气(Nash, 1972)。由于员工很容易获悉同事的薪水,所以在选择薪酬系统时,公平是至关重要的。在组织中,雇主需要和员工进行良好的沟通,确保他们充分理解薪酬决定,以保持高昂的士气和员工低流动率。建立成功的薪酬体系,并正确评估组织中不同的工作可以采用四种方法,即工作排列、工作分类、计分系统和因素比较。

3.2 外部公平

外部公平的一个简单定义是在与其他公司雇员作比较的情况下,员工对自身工作条件和报酬的看法。"外部公平"这个术语是从工作的市场价值角度来描述薪酬的公平性和竞争力的。考虑薪酬的外部公平问题,雇主需要研究竞争对手支付了什么样的薪酬来吸引和留住那些具有类似技能并承担相似职责的未来员工。由于种种原因,管理人员为了实现公司进一步生存的目的,会使用补偿这一薪酬工具。企业可以根据业务需要、目标和现有资源调整薪酬。外部公平是指企业的薪酬至少要等于市场薪酬,也称匹配策略。雇主的目标应该是支付必要的薪酬,以吸引、留住和激励大量的合格员工。实现这一目标需要有竞争力的基本工资计划。离职率数据和离职面谈有助于确保薪酬的竞争力和公平性。

4. 岗位评价

岗位评价与薪酬管理密切相关。理解并识别岗位的重要性顺序是很重要的。岗位评价是指在组织内对工作进行系统评估的过程,以确定工作的价值,并确保同工同酬的原则得以遵循。在英国,差别地对待雇员的工资、福利、就业条件和晋升机会是违法的。公司可以采取岗位评价这一方法来消除歧视,并确保工作得到公平报酬。岗位评价系统对于管理者决定给谁发多少薪酬起着至关重要的作用。岗位评价为工作分级、薪酬结构设计、结构内工作评级、职位及薪酬管理等方面提供了基础性依据。有人说,公平性和客观性是评估每一位员工工作性质和规模的核心原则。

岗位评价主要有三种方法:(1)排序法,(2)分类法,(3)因素比较法或评分法。这里对三种方法做了基本描述,但这些方法在实践中会存在许多变化。

4.1 排序法

排序法也许是最简单的岗位评价方法。根据这种方法,将员工对组织的价值或贡献大小从高到低排序。企业也可以根据工作的相对难度对工作进行排序。利用排序法,企业将工作作为整体,而不是根据工作中的某个重要因素来进行评价。显然,排名第一的工作价值最高,排名最后的工作价值最低。通常,每个部门先进行职位排序,然后综合各部门职位排序再形成整个企业的工作排序。薪酬的变动取决于雇员所从事的工作性质的变化。这种排序法简单易懂,易实施,适合于小型企业。然而,这种简单的排序法对大型企业不利,因为在大型、复杂的企业中对工作岗位进行排序很难。此外,这种排序实质上是很主观的,可能会得罪许多员工。

4.2 分级法

根据该方法,企业需要设定预定数量的岗位或岗位类别,并将所有的工作岗位归入这些类别中。这种方法将工作归入岗位类别或岗位级别。岗位类别可以包括办公室、文书、管理人员、人事，等等。下面是有关办公室工作岗位级别的简要说明：

Ⅰ级——管理人员。此类别下的进一步分类可能是办公室经理、副经理、办公室主任、部门主管等；

Ⅱ级——熟练工人。这一类别下的工作岗位可能包括采购助理、出纳、收款员等；

Ⅲ级——半熟练工人。这一类别下的工作岗位可能有速记打字员、机器操作工人、接线员等；

Ⅳ级——非熟练工人。这一类别下的工作岗位可能包括苦工、信使、家政人员，文员，办公室勤杂工等。

与前面的排序法相比，评级法主观性较低。这个评价系统易于理解，几乎所有员工都能毫不犹豫地接受。赞成这种方法的一个强有力的观点是，它考虑到了工作的所有因素。该系统可以有效地用于评定各种工作。

4.3 因素比较法或评分法

这种方法广泛地应用于大中型企业中，而且被认为是可靠、系统的工作评价方法之一。在这种方法中，工作是以关键因素来体现的。在按重要性顺序排列每个因素后，对每个工作因素进行赋分。分数的总和决定了该工作的工资水平。具有相似积分的工作被归入相似的工资级别。其涉及的程序可以理解为：

• 选择关键工作因素，确定被鉴定工作的共同因素，如技能、努力、职责等；

• 将每个主要因素划分为若干子因素，按重要性顺序明确地定义和表述每个子因素，最好按级别进行。

评分系统中最常见的因素是：（1）技能（注：关键因素）：学历和培训资历、经验的广度或深度、社交技能、解决问题的能力、运用决定权或判断力的程度、创造性思维；（2）职责/责任：职责的广度、专业程度、工作复杂性、自由行动的程度、下属员工的数量和性质、设备/装置的问责程度、产品/材料的责任范围；（3）精力：工作的脑力要求、体力要求、潜在的压力程度。

找到分配给每份工作的最高分（注：将该工作的关键因素和子因素赋分累加），这将有助于确定工作的相对价值。例如，分配给银行高级职员的最高分为540分。在将关键因素和子因数分值相加后，工作评估委员会可能会给银行经理工作赋予650分。这样，这项工作就被评估为更高级别的工作。

一旦计算出工作的价值总分，就可以将这些分值转化为货币价值，并密切留意小时工资率或日工资率。通常企业会进行工资调查来收集某些关键工作的工资信息。

Unit 9

Text A

Incentives

Incentive is an act or promise for greater action. It is also called as a stimulus to greater action. Incentives are something which are given in addition to wages. It means additional remuneration or benefit to an employee in recognition of achievement or better work. Incentives provide a spur or zeal in the employees for better performance. It is a natural thing that nobody acts without a purpose behind. Therefore, a hope for a reward is a powerful incentive to motivate employees.

1. Importance of Incentive Plans

Incentive plans are formalized approaches to offering recognition and reward to employees for meeting pre-established goals or objectives. Incentives may include cash bonuses, profit sharing, additional paid vacation time or any range of prizes such as gift cards, corporate merchandise or other products or services. To be effective, incentives must be clearly defined and considered as a viable, valuable reward for the associated workload.

Motivational tool. Incentive programs motivate employees to push and challenge themselves to achieve higher degrees of productivity. This ultimately translates to increased earnings for your company. When incentive plans are in place, employees recognize that significant effort on their behalf will be acknowledged and rewarded. This can increase the amount of time, effort and energy a staffer is willing to put forth on your company's behalf.

Promoting teamwork. Incentive plans tied to teamwork or group initiatives can help promote collaborative work efforts in your business. Staffers working in teams that collectively rely on each others' productivity for the group to receive a bonus or award may support and encourage each other to perform at top levels. Peer pressure may also encourage additional degrees of performance from underperforming staffers who don't want to let their team members down.

Morale boosters. Incentive plans have the potential to raise morale and increase job satisfaction in a company. Employees see a direct correlation between their work effort and their earning potential. Higher workplace morale can decrease turnover, which saves your company money associated with recruiting, hiring and training new staffers. Additionally, staffers with high levels of job satisfaction often exhibit lower degrees of absenteeism, which can also help improve a company's bottom line.

Service levels. Employees competing for or striving to meet the goals of an incentive plan may provide higher degrees of service to your customers. This can encourage repeat business, improve customer satisfaction and enhance your company's reputation. Improved service levels can also encourage referral business as well as positive word-of-mouth advertising.

For an incentive program to be effective, goals and objectives should be clearly defined for staffers. Workload should also be equitably distributed, or it could create resentment if staffers feel they have to carry slow or poor-performing team members. Consider both individual and group incentives to promote the concepts of solo effort and teamwork.

2. Monetary & Non-Monetary Incentives

Incentives can be defined as monetary or non-monetary reward offered to the employees for contributing more efficiency. Incentive can be extra payment or something more than the regular salary or wage. Incentive acts as a very good stimulator or motivator because it encourages the employees to improve their efficiency level and reach the target. The two common types of incentives are monetary or financial incentives and non-monetary/non-financial incentives.

2.1 Monetary or Financial Incentives

The reward or incentive which can be calculated in terms of money is known as monetary incentive. These incentives are offered to employees who have more physiological, social and security needs active in them. The common monetary incentives are as follows:

Pay and allowances. Regular increments in salary every year and grant of allowance act as good motivators. In some organizations pay hikes and allowances are directly linked with the performance of the employee to get increment and allowance employees perform to their best ability.

Profits sharing. The organization offers share in the profits to the employees as a common incentive for encouraging the employees for working efficiently. Under profits sharing schemes generally the companies fix a percentage of profits, and if the profits exceed that percentage then the surplus profits are distributed among the employees. It encourages the employees to work efficiently to increase the profits of the company so that they can get share in the profits.

Co-partnership/Stock option. Sharing the profit does not give ownership right to the employees. Many companies offer share in management or participation in management along with share in profit to its employees as an incentive to get efficient working from the employees. The co-partnership is offered by issue of shares on exceeding a fixed target.

Bonus. Bonus is a onetime extra reward offered to the employee for sharing high performance. Generally, when the employees reach their target or exceed the target, they are paid extra amount called bonus. Bonus is also given in the form of free trips to foreign countries, paid vacations or gold, etc. Some companies have the scheme of offering bonus during the festival times.

Commission. Commission is the common incentive offered to employees working under sales department. Generally the sales person gets the basic salary and also commission with the efforts put in by them. More orders mean more commission.

Suggestion system. Under suggestion system the employees are given reward if the organization gains with the suggestion offered by the employee. For example, if an employee suggests a cost saving technique, then extra payment is given to the employee for giving that suggestion. The amount of reward or payment given to the employee under suggestion system depends on the gain or benefit which organization gets with that suggestion. It is a very good incentive to keep the initiative level of employees high.

Productivity linked with wage incentives. These are wage rate plans which offer higher wages for more productivity. Under differential piece wage system efficient workers are paid higher wages compared to inefficient workers to get higher wages workers perform efficiently.

Retirement benefits. Some organizations offer retirement benefits such as pension, provident fund, gratuity, etc. to motivate people. These incentives are suitable for employees who have security and safety need.

Perks/Fringe benefits/perquisites. It refers to special benefits such as medical facility, free education for children, housing facility, etc. These benefits are over and above salary. These extra benefits are related with the performance of the employees.

2.2 Non-Monetary/Non-Financial Incentives

Money is not the only motivator, and the employees who have more of esteem and self actualization in them get satisfied with the non-monetary incentives only. The incentives which cannot be calculated in terms of money are known as non-monetary incentives. Generally, people working at high job position or at high rank get satisfied with non-monetary incentives. The common means or ways of non-monetary incentives are as follows:

Status. Status refers to rank, authority, responsibility, recognition and prestige related to job. By offering higher status or rank in the organization managers can motivate employees having esteem and self-actualization need active in them.

Organizational climate. It refers to relations between superiors and subordinates. These are the characteristics which describe an organization. These characteristics have direct influence over the behavior of a member. A positive approach adopted by manager creates better organizational climate whereas negative approach may spoil the climate. Employees are always motivated in the healthy organizational climate.

Career advancement. Managers must provide promotional opportunities to employees. Whenever there are promotional opportunities, employees improve their skill and efficiency with the hope that they will be promoted to a higher level. Promotion is a very big stimulator or motivator which induces people to perform to their best level.

Job enrichment/Assignment of challenging job. Employees get bored by performing routine job. They enjoy doing jobs which offer them variety and opportunity to show their skill. By being offered challenging jobs, autonomy to perform job and interesting jobs, employees get satisfied and they are motivated. Interesting, enriched and challenging job itself is a very good motivator or stimulator.

Employee's recognition. Recognition means giving special regard or respect which satisfies the ego of the subordinates. Ego-satisfaction is a very good motivator. Whenever the good efforts or the positive attitudes are shown by the subordinates, it must be recognized by the superior in public or in presence of other employees. Whenever if there is any negative attitude or mistake is done by subordinate, it should be discussed in private by calling the employee in cabin. Examples of employee's recognition are congratulating employee for good performance, displaying the achievement of employee, giving certificate of achievement, distributing mementos, gifts, etc.

Job security. Job security means life time bonding between employees and organization. It means giving permanent or confirmation letter. Job security ensures safety and security need but it may have negative impact. Once the employees get job secured, they will lose interest in job. Job security must be given with some terms and conditions.

Employee's participation. It means involving employee in decision making especially when decisions are related to workers. Employees follow the decision more sincerely when these are taken in consultation with them. For example, if target production is fixed by consulting employees, then they will try to achieve the target more sincerely.

Autonomy/Employee empowerment. It means giving more freedom to subordinates. This empowerment develops confidence in employees. They use positive skill to prove that they are performing to the best when freedom is given to them.

3. Individual & Group Incentives

Individual incentive plans and group incentive plans both have a similar goal. They strive to provide an incentive that will drive the right kind of performance for the company. For the company to determine the best incentive options, they must know their goals and ensure those goals are within the individual's ability to impact. Here outlined are some of the considerations when determining whether individual or group incentive plans are most appropriate.

Identification. An individual incentive plan is intended to reward individual workers based on reaching certain performance goals. A common example is giving a salesperson a bonus for reaching a specified production level or providing additional compensation to a factory worker for producing a desired number of goods during his shift. Group incentive plans are designed to reward each member of a team or an organization for a joint accomplishment such as improving profitability or reducing expenses.

Suitability. An individual incentive plan is typically more appropriate where a worker's productivity does not depend on the performance of others, such as a salesperson who works independently and has complete control over outcomes. Group incentive programs can be suitable where individual contributions are more difficult to measure. An example is a profit-sharing program where all workers are rewarded based on the company's ability to reach an overall profitability goal.

Group Incentive Considerations. Group incentive programs can foster an atmosphere of teamwork and cooperation in an organization. Top performers may be more willing to help those who are struggling or are new to the organization when rewards are based on the performance of the group as a whole. On the other hand, top performers may come to resent underachievers that they view as unwilling or unable to make an equal contribution to the effort.

Individual Incentive Considerations. A major benefit of individual incentive programs is that they reward top performers for their efforts and can serve as a motivating force for goal-oriented employees. They may also help to motivate underachievers who previously may not have seen the purpose in putting forth extra effort. Potential drawbacks include the creation of a "dog eat dog" work environment where every worker puts her interests ahead of those of her co-workers and workers pushing the boundaries of ethical behavior to reach their goals, such as a salesperson who lies to prospects just to make a sale.

New Words

stimulus ['stimjuləs] *n.* 刺激物，刺激因素
remuneration [ri,mju:nə'reiʃən] *n.* 工资；酬金
spur [spə:] *n.* 激励因素
zeal [zi:l] *n.* 热情；热忱
formalize ['fɔ:məlaiz] *v.* 使正式，形式化
merchandise ['mə:tʃəndaiz] *n.* 商品，货物
viable ['vaiəbl] *adj.* 切实可行的
workload ['wə:kləud] *n.* 工作量，工作负担
collaborative [kə'læbəreitiv] *adj.* 协作的，合作的;
underperform [,ʌndəpə'fɔ:m] *v.* 表现不佳，工作不如预期（或同行）
booster ['bu:stə] *n.* 支持者；助推器；辅助药剂

correlation [,kɔri'leiʃən] *n.* 相关性，相互关系
exhibit [ig'zibit] *v.* 展示，表现；展览，陈列
strive [straiv] *v.* 努力，力求
reputation [,repju'teiʃən] *n.* 声誉，名声，名气
referral [ri'fə:rəl] *n.* 推荐；转送，送交
word-of-mouth [wə:d-əv-mauθ] *adj.* 口述的，口头传达的
resentment [ri'zentmənt] *n.* 怨恨，愤恨
solo ['səuləu] *adj.* 单独的
monetary ['mʌnitəri] *adj.* 货币的，金钱的
stimulator ['stimjuleitə] *n.* 刺激物，刺激者
motivator ['məutiveitə] *n.* 促进因素，激发因素
increment ['inkrimənt] *n.* 定期的加薪；增量，增额

grant [grɑːnt] v. 授予，承认；同意，准许
co-partnership [kəu-'pɑːtnəʃip] n. 合伙
commission [kə'miʃən] n. 佣金
gratuity [grə'tjuːiti] n. 小费；赏钱
perquisite ['pəːkwizit] n. 额外补贴；临时津贴；（随职位而得到的）好处；利益
esteem [i'stiːm] n. 尊敬，尊重
self-actualization [self-ˌæktʃuəlai'zeiʃən] n. 自我实现
prestige [pre'stiʒ] n. 声誉；威望，声望
spoil [spɔil] v. 损坏，糟蹋；宠坏（孩子等）
induce [in'djuːs] v. 引起；引诱
autonomy [ɔː'tɔnəmi] n. 自治，自治权
ego ['iːgəu] n. 自我；自我意识

memento [mə'mentəu] n. 遗物，纪念品
confirmation [ˌkɔnfə'meiʃən] n. 证实，证明；确认
empowerment [im'pauəmənt] n. 授权，许可
compensation [kɔmpen'seiʃən] n. 补偿，赔偿
profitability [ˌprɔfitə'biləti] n. 获利（状况），盈利（情况）
foster ['fɔstə] v. 促进；培养，抚育
resent [ri'zent] v. 怨恨，愤恨；厌恶
underachieve [ˌʌndərə'tʃiːv] v. 未能充分发挥潜力；工作或学习成绩不良
goal-oriented [gəul-'ɔːrientid] adj. 面向目标的

 **Phrases**

in addition to 除……之外
in recognition of 为了承认或认可，为酬答
cash bonus 现金分红
put forth 提出；产生
on one's behalf 代表某人
peer pressure 同侪压力；同辈压力，同龄人压力
compete for （为……）争夺，竞争
monetary incentive 金钱刺激，鼓励
pay hike 加薪，涨工资
profit sharing 分红制
stock option 优先认股权

ownership right 产权
piece wage system 计件工资制
provident fund 公积金
fringe benefit 小额利益；附加福利
medical facility 医疗设施
over and above 除……之外
in presence of 在……的面前
in private 秘密地；私下地
confirmation letter 确认书
view as 视为，看作
motivating force 动力
put forth extra effort 付出额外的努力

Unit 9

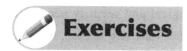

Exercises

EX. 1 Answer the following questions according to the text.

1. What does incentive mean?
2. What may incentives include?
3. How can incentive plans promote teamwork in an organization?
4. What is monetary incentive?
5. Which type of monetary incentive can encourage employees to work efficiently to increase the profits of the company?
6. What is suggestion system?
7. What kind of employees are more likely to get satisfied with non-monetary incentives?
8. Which form of incentive can prevent the employees from getting bored due to performing routine job?
9. How should the supervisors recognize the good efforts or the positive attitude shown by the subordinates?
10. What are potential drawbacks of individual incentives?

EX. 2 Translate the following terms or phrases from English into Chinese and vice versa.

1. cash bonus
2. fringe benefit
3. monetary incentive
4. pay hike
5. piece wage system
6. 分红制
7. 公积金
8. 优先认股权
9. *adj.* 协作的，合作的
10. *n.* 补偿，赔偿

EX. 3 Translate the following text into Chinese.

Money is an important motivator. Common uses of money as incentive are in the form of wages and salaries, bonus, retirement benefits, medical reimbursement, etc. Management needs to increase these financial incentives making wages and salaries competitive between various organizations so as to attract and hold force.

Money plays a significant role in satisfying physiological and security/social needs. As money is recognized as a basis of status, respect and power, it also helps satisfy the social needs of the people. It is important to mention that once the physiological and security needs are satisfied, money ceases to be motivator. Money then becomes, what Herzberg termed, hygiene and maintenance factor.

The presence of hygiene factor, of course, prevents job dissatisfaction but do not provide "on the job satisfaction" to the employees in the organization. In such case, money cannot be considered as motivator. Then, in order to motivate employees, according to Herzberg, it is necessary to provide other incentives for the satisfaction of ego, status, and self-actualization needs.

EX. 4 Fill in the blanks with the words given below.

reinforce	appreciated	contributions	indicate	foster
recognition	transparent	random	motivation	eventually

Managers Are Encouraged to Provide Incentives on a Daily Basis

In addition to company programs or incentive processes, managers have the opportunity every day to provide incentives for employees. A simple thank you, even asking the employee how they spent their weekend to __1__ care and interest, doesn't cost anything and goes a long way in helping employees experience positive workplace morale.

Gifts that are provided for specific achievements such as releasing a product or making a large sale should be __2__ and frequent. You want to create an environment in which employees feel that __3__ and incentives are available for good work and that they are not a scarce resource.

You also want to avoid doing the same thing every time because those incentives __4__ become entitlements. Once they are entitlements, they lose their power to recognize employees or to communicate and __5__ the behaviors the employer wishes to encourage.

Incentives can help employers reinforce with employees the kinds of actions and __6__ that will help the organization succeed. Used effectively, incentives help build __7__ and engagement. Employees want to be part of something that is bigger than themselves.

Employers need to use more incentives to help build employee morale and to ensure that employees feel __8__ for their contributions. Distributed appropriately, in a __9__ manner that employees understand, you can't go wrong with incentives to praise and thank employees for their performance and contributions.

Incentives provide a powerful, affirming recognition. Do more of it to __10__ your organization's success.

Text B

Employee Benefits

Employee benefits are indirect means of compensating workers; employees receive these benefits above and beyond their wages. Unlike wages alone, benefits foster economic security and stability by insuring beneficiaries against uncertain events such as unemployment, illness, and injury. Furthermore, some benefit programs serve to protect the income and welfare of families. A common distinction between direct forms of employee compensation, such as wages, and indirect compensation, or benefits, is that the former creates an employee's standard of living, whereas the latter protects that standard of living.

The range of employee benefits includes education, employee incentive, family, government, health, lifestyle, recreational, retirement, savings, and transportation benefits. While some benefits, such as government sanctioned ones, are mandatory, others are supplementary or optional at the discretion of employers. The availability of these supplementary benefits, health insurance and pension coverage in particular, is dependent on a number of factors, but most importantly on the size of a company.

1. Why to Keep Employee Benefits

Along with the basic morale reasons for keeping employee benefits, there are some other reasons that a business owner should be aware of, including:

Tax credits. If an employer offers health care plans including dental or company-paid premium life insurance plans, these are expenses that can help an organization at tax time. In addition, for employees, most health-care plans are pre-tax programs meaning the employee's share of the premium is deducted and then federal and state taxes are deducted based on a subtotal.

Retirement credits. Depending upon retirement plan, a business owner can also reap tax credit rewards and so can his employees. Speak with a tax professional on the best retirement program to initiate.

Employee packages. When employees are hired, they may not be initially excited or pleased about their base wage. By keeping employee benefits, a business owner can throw the cost the company will be enduring into their total employee compensation package to show them how much the company is really investing on their behalf.

Lower turnover rate. Ask most employees what is the most employee benefit they desire and the answer will be medical benefits. If employers understand the importance of employee benefits and keep them, they will have less employee turnover and employees will stay where they are getting the best package.

2. Types of Benefits

While some benefits are mandatory, those required by federal or state legislation, the majority are supplementary. With supplementary benefits, employers choose whether or not to offer them. Mandatory benefits provide economic security for employees who lack income as a result of unemployment, old age, disability, poor health, or other factors. Supplementary benefits not only serve as safety nets for employees, but also as incentives to attract employees and to encourage employee loyalty.

The primary role of employee benefits is to provide various types of income protection to groups of workers lacking income. Such income protection offers individual security and societal economic stability. Five principal types of income protection delivered by benefits are disability income replacement, medical expense reimbursement, retirement income replacement, involuntary unemployment income replacement, and replacement income for survivors. Different mandatory and voluntary elements of each of these categories are often combined to deliver a benefit package to a group of workers that complements the resources and goals of the organization supplying the benefits.

2.1 Disability Income Replacement

Benefits that provide disability income replacement include government programs such as social security and workers' compensation. The bulk of these benefits are mandatory, although numerous supplementary plans, most of which are tax favored, exist. Most organizations seek to assemble a disability package that will provide adequate safeguards, yet not act as a disincentive to return to work. A common objective is long-term income reimbursement of 60 percent of pay, which is preceded by higher levels of reimbursement, often as much as 100 percent during the first six months of disability. Long-term disability pay typically ends at retirement age (when pension payments begin), or when the worker recovers or finds another job. In addition, supplementary benefits such as disability insurance helps employees weather periods without pay due to disabilities not covered by government programs.

Other disability related incentives may include sick pay, including cash awards for unused sick days at the end of the year. Employers may vary the quality of their disability package with different copayment options, limits on payments for voluntary coverage, and extended coverage for related health insurance, life insurance, and medical benefits related to the disability.

2.2 Medical Expense Reimbursement

Medical expense reimbursements are one of the most expensive and important supplementary benefits. The two primary types of voluntary medical coverage options are fee-for-service plans and prepaid plans. In addition to voluntary plans, government-backed health-care plans, such as Medicare and Medicaid, serve as safety nets to furnish medical coverage to select groups of society and to those least able to afford other types of health insurance.

Under traditional fee-for-service plans, the insurer pays the insured directly for any hospital or physician costs for which the insured is covered. Under a prepaid plan, insurance companies arrange to pay health care providers for any service for which an enrollee has coverage. The insurer effectively agrees to provide the insured with health-care services, rather than reimbursement dollars. Prepaid plans offer the advantages of lower costs, which results in reduced administrative expenses and a greater emphasis on cost control. The most common type of prepaid plan is the health maintenance organization.

Most plans cover basic costs related to hospitalization, including room and board, drugs, and emergency-room care, professional care, such as physician visits, and surgery, including any procedures performed by surgeons, radiologists, or other specialists. More comprehensive plans provide greater coverage, especially of miscellaneous services not encompassed in basic plans, such as medical appliances and psychiatric care. The most inclusive plans eliminate deductible and coinsurance requirements, and may even cover dental, vision, or hearing care.

There are several specific methods that companies can use to vary the level of voluntary benefits provided in their medical benefit packages. For instance, employers may offer a high-deductible coverage plan as a way of lowering the cost of a plan (the deductible is the amount of initial costs covered by the insured before reimbursement begins). Likewise, different levels of coinsurance and copayments are usually available. For example, a beneficiary may be required to cover 10 percent of all costs incurred after the deductible amount up to a total of $100,000 (for a total payment by the insured of $10,000). A more expensive plan may reduce the beneficiary's share of those costs to 5 percent, or even zero. The total limit on insurer payments can also be adjusted. An individual lifetime maximum of $250,000 to $1 million is common.

Auxiliary medical-related employee benefits include wellness programs that teach and encourage exercise, weight control, how to stop smoking, and similar health benefits. Many companies also provide financial incentives for workers who achieve specific health-related goals, such as a certain height-to-weight ratio.

2.3 Retirement Income Replacement

Companies provide retirement-related employee benefits through three avenues: social security, pension plans, and individual savings. Social security mandates that workers and employers jointly fund an account that is managed by the federal government. The combined contribution totals about 15 percent of a worker's total salary. The money is placed in the fund, and most of it is invested in interest-paying securities and bonds backed by the government. The government pays benefits to beneficiaries when they reach retirement age. The amount of expected benefits varies by age, with younger contributors expected to receive at least a meager portion of their and their employer's total contribution. Approximately 50 million people receive social security benefits, while 135 million workers pump money into the program through wage deductions.

Pension plans are primarily financed by employers. Unlike the social security fund, funds created by private employers are subject to strict government controls designed to ensure their long-term existence. The two major categories of pension funds are defined benefit and defined contribution. Defined-benefit programs represent the traditional approach where workers are assured a determined income level (given expected social security disbursements) at retirement.

The company finances the worker's account and manages the investments. In contrast, defined-contribution plans utilize investment techniques such as stock and bond purchases with an amount of money defined by the employer. Companies make regular contributions to workers' accounts through those different instruments, and may also integrate employee contributions. The employee simply receives the value of the contributions, with interest, at retirement. The obvious benefits are deferred taxes and flexibility in comparison to defined-benefit programs.

Other pension-related programs include profit-sharing pensions, money purchase pensions, 401(k) pensions, and target-benefit pensions. 401(k) programs receive contributions from both employers and employees—employers generally match employee contributions. These programs allow the beneficiary to determine how much to save annually and they shelter employee savings from taxes until money is drawn from them. Furthermore, employees have the option of receiving monthly payments or lump sums after retirement with 401(k)s.

The third type of retirement benefit offered by many employers is supplementary individual savings plans. These plans include various tax favored savings such as individual retirement accounts (IRAs) and investment options. Employers may also provide retirement benefits such as retirement counseling, credit unions, investment counseling, and sponsorship of retiree clubs and organizations.

2.4 *Involuntary Unemployment Income Replacement*

Most employers choose to offer some form of protection against involuntary termination as a benefit to employees. In addition, termination benefits are required under various circumstances by collective bargaining agreements and state and federal laws. *The Federal Unemployment Tax Act*, for example, regulates taxes collected and sets minimum limits on unemployment benefits for all 50 states. The law, however, allows states to determine their own specific policies within the guidelines of the act. Unemployed people may receive roughly 35 percent of their weekly wages for a minimum of 26 weeks.

A common unemployment benefit provided by employers is severance pay, which may take the form of a lump sum or continuing payments. In addition, some industries provide supplemental unemployment pay plans. These are employer-funded accounts designed to ensure adequate and regular payments to workers, usually members of labor unions, during periods of inactivity.

Because of the increase in employee layoffs caused by corporate restructuring during the 1980s and 1990s, many companies have initiated benefit plans that help their terminated workers find new jobs. These programs help workers to develop new skills, learn job-seeking techniques, relocate to new regions, and pay for professional outplacement assistance. At the executive level, some workers receive "golden parachutes", or similar severance packages. These benefits ensure that if the executive is terminated as a result of a hostile takeover or some other unforeseen event, he or she will receive a preset sum or allowance.

2.5 *Replacement Income for Survivors*

Like disability compensation, benefits for the survivors of deceased employees are comprised primarily of mandatory social security and workers' compensation benefits. Eligibility for such mandatory benefits is determined by factors such as age, marital status, and parental responsibilities. In addition, however, a plethora of different privately financed benefits are available for employers, most of which have a tax favored status. Most plans are set up to make payments to a beneficiary designated by the employee. Payment levels are usually contingent on the cause of death. For example, survivors of a worker killed while on the job would likely receive much more than survivors of an employee who died at home or on vacation. A common survivorship benefit is some form of term life insurance that takes advantage of tax preferences and exemptions. Those plans often allow employees to contribute, thus significantly raising the expected payoff at death.

3. Employee Benefits Legal Compliance

While employers largely have discretion to choose what benefits to offer their employees, and how, employee benefits are also highly regulated by law. Thus, as employers explore the employee benefits section, they should keep the following ideas in mind:

• Which benefits must be provided by law to employees, such as family and medical leave and continuation of health coverage, and which benefits are voluntary.

• For each benefit, determining who is a covered employer, and who is a covered employee, keeping in mind whether your workers are properly classified as independent contractors or employees.

• Knowing whether the benefits you provide are regulated by federal and/or state law. For example, health coverage and retirement plans, while optional, are both governed by the Federal *Employee Retirement Income Security Act* (ERISA). Health insurance is further subject to a variety of other federal laws, including *the Affordable Care Act* (Health Care Reform), and state laws that add to or expand federal law.

• Finally, employers should understand the tax consequences of employer-provided benefits, such as cafeteria plans.

New Words

compensate ['kɔmpənseit] v. 补偿，赔偿；付报酬	**supplementary** [ˌsʌpli'mentəri] adj. 补充的，附加的；增补的
beneficiary [beni'fiʃəri] n. 受惠者，受益人	**optional** ['ɔpʃənəl] adj. 可选择的；随意的，任意的
welfare ['welfeə] n. 福利，福利事业	**availability** [əˌveilə'biləti] n. 可利用性；有效，有益
sanction ['sæŋkʃən] v. 批准，支持	
mandatory ['mændətəri] adj. 法定的，义务的，强制性的	**premium** ['primjəm] n. 保险费；额外费用，附加费

deduct [di'dʌkt] v. 扣除，减去；演绎
subtotal ['sʌbtəutl] n. 小计 v. 求和 adj. 几乎全部的
initiate [i'niʃieit] v. 发起，开始，创始
legislation [,ledʒis'leiʃən] n. 立法，制定法律；法律，法规
majority [mə'dʒɔrəti] n. 大多数，多数派；法定年龄
disability [,disə'biləti] n. 残疾
societal [sə'saiətəl] adj. 社会的
reimbursement [,ri:im'bə:smənt] n. 补偿，赔偿；退还，偿还
involuntary [in'vɔləntəri] adj. 非自愿的；无意的，不由自主的
survivor [sə'vaivə] n. 幸存者
bulk [bʌlk] n. 大量；（大）体积，大块
assemble [ə'sembl] v. 装配，组合；集合，收集
disincentive [,disin'sentiv] n. 抑制因素，使意图挫折的事物
copayment [kəu'peimənt] n. 雇主给予雇员的医疗保险补助金
fee-for-service ['fi:-fə'-sə:vis] n. （一次一付的）医疗费
enrollee [in,rəu'li:] n. 入伍者；入会者；入学者
hospitalization [,hɔspitəlai'zeiʃən] n. 住院治疗
radiologist [,reidi'ɔlədʒist] n. 放射线学者
miscellaneous [misə'leiniəs] adj. 多方面的；混杂的；各种各样的
psychiatric [saiki'ætrik] adj. 精神病学的；精神病治疗的
deductible [di'dʌktəbl] adj. 可扣除的

coinsurance [kəuin'ʃuərəns] n. 共同保险，共同担保
incur [in'kə:] v. 招致，引起；遭受
auxiliary [ɔ:g'ziljəri] adj. 辅助的，备用的；附加的
bond [bɔnd] n. 债券；纽带，联系
meager ['mi:gə] adj. 贫乏的，不足的
deduction [di'dʌkʃən] n. 扣除，减除；推演，推理，演绎
assure [ə'ʃuə] v. （英）给……保险；向……保证
disbursement [dis'bə:smənt] n. 支付，支出
integrate ['intigreit] v. 使一体化，使整合
sponsorship ['spɔnsəʃip] n. 赞助；发起，倡议
severance ['sevərəns] n. 补偿金
supplemental [,sʌpli'mentl] adj. 补足的，追加的
inactivity [,inæk'tivəti] n. 不活动；不活跃，不活泼
outplacement ['aut,pleismənt] n. (被解雇后的)新职介绍
hostile ['hɔstail] adj. 怀有敌意的，敌对的；不利的
decease [di'si:s] v. 亡故，死亡 n. 死亡
eligibility ['elidʒəbiləti] n. 合格，有资格
plethora ['pleθərə] n. 过多，过剩
survivorship [sə'vaivəʃip] n. 幸存，残存；[法律]遗产享有权
exemption [ig'zempʃən] n. 免除（税）
continuation [kən,tinju'eiʃən] n. 继续，延续

Unit 9

pension coverage 养老金覆盖范围
tax credit reward 税收信用奖励
compensation package （公司发给员工的）薪酬包（通常包括基本工资、奖金、福利计划及长期激励等）
turnover rate 流动率；周转率
medical benefit 医疗津贴
safety net 安全网
social security 社会保障，社会保险
tax favored 税收优惠
disability insurance 残疾保险
life insurance 人寿保险，（保险公司偿付的）人寿金
medical expense reimbursement 医疗费用报销
medical coverage 医疗保险

health maintenance organization 保健组织
medical benefit package 医疗福利
pump... into 把……注入；用泵把……抽入
be subject to 服从；以……为条件
in comparison to 与……相比
lump sum 总金额
take the form of 采取……的形状，表现为……的形式
be comprised of 由……组成
marital status 婚姻状况
be contingent on 视……而定，随……而定
tax preference 税收优惠
tax exemption 免税
legal compliance 遵守法律，守法
be classified as 被分类为

401K　401K 计划也称 401K 条款，始于 20 世纪 80 年代初，是一种由雇员、雇主共同缴费建立起来的完全基金式的养老保险制度
IRAs (Individual Retirement Accounts) 个人退休账户
FUTA (*the Federal Unemployment Tax Act*)《联邦失业税法》
ERISA (*Employee Retirement Income Securities Act*)《雇员退休收入保障法》
ACA (*the Affordable Care Act*)《平价医疗法案》
HCR (Health Care Reform) 医疗改革

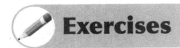

EX. 5 Fill in the following blanks with the information from Text B.

1. Usually, employees can receive two categories of benefits: some are mandated by government and others are _____.

2. _____ provide economic security for employees who lack income as a result of unemployment, old age, disability, poor health, or other factors.

3. Benefits that provide disability income replacement include government programs such as _____.

4. _____ are one of the most expensive and important supplementary benefits.

5. Usually, there are three approaches employed by companies to provide retirement-related benefits for their employees, which are _____.

6. Defined contribution is one major category of pension funds and defined-contribution plans utilize _____ such as stock and bond purchases.

7. _____ include various tax favored savings such as individual retirement accounts (IRAs) and investment options.

8. A common unemployment benefit provided by employers is _____, which may take the form of a lump sum or continuing payments.

9. A common survivorship benefit is some form of _____ that takes advantage of tax preferences and exemptions.

10. As employers explore the employee benefits section, they should bear in mind that health coverage and retirement plans are both governed by the federal _____.

Supplementary Reading

Text	Notes
Strategies to Motivate Employees Motivation is what causes us to act. Motivation activates[1], directs and sustains our goal driven behaviors, from a basic act such as obtaining food to a more sophisticated[2] act such as obtaining a Ph.D. or becoming an entrepreneur. At our core people are motivated by our biological/physiological, social,	[1] activate ['æktiveit] v. 使活动，起动，触发 [2] sophisticated [sə'fistikeitid] adj. 复杂的；精致的

emotional and cognitive needs. Very often our biological needs motivate us initially before our emotional, social and cognitive needs assert themselves especially as we gain new experiences and form bonds with others.

People are complex and it is not always enough to satisfy basic biological or even emotional, social and cognitive needs. It is the interplay[3] between all of these factors, coupled with an individual's own experiences and perceptions that drive individual motivation.

Motivations can be described as intrinsic or extrinsic. Intrinsic meaning arising from within and extrinsic from outside. Extrinsic rewards are often described as material rewards such as a trophy[4] or award including recognition or praise. And intrinsic motivations arise from internal factors such as the desire to climb a mountain or complete a complicated task. But at the end of the day both internal and external motivation are fueled by the individual's own goal driven needs.

As an employer you can provide your employees with the ability to satisfy some of their needs. You can provide them with financial rewards that allow them to meet their biological/physiological needs and also meet their other needs as finances are often useful in satisfying social, emotional and cognitive needs. If you pay an employee well enough, you may be satisfying their need for recognition and increasing their ability to satisfy social needs.

But while money can be a way to motivate employees, it is a blunt[5] instrument and does not work the same with all people and in some cases motivating with money is unsustainable[6] and for every one who it motivates, there may be a corresponding[7] person who is demotivated[8] by the lack of a financial incentive.

Once basic needs are met, most people are more motivated by social, emotional and cognitive factors over basic biological ones. Motivations can be sophisticated in their nuances[9] but often they do come back to a desire to fit in, be accepted and not alone (social), not be afraid, sad or lonely or to be happy (emotional) and to learn, challenge oneself, become adept[10] and masterful at something (cognitive). Employees who feel valued are more likely to work hard and work happy.

[3] interplay ['ɪntə(ː)'pleɪ] *n.* 相互作用

[4] trophy ['trəʊfi] *n.* 奖品

[5] blunt [blʌnt] *adj.* 直率的，迟钝的

[6] unsustainable [ˌʌnsəs'teɪnəbl] *adj.* 不能持续的，无法支撑的

[7] corresponding [ˌkɒrɪs'pɒndɪŋ] *adj.* 相当的，相应的；一致的

[8] demotivate [diː'məʊtɪveɪt] *v.* 使……失去动力，使消极

[9] nuance [njuː'ɑːns] *n.* 细微差别；细微的表情

[10] adept [ə'dept] *adj.* 精于……的，擅长于……的

However, instilling[11] motivation isn't easy. There isn't any single strategy that can magically motivate all your employees at once and keep them motivated throughout their employment. Everyone is unique, with unique values and ideas, and if you want to be successful in instilling company-wide motivation, you have to find multiple strategies to reach each individual. Here are six motivation strategies that can help you keep your work force happy and driven to succeed.

1. Individual Attention Matters

While teamwork is an important element of company success, and grouping your employees together has advantages in building that "team" mentality[12], nothing beats individual attention when it comes to individual motivation. In large corporations, this is especially true, since employees can feel isolated or unrecognized in a vast sea of workers. Taking a moment to speak to an individual alone and personally can make him or her feel truly appreciated.

The best way to go about this is to offer direct praise when an individual exceeds performance goals or does some exemplary[13] work. Not only does this make the employee feel recognized and appreciated, it also reinforces[14] the positive behavior for the entire workforce. But the importance of individual attention extends beyond simple praise. If someone is underperforming, or is overwhelmed[15] by a specific duty, take him/her aside for some personal coaching or one-on-one talks that can help that employee work through his/her problems. This type of individual attention demonstrates that you care about the individual behind the work as much as the work itself, and that you're willing to take extra steps[16] to make the individual feel comfortable.

2. Advancement Opportunities Are Enticing

People tend to feel stifled[17] when their job becomes repetitive[18] or stagnant[19]. Going too long in the same position, with no changes or hope for change, will eventually demotivate even the most ambitious employees.

However, if you offer opportunities for advancement and improvement, your employees will be motivated to work harder. As a simple example, promoting from within rather than

---

[11] **instill** [in'stil] v. 逐渐使某人获得（某种可取的品质）；逐步灌输

[12] **mentality** [men'tæləti] n. 心理，思想；精神力

[13] **exemplary** [ig'zempləri] adj. 示范的，典型的

[14] **reinforce** [,ri:in'fɔ:s] v. 加固，强化；增援

[15] **overwhelm** ['əuvə'welm] v. 压倒，压垮；淹没，覆盖

[16] **take extra step**: 采取额外的步骤

[17] **stifle** ['staifl] v. 使窒息；扼杀；抑制

[18] **repetitive** [ri'petətiv] adj. 重复的，反复的

[19] **stagnant** ['stægnənt] adj. 不流动的，停滞的；不景气的

hiring outside experts can have a profound effect on your company's overall morale. But advancement doesn't always have to come with a raise and a new job title. Offering new training or education opportunities for your employees is also motivating, as is offering new responsibilities to those willing to take them on. Help your employees grow and change in their own ways, and they'll be far more excited about working for you.

3. Leaders Set the Example

As a leader within your organization, people are going to look to[20] you to set an example for the rest of the group. You're going to be setting a tone[21], a work ethic[22], and a set of values for the company whether you mean to directly or not, and setting the right example can have a meaningful effect on the mentality of your group. For example, if you work hard and stay optimistic about everything, even in the face of enormous challenges, your employees will be likely to do the same. If you set an example of positivity and understanding, your workers will mirror[23] you, and the entire culture of the work environment will become more motivating.

In larger organizations, it's important to convey this idea to all the leaders who work individually with others, especially bosses and supervisors. Having consistent good examples across the board can dramatically alter the landscape of your workplace.

4. Environmental Motivators Can Make or Break You

How you shape your work environment has a major effect on your team's mentality. There's no right or wrong way to go about this, since every company is going to have a different culture, but it is important to include both opportunities to "get away" from the traditional work environment and pieces of color or flair[24] that make the office interesting. For example, some companies have torn down their cubicle walls in an effort to make a more open, team-based workspace. If this is too extreme for your company culture, implementing something simple like a decked-out break room could be just as effective.

Stereotypical[25] motivational posters aren't going to instantly motivate your team every day, but including pictures, quotes, and artwork on the walls of the office can inspire

[20] look to: 指望，依赖
[21] set a tone: 定下基调
[22] work ethic: 职业道德

[23] mirror ['mirə] v. 反映，反射

[24] flair [fleə] n. 天赋，才华；鉴别力

[25] stereotypical [ˌsteriə'tipikəl] adj. 典型的，带有成见的

creativity and make the office feel like a much more human, organic place to work. It's much easier to become and stay motivated when you feel comfortable in your workplace.

If you're ever concerned about the effectiveness of your workplace, ask around. Chances are your employees will tell you directly if they feel like your office is dull or uninspiring.

5. Socialization Makes People More Committed

Most people try to separate their personal and professional lives, and it's usually for the best. Trying to make everyone in the office best friends is a bad idea for a number of reasons, but that doesn't mean they shouldn't have meaningful conversations outside of a typical work environment. Being friendly with your work force builds bonds and a collective sense of teamwork, and makes work seem less machine-like and more like an organic team effort.

You can prompt people to socialize with each other more by holding team-based events. They can be outside gatherings, like parties or group activities, or something simpler like group lunches at which people are encouraged to let their hair down and talk casually to one another.

6. Transparency[26] Is the Key to Communication

Creating an environment of transparency, where you speak openly about your business to your employees and they feel comfortable coming to you with anything that's on their minds can do wonders for the collective motivation of your workplace. That's because transparency builds trust; when people understand that you aren't hiding anything, and that you'll listen to anybody, they're far more likely to respect you as an authority and appreciate you as a leader. It also opens interdepartmental channels, giving employees and supervisors greater clarity and more opportunities to openly communicate. Employees are more comfortable bringing up what they like and don't like, and there are more chances to nip[27] potential problems in the bud by calling them out.

Something as simple as an "open door policy" will, over time, make people feel more appreciated, more heard, and more valued. It also opens new lines of communication, and can improve your performance as a team.

[26] transparency [træns'pεərənsi] n. 透明度

[27] nip [nip] v. 夹，捏；阻止；剪断

People are unique and unpredictable, with individual desires and complicated ideals. No matter how perfectly it all plays out in your head, no single strategy can ever hope to please all your workers all at once. As you work to find the best motivators for your team, remember that you're going to need to make adjustments and changes as you discover what works and what doesn't. Perfect your motivation strategy as you get to know the individuals in your company, and they'll reward you with greater dedication[28] and a confident vision for the future.

[28] dedication [ˌdediˈkeiʃən]
n. 奉献，贡献

参考译文（Text A）

激 励

激励是一种行为或承诺，激发更大的行动，也叫作激发更大行动的动力。激励是除了工资之外的奖酬形式。它指员工的额外报酬或福利，以表彰其成就或良好的工作表现。激励为员工提供动力或激情，并提高其绩效。每个人的行为都有目的，这很自然。因此，给予奖励是激发员工积极性的有力的激励方式。

1. 激励计划的重要性

激励计划是认可和奖励完成既定目标的员工的形式化方法。激励可能包括现金红利、分红、额外的带薪休假或奖品，如礼品卡、公司商品或其他产品或服务。为了使之有效，必须明确地将激励界定为对相关工作量给予的可行的、有价值的奖励。

激励工具。激励计划激励员工推动并挑战自己，达到更高的生产力水平，从而最终实现公司收入的增加。实施激励计划，员工能认识到他们付出的努力将被认可和奖励。这样，为了公司的利益，他们愿意付出更多的努力，投入更多的时间和精力。

促进团队合作。与团队合作或团队活动挂钩的激励计划有助于促进企业内员工协作。在团队中工作的员工需要共同依靠相互的生产力来获得团队奖金或奖励，因此，他们会互相支持和鼓励，把工作做到最好。同侪压力也可能会鼓励那些不想让团队成员失望的、表现不佳的员工有额外的工作表现。

提高士气。激励计划有可能提高公司士气和员工工作满意度，因为员工能看到他们的努力工作和可能性收入直接相关。较高的职场士气可以减少员工流动量，从而节省公司因招聘、雇用和培训新员工产生的费用。此外，工作满意度高的员工往往缺勤率较低，这也有助于达到公司的基本要求。

提高服务水平。争取或努力实现奖励计划的员工可能为客户提供更高水平的服务。这可以增加回头生意，提高客户满意度和公司的声誉。服务水平的提高还可以促进业务推广，促进正面的口碑宣传。

为了使激励计划有效，应该对员工明确界定激励目标，公平分配工作量。否则，如果员工背上了工作缓慢、表现不佳这些包袱的话，会有不满情绪。所以，务必要考虑对个人和团体进行双重激励，以促进个人努力和团队合作相结合的理念。

2. 金钱和非金钱激励

激励可以定义为向高效员工提供的金钱和非金钱奖励。奖励可以是额外收入，或是除了固定薪水、工资以外的收入。激励起着很好的刺激和推动作用，能鼓励员工提高工作效率，实现目标。两种常见的激励方式是：金钱或财务激励、非金钱或非财务激励。

2.1 金钱或财务激励

可以用钱来计算的奖励或激励称为金钱激励。这些激励措施提供给有更多生理、社会和安全需求的员工。常见的金钱激励措施有：

工资和津贴。每年定期的加薪、发放津贴都有良好的激励作用。在一些企业，加薪和津贴与员工业绩直接挂钩。因此，为了加薪并获得津贴，员工会尽全力干好工作。

分红制。企业将一部分利润分给员工，这是一种激励员工高效工作的常见激励措施。一般来说，实行分红制时，公司会确定利润比例。如果利润超过这个比例，剩余利润就分配给员工。这种激励措施能鼓励员工有效地工作，促进公司利润增长，从而使他们自己能够得到分红。

有限合伙或股票期权。分红并没有赋予员工所有权，因此许多企业将一部分管理权、参与管理权以及一部分利润分给员工，激励他们高效工作。有限合伙权是通过发行超过固定利润的股票形式来提供的。

奖金。奖金是给高绩效员工的一次性额外奖励。一般情况下，当员工达到目标或超过目标时，他们就会得到额外的奖金。奖金还以免费出国、带薪休假或黄金等形式发放。有些公司还制定了节日期间奖金发放的方案。

提成。提成是提供给销售员工的常见激励措施。一般来说，销售人员有基本工资，并能通过努力获得提成。订单越多，提成越多。

建议制。在建议制度下，如果企业因采取某个员工的建议而获利，那么该员工就会得到奖励。例如，如果一名员工提议了一个节约成本的技术，那么提出建议的这名员工可以获得额外的报酬。在建议制度下，给予员工的奖励或报酬额度取决于该建议为企业带来的收益或利润。建议制是个很好的激励措施，它可以使员工保持较高的主动性。

生产力与工资激励挂钩。基于工资计划，生产率越高，薪水越高。在特定的计件工资制下，高效员工比低效员工得到更高的工资。因此，员工会高效地工作来争取更高的工资。

退休金。一些企业用退休金来激励员工，如养老金、公积金、抚恤金等。这些激励措施适用于有安全需求的员工。

津贴福利。它指的是一些特殊福利，如医疗、免费儿童教育、住房等福利。这些福利都是工资以外的。这些额外的福利都与员工的绩效挂钩。

2.2 非金钱或非财务激励

金钱不是唯一的激励因素。那些有较强自尊心、较强自我实现欲望的员工会对非金钱激励感到满足。不能以金钱来计算的激励称为非金钱激励。一般来说，高职位或高级别员工对非金钱奖励会感到满意。非金钱激励的常见方式有：

地位。地位是指与工作相关的职位、权力、责任、声誉和声望。在组织中，管理者可以通过提供更高的职位和地位，激励有自尊心和自我实现欲望的员工。

企业氛围。它指的是上司和下属之间的各种关系。这些关系是组织的特性，会直接影响员工的行为。管理者的积极做法会创造出更好的企业氛围，而消极的做法可能会破坏气氛。健康的组织气氛会激发员工的工作热情。

职业发展。管理者必须给员工提供晋升机会。每当有晋升机会时，员工都会提高他们的技能和工作效率，希望能晋升到更高职位上。职位晋升是一个很大的刺激因素或激励因素，它促使员工发挥出最佳水平。

工作丰富化或具有挑战性的工作分配。如果总是进行日常的工作，员工就会感到厌倦。他们喜欢做一些能改变他们、有机会展示技能的工作。被分配一些具有挑战性的工作、拥有工作的自主权以及完成一些有趣的工作，员工会得到满足，并受到激励。有趣、充实和富有挑战性的工作本身就是非常好的激励或动力因素。

员工认可。认可意味着给予下属特殊的关注或尊重，以满足他们的自我。满足自我是非常好的激励因素。当下属表现很出色，态度很积极时，上级应该在公共场合或在其他员工面前对他给予表扬；如果下属态度消极或做错了事，可以将这名员工叫至隔间私下交谈。认可员工的方式可以是祝贺员工取得好业绩、展示员工的成就，发放成绩证书、纪念品、礼品等。

工作保障。工作保障是员工与组织之间的终身联系，意味着给予员工永久性的确认书。工作保障确保了员工安全和保障需要，但可能会产生负面影响。一旦员工获得了有保障的工作，他们就失去了工作兴趣。因此，工作保障必须要有一些条款和条件。

员工参与。员工参与是指员工参与决策的制定，特别是当决策涉及员工时。如果这些决策是在和员工商议后制定的，员工会更真诚地遵守并执行这些决策。例如，如果生产目标是通过咨询员工来确定的，那么员工将更加努力地去实现该目标。

自主权或员工赋权。自主权意味着给下属更多的自由，赋权增强了员工的信心。员工会用良好的工作技能来证明如果有了自由，他们会有最佳的表现。

3. 个人与团体激励

个人激励计划和团体激励计划有相似的目标。它们都力求通过奖励来促进公司业绩发展。为了给公司确定最佳的激励方式，激励计划必须明确目标，并确保这些目标是在个人能力范围之内的。在此，在确定个人激励计划或团体激励计划是否恰当时，需要考虑如下问题：

识别。个人激励计划旨在奖励达到特定业绩目标的员工个人。常见的就是，给达到规定销售业绩的销售人员发奖金，或给工厂工人额外的报酬，因为他在轮班期间生产了所需数量的产品。团体激励计划旨在奖励团队或组织中的每个成员，因为他们取得了共同的成就，如提高了盈利或降低了成本。

适用性。当员工的生产力不依赖于其他员工的业绩表现时，个人激励计划通常更合适，如独立工作的、并能完全控制工作成效的销售人员。在难以衡量个人贡献的情况下，团体激励计划更适用，分红制就是其中之一。由于公司能够实现整体的盈利目标，所有的员工都能得到奖励。

　　团体激励考虑因素。团队激励计划可以促成组织中的团体协作和合作氛围。当奖励是基于团队的整体业绩时，最优秀的员工可能更愿意去帮助那些工作吃力的员工或新员工。另外，最优秀的员工可能会对那些他们认为不愿意或无法做出同等贡献的表现不佳的团队员工表示不满。

　　个人激励考虑因素。个人激励计划的主要好处是，这类激励计划能奖励优秀员工所付出的努力，并能成为目标导向型员工的工作动力。这类激励计划还有助于激励那些表现不佳的员工，因为这类员工以前看不到付出额外努力的意义所在。个人激励计划潜在的缺点是，会创造一个"狗咬狗"的工作环境。在这种环境下，每个员工都把自己的利益放在同事的利益之前。个人激励计划潜在的缺点还包括，一些员工为达到目的，不顾职业道德底线，如销售人员为了销售对潜在的客人说谎。

Unit 10

Text A

Labor Relations Management

1. Definition of Labor Relations Management

Labor relations management is the study and practice of managing unionized employment situations. In academia, labour relations is frequently a subarea within industrial relations, though scholars from many disciplines—including economics, sociology, history, law, and political science—also study labor unions and labor movements. In practice, labor relations management is frequently a subarea within human resource management. Courses in labor relations management typically cover labor history, labor law, union organizing, bargaining, contract administration, and important contemporary topics.

Labor relations can refer broadly to any dealings between management and workers about employment conditions. Most commonly, however, labor relations refer to the continuous relationship between a union representing the collective interest of workers and the organization's management. This relationship focuses primarily on union and management rights, a written contract and the interpretation of the written contract.

2. Labor Relations Managers

A labor relations manager works as a conduit between management and employees to guarantee the satisfaction of both groups. He may deal with union or non-union employees and is often employed by government agencies. Both small and large companies usually employ these types of managers. People in this profession frequently teach on the subject at the college level or serve as independent consultants for profit and non-profit firms.

To be competent in this position, a labor relations manager is generally required to be well informed on the most recent labor and wage laws in the region in which he works. He is frequently expected to interpret changes in policies for management and employees as well as explain the language and subtext of contracts. In some situations, he is designated to represent management's viewpoints to union representatives.

Conflict resolution is normally a large part of a labor relations manager's job. Before a relatively minor issue elevates into a full-blown workplace complaint, he typically intercedes to mediate the situation. This intervention often prevents work disruption, lawsuits or strikes. It frequently requires the manager to communicate with a variety of players, including government agencies, unions, employees and management.

If a labor relations manager works for a government agency at a local or regional level, his job may concentrate more on issues specific to government employees. These topics regularly include job classifications, labor laws and guidelines and rules that relate to workplace safety codes, wages, hourly workers and general fair employment practices. Some managers conduct research on economics, workplace communications and labor laws and compile statistics for government agencies.

The daily job duties of a labor relations manager are usually consistent whether he works in the private or public sector. He is commonly required to document all workplace activities that involve labor topics or workplace communications. As he is frequently expected to attend meetings of both employee and management representatives, the manager is often required to be objective in his observations and reports. Statistical reports based on labor relations activities are commonly expected from a person with this job.

A successful labor relations manager is typically a good listener who is reputed to be fair-minded and empathetic to all parties. His organizational skills are important, as he is normally inundated with paperwork and files relating to a number of issues that may remain open for discussion for weeks or months. Excellent oral and written communications skills are considered a plus.

A bachelor's degree in business administration, labor relations or human resources is generally required to qualify for this position. Senior level positions in labor management may require a master's degree in a related concentration. Experience as a union representative, shop steward or human resources manager is preferred.

3. Survey of Employee Satisfaction

An employee satisfaction survey is one method for employers to discover how employee centered their business is. Such a survey, which is usually conducted anonymously, gauges the level of employee contentment by asking questions of employees on a number of fronts that could have to do with training, development, effective management, lack of discrimination, compensation, and work environment or peer relationships. Many employers look to these surveys especially if they are having difficulty retaining workers, but they may also be interested in hearing from employees to get ideas on how to improve relationships between employees and employers.

There are lots of different ways in which an employee satisfaction survey might be conducted. Often the employer works with people like independent human resource consultants who actually administer the survey and then interpret the results for the company. A slightly less expensive approach is to conduct online surveys where findings suggest certain pre-determined remedies. When companies can afford the more expensive scenario, it may prove most helpful because any solutions will be tailored to the specific company and its employees.

One of the things of greatest concern to an employee who is asked to participate in a survey is whether results will be kept confidential. In the best surveys they are confidential, but anyone concerned about this should get verification, preferably in writing, that negative comments on an employee satisfaction survey cannot be used in punitive ways. When a company is truly interested in increasing satisfaction, they should hear not just good reviews but also bad ones. With only positive comments, they will have nothing to improve. To get these results, employers should use surveys that guarantee confidentiality of responses, or they may just end up with dishonest statements that aren't productive.

The quality of the employee satisfaction survey is probably best determined by how it helps the company make improvements that increase satisfaction. When employers aren't willing to make real changes, there isn't much point in having a survey. Employees tend to know what their co-workers have to say about work, and most can identify several problem areas creating things like poor worker retention. If they don't see such areas improved over time after a survey, retention could sink lower, though other factors like a poor job market may keep workers at jobs they really don't like.

While an employee satisfaction survey should lead to improvements in the workplace, individual employees also need to be realistic about what improvements they'll see. What gets improved depends on the number of employees that all listed a mutual concern. One individual may have legitimate grievances with an employer that not everyone else shares, and the employer's failure to address individual concerns is usually because they are trying to take the steps that would satisfy the most employees at once. Workers who feel comfortable in their work environment might attempt to address legitimate personal issues with management.

4. Employee Satisfaction Enhancement

Employee satisfaction is a measure of how happy workers are with their jobs and working environment. Keeping morale high can be of tremendous benefit to any company, as happy workers are more likely to produce more, take fewer days off, and stay loyal to the company. There are many efficient ways involved in improving or maintaining high satisfaction rates, which wise employers would do well to implement.

Employee orientation. One of the best ways to have satisfied employees is to make sure they're pleased from the get-go. Offering a thorough orientation will ensure that the expectations are realistic and that new staffers don't come in with rose-colored glasses that will quickly fade. Proper onboarding encourages positive attitudes and can reduce turnover.

Positive work environment. An upbeat workplace is a necessity. If the workspace isn't positive, you can't expect the workers to be. Encouraging one another, avoiding micromanagement, giving positive feedback and ensuring criticism is constructive are all ways to keep the environment a place where employees can do more than survive, and they can thrive!

Provide competitive benefits. Fair wages are important, but competitive benefits are also critical to keeping your workforce satisfied. If your benefits package is thin, employees may look for other opportunities with firms that are more generous. Beyond insurance, benefits such as flex time, paid holidays and personal days are important factors to employee satisfaction.

Workforce engagement. Employees that don't find their work interesting or don't feel they are contributing to the mission of the firm will not be engaged. For employees to be satisfied, they must feel like they are part of something bigger than just what their individual work tasks are. Include staffers in goal setting and how they fit in the corporation fabric to increase engagement and satisfaction.

Develop skills. Everyone needs something to working toward. Stagnation is unfulfilling. Employees have more potential than their current level of functionality. Encouraging employees to fulfill that potential will increase engagement and satisfaction. Whether it's training opportunities, mentoring, online courses or external training, always encourage staff to improve their skills.

Recognition and rewards. Employees enjoy an attaboy and it need not be a public show to mean something to employees. Encourage supervisors and managers to acknowledge employees deeds on a daily basis. Also implement a formal program company-wide to recognize top achievers in every job category. Healthy competition can boost morale, encourage hard work and increase satisfaction and retention.

Track job satisfaction. Don't sit back and just hope that employees are satisfied—put some data behind it. Offer anonymous online surveys or mobile surveys to effectively track how employees feel about benefits, recognition, supervisor feedback and other aspects that contribute to employee satisfaction. This allows you to improve, tweak and monitor satisfaction levels to reduce turnover and save the company money.

HR professionals have one of the most challenging jobs in a business because your job is considering everyone else's job and how well they like it, how likely they are to quit or how their attitude affects co-workers. Increasing employee satisfaction through these and other measures can make your job (and everyone else's) more satisfying and fulfilling.

5. Labor Disputes

Labor disputes refer to controversy between an employer and its employees regarding the terms (such as conditions of employment, fringe benefits, hours or work, tenure, wages) to be negotiated during collective bargaining, or the implementation of already agreed upon terms.

A labor dispute is a conflict which arises over the terms negotiated in collective bargaining agreements mediated by a union. Labor disputes can occur while the union is working with the employer to negotiate an agreement, or when an already established agreement is violated. If labor disputes escalate, they can develop into strikes, in which the employees do not report for work until the dispute is resolved. This can become extremely costly very quickly and can

Unit 10

lead to situations in which governments may be forced to intervene. Thus, workers, unions, and employers all want to avoid labor disputes. Once labor disputes arise, the following effective resolutions need to be implemented.

Labor arbitration. Labor arbitration is an informal adjudicative process in which labor and management empower an arbitrator to issue a final and binding award based on evidence submitted in a hearing. The authority for appointment as a labor arbitrator arises from the collective bargaining agreement.

Grievance mediation. The vast majority of grievances are settled prior to labor arbitration. Labor-management is increasingly considering mediation as an alternative to arbitration. We are accomplished mediators of labor grievances. We have mediated numerous labor grievances concerning discipline and contract interpretation.

Neutrality agreements. Neutrality agreements are increasingly accepted as a tool to set the ground rules for union organizing conduct. We conduct union recognition and ratification elections, union card checks, and arbitrates disputes arising from neutrality agreements.

Interest-based negotiations. The negotiation of labor and employment agreements is increasingly complex. Traditional bargaining is often about relative power and willingness to use it against each other, often at the expense of a better agreement or even the relationship. We utilize interest-based problem solving as a process that enables negotiators and leaders to become joint problem-solvers. The process assumes that mutual gains are possible, that solutions which satisfy mutual interests are more durable, and that parties should help each other achieve a positive result.

Grievances and conflicts are an inevitable part of the employment relationship. The objective of public policy is to manage conflict and promote sound labor relations by creating a system for the effective prevention and settlement of labor disputes. Labor administrations typically establish labor dispute procedures in national legislation. A key objective of effective systems is to ensure that wherever possible, the parties to the dispute resolve it through a consensus-based process such as conciliation and mediation, before reverting to arbitration and/or adjudication through a tribunal or labour court.

New Words

unionize [ˈjuːnjənaɪz] v. （使）加入工会，（使）成立工会
sociology [ˌsəʊsiˈɒlədʒi] n. 社会学；群体生态学
continuous [kənˈtɪnjuəs] adj. 连续的，延伸的

collective [kəˈlektɪv] adj. 集体的，共同的；集合的
interpretation [ɪnˌtɜːprɪˈteɪʃən] n. 理解，解释
conduit [ˈkɒndjuɪt] n. 通道；导管；水道，沟渠

consultant [kən'sʌltənt] *n.* 顾问，咨询者

subtext [sʌb'tekst] *n.* 潜在的意思，潜台词

designate ['dezigneit] *v.* 指定；标明；把……定名为

viewpoint ['vju:,pɔint] *n.* 观点，看法

elevate ['eliveit] *v.* 变高，提高，提升，举起；鼓舞

full-blown [ful-'bləun] *adj.* 全面的；盛开的，成熟的

complaint [kəm'pleint] *n.* 投诉，控告；抱怨，诉苦

intercede [,intə'si:d] *v.* 仲裁，调解；说情

mediate ['mi:dieit] *v.* 调停，调解，斡旋

strike [straik] *n.* 罢工，打击

fair [fɛə] *adj.* 公平的，合理的；晴朗的；美丽的

compile [kəm'pail] *v.* 编译，编制；汇编

consistent [kən'sistənt] *adj.* 一致的；连续的，不矛盾的

repute [ri'pju:t] *v.* 认为，以为 *n.* 名声，名气，声望

fair-minded ['fɛə-'maindid] *adj.* 公正的，公平的

empathetic [,empə'θetik] *adj.* 感情移入的，移情作用的

inundate ['inʌndeit] *v.* 淹没，泛滥

anonymously [ə'nɔnimənsli] *adv.* 用匿名的方式

discrimination [dis,krimi'neiʃən] *n.* 歧视；辨别，区别

confidential [kɔnfi'denʃəl] *adj.* 机密的，秘密的；表示信任的

verification [,verifi'keiʃən] *n.* 核实，证明，证实

punitive ['pju:nitiv] *adj.* 处罚的，惩罚性的；令人受苦的

confidentiality [,kɔnfi,denʃi'æləti] *n.* 机密性

legitimate [li'dʒitimit] *adj.* 合法的，合理的；正规的

grievance ['gri:vəns] *n.* 不满，牢骚；委屈，苦衷

get-go [get-gəu] *n.* 开端，开始

onboarding ['ɔn'bɔ:diŋ] *n.* 入职

upbeat ['ʌpbi:t] *adj.* 积极乐观的，愉快的，高兴的

necessity [ni'sesəti] *n.* 必需品；必要（性）

competitive [kəm'petətiv] *adj.* （薪水、价格等）有竞争力的；比赛的

flextime ['flekstaim] *n.* 弹性工作时间

stagnation [stæg'neiʃən] *n.* 停滞；不景气

unfulfilling [ʌn'fulfiliŋ] *adj.* 不称心的，不能使人满足的

attaboy ['ætəbɔi] *int.* [口]好小子；好样的

boost [bu:st] *v.* 增加；促进，提高

tweak [twi:k] *v.* 微调；拧，扭

controversy ['kɔntrəvə:si] *n.* 争议，（公开的）争论

tenure ['tenjə] *n.* 终身职位；任期

negotiate [ni'gəuʃieit] *v.* 谈判，协商，交涉

violate ['vaiəleit] *v.* 违反，侵犯

Unit 10

escalate [ˈeskəleit] v. （使）逐步升级；（使）逐步上升；（使）逐步扩大
adjudicative [əˈdʒuːdiˌkeitiv] adj. 有判决权的，（法院）宣告的
arbitrator [ˈɑːbitreitə] n. 仲裁员，仲裁人，公断人
binding [ˈbaindiŋ] adj. 有约束力的，应履行的
mediation [ˌmiːdiˈeiʃən] n. 调停，调解，斡旋
accomplished [əˈkɔmpliʃt] adj. 才华高的，技艺高超的，熟练的
mediator [ˈmiːdieitə] n. 调解人，调停者

neutrality [njuːˈtræləti] n. 中立，中立地位
ratification [ˌrætifiˈkeiʃən] n. 正式批准，认可；承认
interest-based [ˈintrist-beist] adj. 基于利益的
consensus-based [kənˈsensəs-beist] adj. 基于一致性的
conciliation [kənˌsiliˈeiʃən] n. 调解，安抚，说服
adjudication [əˌdʒuːdiˈkeiʃən] n. 判决，宣判
tribunal [triˈbjuːnl] n. 法庭，法院；裁决

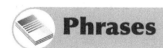

Phrases

conflict resolution 冲突解决，矛盾解决
concentrate on 专心于，把思想集中于
job classification 工作分类
safety code 安全法则，安全规程
be inundated with 充斥着
business administration 经营管理
qualify for 有资格，合格
shop steward 工会代表
tailor to 根据……调整
stay loyal to 对……保持忠诚

employee orientation 员工入职培训
on a daily basis 每天
sit back 袖手旁观，不采取行动
labor dispute 劳资纠纷
labor arbitration 劳动仲裁
the vast majority of 绝大部分
prior to 在……之前的
neutrality agreement 中立协议
set the ground rules for 为……制定基本规则
revert to 回复，归还

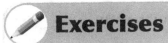

EX. 1 Answer the following questions according to the text.

1. What relationship does labor relation commonly refer to ?
2. To be competent in his/her position, what information is a labor relations manager generally required to know?
3. What is a successful labor relations manager typically like?
4. What is one of the greatest concerns to an employee who is asked to participate in an employee satisfaction survey?
5. What factor best determines the quality of the employee satisfaction survey?
6. What will a thorough employee orientation ensure?
7. What do the employers effectively track by offering anonymous online surveys or mobile surveys?
8. What do labor disputes refer to?
9. What is labor arbitration?
10. Which resolution is being increasingly considered as an alternative to arbitration to resolve the labor conflicts?

EX. 2 Translate the following terms or phrases from English into Chinese and vice versa.

1. shop steward   1. _____
2. conflict resolution   2. _____
3. neutrality agreement   3. _____
4. employee orientation   4. _____
5. binding   5. _____
6. *adj.* 有竞争力的   6. _____
7. *n.* 调解，安抚，说服   7. _____
8. *n.* 歧视；辨别，区别   8. _____
9. *vi.* 谈判，协商，交涉   9. _____
10. 劳资纠纷   10. _____

EX. 3 Translate the following text into Chinese.

Job satisfaction is a business term that refers to a person's contentment with his or her job. Numerous factors can contribute to an employee's satisfaction or dissatisfaction in the workplace. Such factors can include the work environment, employee relations, and salary. Although an individual's perception of his own job contentment is usually subjective, there are methods that employers can use to quantify responses to employee surveys and other similar measurement

Unit 10

tools. They can then implement measures to help foster job satisfaction among workers. Ultimately, though, it may be up to individual employees to ensure their own contentment.

Over time, different theories have evolved regarding the perceived connections between job satisfaction and other variables such as workplace productivity. According to some human resources professionals, for instance, employee satisfaction typically leads to increased motivation, which then results in improved performance. Some studies have shown, however, that this is not necessarily the case; they have concluded that job satisfaction and productivity might both be associated with another variable such as an employee's personality, but that satisfaction alone does not necessarily cause higher productivity.

EX. 4) Fill in the blanks with the words given below.

| positive | data | determining | monitors | assess |
| customized | observer | common | sophisticated | effective |

Different Methods of Measuring Job Satisfaction

Different methods for measuring job satisfaction include using surveys, interviewing employees and monitoring performance targets. __1__ which method to use depends on the level of complexity or underlying issues the business feels could be causing the dissatisfaction.

Surveys are a __2__ method of measuring job satisfaction. A survey can __3__ satisfaction in the areas of pay, promotion, supervision, tasks and co-workers. While standard surveys are available for businesses, a __4__ survey that is tailored to a business's own needs and industry may be more __5__ .

Interviewing employees as a method of measuring job satisfaction is mostly useful in organizations that have __6__ relationships with employees and believe the problem is too __7__ to be understood with a survey.

Monitoring performance targets is a method of measuring job satisfaction that requires a business to be an active __8__ . With this method, management __9__ employee satisfaction by using standard criteria, such as achieving bonuses, participating in optional programs and performance in reaching goals. This method provides indirect __10__ on the levels of job satisfaction.

Text B

Collective Bargaining

1. What Is Collective Bargaining?

Collective bargaining is a process of negotiation between employers and a group of employees aimed at agreements to regulate working salaries, working conditions, benefits, and other aspects of workers' compensation and rights. The interests of the employees are commonly presented by representatives of a trade union to which the employees belong. The collective agreements reached by these negotiations usually set out wage scales, working hours, training, health and safety, overtime, grievance mechanisms, and rights to participate in workplace or company affairs.

The union may negotiate with a single employer (who is typically representing a company's shareholders) or may negotiate with a group of businesses, depending on the country, to reach an industry-wide agreement. A collective agreement functions as a labor contract between an employer and one or more unions. Collective bargaining consists of the process of negotiation between representatives of a union and employers (generally represented by management, or, in some countries such as Austria, Sweden and the Netherlands, by an employers' organization) in respect of the terms and conditions of employment of employees, such as wages, hours of work, working conditions, grievance procedures, and about the rights and responsibilities of trade unions. The parties often refer to the result of the negotiation as a collective bargaining agreement (CBA) or as a collective employment agreement (CEA).

2. What Is Good Faith Bargaining?

Good faith bargaining is the cornerstone of effective labor management relations. It means that both parties communicate and negotiate, that they match proposals with counter proposals, and that both make every reasonable effort to arrive at an agreement. It does not mean that one party compels another to agree to a proposal. Nor does it require that either party make any specific concessions (although as a practical matter, some may be necessary).

The collective bargaining process requires that the parties, including those that qualify as joint employers, negotiate in good faith. This means that both parties must enter the bargaining process with a real intent to reach a fair written agreement and use their best efforts to achieve this goal. This includes:

• meeting at reasonable times and in reasonable locations;

• adequately responding to union requests for information relevant to its role as a bargaining representative;

• conferring on mandatory bargaining subjects such as wage and hour, benefits, discipline and other terms.

Neither party can request or require the other party to agree to any terms that violate *the National Labor Relations Act* (NLRA) and/or the federal or state anti-discrimination laws.

However, when is bargaining not in good faith? As interpreted by the NLRB and the courts, a violation of the requirement for good faith bargaining may include the following:

Surface bargaining. Going through the motions of bargaining without any real intention of completing a formal agreement.

Inadequate concessions. Unwillingness to compromise, even though no one is required to make a concession.

Inadequate proposals and demands. The NLRB considers the advancement of proposals to be positive factor in determining overall good faith.

Dilatory tactics. The law requires that the parties meet and "confer at reasonable times and intervals". Obviously, refusal to meet with the union does not satisfy the positive duty imposed on the employer.

Imposing conditions. Attempts to impose conditions that are so unreasonable as to indicate bad faith.

Making unilateral changes in conditions. This is a strong indication that the employer is not bargaining with required intent of reaching an agreement.

Bypassing the representative. The duty of management to bargain in good faith involves, at a minimum, recognition that the union representative is the one with whom the employer must deal in conducting negotiations.

Committing unfair labor practices during negotiations. Such practices may reflect poorly upon the good faith of the guilty party.

Withholding information. An employer must supply the union with information, upon request to enable it to understand and intelligently discuss the issues raised in bargaining.

Ignoring bargaining items. Refusal to bargain on mandatory item (one must bargain over these) or insistence on a permissive item (one may bargain over these).

3. Collective Bargaining Process

Collective bargaining generally includes negotiations between the two parties (the employees' representatives and the employers' representatives). Collective bargaining consists of negotiations between an employer and a group of employees that determine the conditions of employment. Often employees are represented in the bargaining by a union or other labor organization. The result of collective bargaining procedure is called the collective bargaining agreement. Collective agreements may be in the form of procedural agreements or substantive agreements. Procedural agreements deal with the relationship between workers and management and the procedures to be adopted for resolving individual or group disputes.

This will normally include procedures in respect of individual grievances, disputes and discipline. Frequently, procedural agreements are put into the company rule book which provides information on the overall terms and conditions of employment and codes of behavior. A substantive agreement deals with specific issues such as pay, overtime premiums, bonus arrangements, holiday entitlements, hours of work, etc. In many companies, agreements have a fixed time scale and a collective bargaining process will review the procedural agreement when negotiations take place on pay and conditions of employment.

The collective bargaining process comprises of five core steps:

Prepare. This phase involves composition of a negotiation team. The negotiation team should consist of representatives of both the parties with adequate knowledge and skills for negotiation. In this phase both the employer's representative and the union examine their own situation in order to develop the issues that they believe will be most important. The first thing to be done is to determine whether there is actually any reason to negotiate at all. A correct understanding of the main issues to be covered and intimate knowledge of operations, working conditions, production norms and other relevant conditions is required.

Discuss. Here, the parties decide the ground rules that will guide the negotiations. A process well begun is half done and this is no less true in case of collective bargaining. An environment of mutual trust and understanding is also created so that the collective bargaining agreement would be reached.

Propose. This phase involves the initial opening statements and the possible options that exist to resolve them. In a word, this phase could be described as "brainstorming". The exchange of messages takes place and opinion of both the parties is sought.

Bargain. Negotiations are easy if a problem solving attitude is adopted. This stage comprises the time when "what ifs" and "supposals" are set forth and the drafting of agreements takes place.

Settlement. Once the parties are through with the bargaining process, a consensual agreement is reached upon wherein both the parties agree to a common decision regarding the problem or the issue. This stage is described as consisting of effective joint implementation of the agreement through shared visions, strategic planning and negotiated change.

4. Impasse in Bargaining

During the collective bargaining process, when parties fail to reach agreements about the terms and conditions of employment, either side can typically make it known that they have reached an impasse, signaling that they are unable to resolve their differences on their own. When collective bargaining negotiations reach an impasse, there are three primary methods used to facilitate the resolution of disagreements. These formal methods of dispute negotiation include mediation, fact-finding, and arbitration.

The formal grievance resolution process of mediation involves the use of neutral third-party mediators who work closely with the parties in order to facilitate an agreement. Individual mediators are usually chosen either by state labor relations boards or through the mutual agreement of local school boards and the bargaining representatives of their employees. Mediators' recommendations are ordinarily not disclosed to the public. While the legal authority of mediators is limited, a number of states require that the parties must exhaust formal mediation efforts before they may proceed to fact-finding, arbitration, or the termination of bargaining altogether.

The second method of dispute resolution adopted when an impasse in bargaining has occurred is fact-finding or advisory arbitration. Fact-finding requires the use of a neutral, third-party intermediary called the fact finder. Similar to mediators, fact finders are chosen by either state labor relations boards or through the mutual agreement of the parties to the bargaining agreement. Fact finders are legally empowered to conduct hearings and collect evidence from all parties associated with the bargaining agreement as well as any other relevant outside sources. While the recommendations put forth by fact finders are not legally binding on the parties to the agreement, their reports are usually made available to the public and in some cases act as a catalyst for the resolution of a dispute.

The third method of dispute resolution when an impasse arises in bargaining is arbitration. In the United States, there is a strong inclination within the legal community to use arbitration as an effective means of setting labor related disputes. As with mediation and fact-finding, arbitrators are selected by either state labor relations boards or through the mutual agreement of the parties to the dispute. However, unlike mediators or fact-finders, arbitrators' decisions are legally binding on all parties to the agreement.

5. Terms of Collective Bargaining Agreements

Collective bargaining agreements are lengthy, detailed legal documents that cover every aspect of the working relationship between workers and management. Like a standard contract, a collective bargaining agreement is divided into articles and clauses. The following are considered "mandatory" subjects covered by all collective bargaining agreements.

Wages and hours. Unions and management must agree on the hourly wages and overtime rules for each job position covered by the agreement.

Fringe benefits. This section includes, but is not limited to, paid and unpaid vacation days, holidays, sick leave, jury duty, maternity leave, health care coverage, pension and other retirement savings plans.

Scope of work. Many collective bargaining agreements go into great detail to describe the scope and responsibility of each job title.

Seniority and promotions. Workers who have been on the job the longest may be entitled to greater benefits (more vacation time, first to be considered for promotion) and some protections (last to be laid off) defined by the agreement.

Grievance procedure. The agreement outlines the dispute resolution process for matters like unfair firings and pay discrepancies. Grievances typically have to be in writing and arbitration, if necessary, chosen by both parties or provided by the Federal Mediation and Conciliation Service.

Disciplinary measures. Union membership doesn't mean you can't be demoted or fired. This section details the acceptable reasons and processes for disciplinary action or termination.

No strike/No lockout. Many collective bargaining agreements contain a clause preventing either side from participating in a strike or lockout while the contract is active. This clause does not hold in cases where one side accuses the other of unfair labor practices.

Union Dues. Most agreements allow for dues to be automatically deducted from employee paychecks. In so-called "open shops", where union membership isn't mandatory for employment, even non-union workers pay a service fee, since they're also covered by union negotiations.

New Words

negotiation [ni‚gəuʃi'eiʃən] n. 协商，谈判；转让

regulate ['regjuleit] v. 控制，管理；调节，调整

cornerstone ['kɔ:nəstəun] n. 奠基石，基础

compel [kəm'pel] v. 强迫，迫使

concession [kən'seʃən] n. 让步，迁就

adequately ['ædikwitli] adv. 适当地，足够地

anti-discrimination ['ænti-dis‚krimi-'neiʃən] n. 反歧视

motion ['məuʃən] n. 提议；手势；示意

intention [in'tenʃən] n. 意图，目的；意向，打算

dilatory ['dilətəri] adj. 迂缓的；拖拉的，延误的

tactics ['tæktiks] n. 战术；策略，手段

unilateral ['ju:ni'lætərəl] adj. 单边的，一方的；片面的

bypass ['baipɑ:s] v. 绕开，忽视

guilty ['gilti] adj. 内疚的；有罪的

withhold [wið'həuld] v. 抑制，克制；扣留，拒绝给予

permissive [pə'misiv] adj. 宽大的；自由的；容许的

substantive ['sʌbstəntiv] adj. 本质的，实质的；大量的

dispute [dis'pju:t] n. （劳资）纠纷；争端

entitlement [in'taitlmənt] n. 授权；应得权益

composition [kɔmpə'ziʃən] n. 组织，构成；合成物

intimate ['intimit] adj. 关系紧密的；亲密的，私人的

brainstorm ['brein‚stɔ:m] v. 集思广益，集体讨论

supposal [sə'pəuzl] n. 想象，推测

consensual [kən'senʃuəl] adj. 经双方同意的，一致同意的

regarding [ri'gɑ:diŋ] prep. 关于，就……而论；至于

impasse [im'pɑ:s] n. 僵局；绝境，死胡同

signal ['signl] n. 信号，暗号；预兆，征象

disclose [dis'kləuz] v. 公开，揭露，使显露，使暴露

exhaust [ig'zɔ:st] v. 耗尽，使筋疲力尽

intermediary [‚intə'mi:diəri] adj. 中间人的；调解的 n. 媒介；中间人，调解人

catalyst ['kætəlist] n. 促进因素

discrepancy [dis'krepənsi] n. 差异；不一致，分歧

demote [di'məut] v. 降级；降职

lockout ['lɔkaut] n. 关闭工厂；停工

due [dju:] n. 应得物；会费

Unit 10

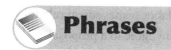

collective bargaining 集体协定，劳资双方就工资等问题谈判
grievance mechanism 诉冤机制
collective agreement 集体协议
in respect of 涉及；关于，在……方面
collective bargaining agreement 劳资谈判合同
good faith bargaining 诚意谈判
counter proposal 反建议
arrive at an agreement 达成协议
make concession 让步
qualify as 取得……资格
with intent to 蓄意，存心；心怀……的意图
confer on 授给，授予
surface bargaining 敷衍性谈判

dilatory tactics 拖延战术
impose on 把……强加于；施加；利用
at a minimum 最低限度；至少
procedural agreement 程序协议
substantive agreement 实质性的协议
overtime premium 加班费
comprise of 由……构成，包括
have intimate knowledge of 对……非常熟悉
opening statement 开场白
associated with 与……相联系，与……有关
maternity leave 产假
be entitled to 有权（做）；有资格（做）
disciplinary measures 纪律措施
accuse sb. of 控告某人……

CEA (Collective Employment Agreement) 集体就业协议
NLRA (*National Labor Relations Act*) 《国家劳工关系法》
NLRB (National Labor Relations Board) 美国全国劳资关系委员会

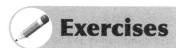

EX. 5 Read the following statements and then decide whether each of them is true or false based on the information in Text B. Write T for True and F for False in the space provided before each statement.

_____ 1. Collective bargaining is a process of negotiation between an employer and an employee aimed at agreements to regulate working salaries, working conditions, benefits, and so on.

_____ 2. A collective bargaining agreement (CBA) or a collective employment agreement (CEA) is often used to refer to the result of collective negotiation.

209

_____ 3. Good faith bargaining is the cornerstone of effective labor management relations, which in the extreme cases, can mean that one party compels another to agree to a proposal.

_____ 4. Although surface bargaining is regarded as a violation of the requirement for good faith bargaining, yet it is indeed an effective bargaining strategy.

_____ 5. Collective bargaining agreements refer to the results of collective bargaining procedure, which may take the form of procedural agreements or substantive agreements.

_____ 6. A procedural agreement deals with specific issues such as pay, overtime premiums, bonus arrangements, holiday entitlements, hours of work, etc.

_____ 7. The collective bargaining process consists of five core steps, including preparing, discussing, proposing, bargaining and settlement.

_____ 8. When collective bargaining negotiations reach an impasse, there are three primary methods used to facilitate the resolution of disagreements, including mediation, accusation, and arbitration.

_____ 9. Since the legal authority of mediators is limited, it is unnecessary for the parties of bargaining to resort to formal mediation before proceeding to fact-finding, arbitration, or the termination of bargaining altogether.

_____ 10. All collective bargaining agreements must cover some "mandatory" subjects, such as fringe benefits, scope of work, grievance procedures and so on.

Supplementary Reading

Text	Notes
Employment Contract An employment contract or contract of employment is a kind of contract used in labor law to attribute rights and responsibilities between parties to a bargain. The contract is between an "employee" and an "employer". It has arisen out of the old master-servant law, used before the 20th century. But generally, the contract of employment denotes[1] a relationship of economic dependence and social subordination[2]. In the words of the controversial[3] labour lawyer Sir Otto Kahn-Freund, "the relation between an employer and an isolated	[1] denote [di'nəut] v. 表示，象征；意思是 [2] subordination [sə,bɔ:di'neiʃən] n. 附属；次级 [3] controversial [,kɔntrə'və:ʃəl] adj. 有争议的，引起争议的，被争论的

employee or worker is typically a relation between a bearer[4] of power and one who is not a bearer of power. In its inception[5] it is an act of submission[6], in its operation it is a condition of subordination, however much the submission and the subordination may be concealed[7] by the indispensable[8] figment[9] of the legal mind known as the 'contract of employment'. The main object of labor law has been, and will always be a countervailing[10] force to counteract the inequality of bargaining power which is inherent[11] and must be inherent in the employment relationship."

1. Benefits of an Employment Contract

A good employment contract is beneficial to both the employee and the employer. It spells out the rights and obligations[12] of each party, protects the job security of the employee and protects the employer from certain risks such as the release[13] of confidential employer information after the term of employment ends. A good employment contract can benefit both the employee and the employer in the following ways:

Term. Most employment contracts set a definite term of employment. This guarantees employees a job as long as they do not violate the terms of the contract, and allows employers to dismiss[14] an employee at the end of the term in jurisdictions[15] that restrict the ability of employers to fire employees. The length of this term should be carefully negotiated.

Termination. A good employment contract will specify exactly what offenses can result in termination of the employee. This helps both parties, because it ensures that the employee knows which activities are required and which are forbidden, thus rendering a serious breach[16] less likely. The labor law of the particular jurisdiction should be consulted to ensure that the terms of the contract do not contradict[17] legal requirements.

Non-competition covenants[18]. If the employee will have access to confidential company information, it is important from the employer's point of view to include a clause preventing the employee from divulging[19] this information to others. An employer might also wish to prevent the employee from working for competitors, although the labor laws of various

[4] bearer ['beərə] *n.* 承担人
[5] inception [in'sepʃən] *n.* 创始，开端
[6] submission [səb'miʃən] *n.* 屈服，服从；谦恭
[7] conceal [kən'si:l] *v.* 隐瞒，遮住
[8] indispensable [ˌindis'pensəbl] *adj.* 不可缺少的；绝对必要的
[9] figment ['figmənt] *n.* 虚构的事物，臆造的事物
[10] countervailing ['kauntəveiliŋ] *adj.* 弥补的，抵消的
[11] inherent [in'hiərənt] *adj.* 固有的，内在的
[12] obligation [ˌɔbli'geiʃən] *n.* 义务，责任；债务
[13] release [ri'li:s] *n.* 发布；发行；释放

[14] dismiss [dis'mis] *v.* 解雇，把……免职
[15] jurisdiction [ˌdʒuəris'dikʃən] *n.* 管辖权；管辖范围

[16] breach [bri:tʃ] *n.* 违背；破坏

[17] contradict [ˌkɔntrə'dikt] *v.* 反驳，驳斥；与……矛盾，与……抵触
[18] covenant ['kʌvinənt] *n.* 协议，协定
[19] divulge [dai'vʌldʒ] *v.* 吐露，泄露

jurisdictions differ on the acceptability[20] of such a clause. In both cases, noncompetition clauses are typically binding on the employee for a certain period (perhaps two or three years) after the employment ends.

Duties. The duties of both the employer and the employee should be clearly spelled out in the employment contract. This section should include employee job duties, salary and benefits and any overtime incentives. The employer's right to transfer the employee to another position should also be included, although if this happens, the employment contract should be amended[21] to reflect the employee's new job duties.

Dispute Resolution. A good employment contract will specify dispute resolution procedures that minimize the time and expense of a courtroom[22] battle that neither party can afford. Arbitration procedures often reduce time and expense, although appeals[23] from arbitration decisions are typically difficult. Some jurisdictions require that employment disputes be brought to a special employment dispute resolution tribunal, in which case, no dispute resolution clause is necessary.

It is imperative that employers have a contract of employment in place for all of their employees—this is not only a statutory[24] requirement, but also good business sense as it essentially lays down[25] a set of ground rules between the two parties.

2. Contents of a Contract of Employment

A contract of employment is made in two identical[26] copies, one for the employee and the other for the employer. At least the following matters are generally recorded in the contract of employment.

• The parties to the contract of employment. Both the employer and employee sign the contract of employment.

• The date of commencement[27] of work.

• Whether the contract is valid for the present or fixed-term.

A contract of employment that is valid for the present is the principal rule. It means that work will continue until the employee resigns or the employer dismisses the employee. An employer must have a justified reason for dismissing an employee. Acceptable reasons for dismissal are specified in *the Employment Contracts Act*. If a contract of employment is valid for the present it means that the employee has a steady or permanent job.

---

[20] acceptability [ək,septə'biləti] n. 可接受性

[21] amend [ə'mend] v. 修订；改良，修改

[22] courtroom ['kɔ:tru:m] n. 法庭，审判室

[23] appeal [ə'pi:l] n. 上诉；呼吁

[24] statutory ['stætjutəri] adj. 法定的，法令的；依照法令的

[25] lay down: 制定、强制性宣称（法律、规则）

[26] identical [ai'dentikəl] adj. 同一的；完全同样的

[27] commencement [kə'mensmənt] n. 开始；毕业典礼

Unit 10

A fixed-term work contract means that the time of commencement and ending of work have been agreed upon. A contract of employment can be made for a fixed-term if there are justifiable grounds for it. Acts and collective agreements determine exactly when fixed-term contracts of employment can be used.

A contract of employment may be fixed-term, for example, for the following reasons: deputyship[28], work experience placement, project work, and peak demand or period.

If a contract of employment is fixed-term, it is binding on both parties for the agreed term unless the possibility of dismissal has been agreed upon. A fixed-term contract can be dissolved [29] only for very weighty reasons:

- probationary[30] period and its duration;
- place of work;
- duties;
- remuneration and its method of payment.

A probationary period can be agreed upon at the beginning of the contract of employment. The probationary period cannot exceed six months. In the fixed-term employment, the probationary period cannot exceed half of the employment contract duration. During this period, the employee can assess whether the work is suitable for them, and the employer can assess whether the employee is suitable for the task. During the probationary period, the employee and the employer can dissolve the contract of employment without a period of notice. The grounds for dissolving the contract of employment during the probationary period must not be discriminating[31]. During the probationary period, the employee is paid normal remuneration[32].

Remuneration is determined according to the collective agreement. If there is no collective agreement in the sector of work, employees are entitled to reasonable remuneration. An employer must not pay remuneration that is less than stipulated[33] in the collective agreement. Remuneration can contain various bonuses. Typical bonuses to remuneration in Finland include experience bonus, overtime pay and extra compensation for shift work.

---

[28] deputyship ['depjutiʃip] n. 代表职务，代理人职务

[29] dissolve [di'zɔlv] v. 消除；解决（问题）

[30] probationary [prəu'beiʃənəri] adj. 试用的，缓刑的

[31] discriminating [dis'krimineitiŋ] adj. 有区别的；有辨别能力的

[32] remuneration [ri,mju:nə'reiʃən] n. 酬金；酬报

[33] stipulate ['stipjuleit] v. （尤指在协议或建议中）规定，约定，讲明（条件等）

Payday is usually once or twice a month. Employers pay remuneration to the employee's bank account. Employees are entitled to receive a payslip[34] that shows the different parts which form the remuneration.

When remuneration is discussed in Finland, what is usually meant is gross salary from which tax, employee and employer's contributions are deducted. The amount that remains for the employee is net salary.

Working hours. The contract must specify regular working hours. Working hours must comply with the working hours act and the collective agreement.

Annual holidays and holiday pay. An employee is entitled to the same remuneration for the holiday period as when working. In addition, an employee is paid holiday pay. The payment of holiday pay is based on the collective agreement. When the contract of employment expires[35], the employee is entitled to holiday compensation for those days for which they have not received holiday or holiday compensation by the end of the contract of employment.

Period of notice[36]. A contract of employment that is valid for the present expires after either the employee's or employer's period of notice. The period of notice signifies the time for the duration of which an employee is obliged to work before the work ends. During the period of notice, all the normal employees' rights and obligations apply to the employee and they receive normal remuneration. If an employer dismisses an employee, they must provide the reason for it. *The Employment Contracts Act* specifies acceptable reasons for dismissal.

[34] payslip ['peislip] n. 工资单

[35] expire [iks'paiə] v. 期满；文件、协议等（因到期而）失效

[36] period of notice: 通知期限

劳动关系管理

1. 劳动关系管理的定义

劳动关系管理是对工会的就业情况所进行的研究和管理。在学术界，许多学科的学者（包括经济学、社会学、历史学、法学和政治学）研究工会和劳工运动，劳动关系也是工

业关系中的一个分支。实际上，劳动关系管理就是人力资源管理中的一个分支。劳动关系管理课程主要包括劳动史、劳动法、工会组织、谈判、合同管理以及重要的当代议题。

从广义上讲，劳动关系可以指管理层和工人之间就雇佣条件产生的任何交往活动或关系。但通常来说，劳动关系指的是代表工人集体利益的工会和组织管理层之间的持续关系。这种关系主要关注的是工会和管理层的权益、书面合同以及对书面合同的解释。

2. 劳动关系经理

为了使双方满意，劳动关系经理在管理层和员工之间起着中介作用。他与工会或非工会雇员打交道，并经常受雇于政府机构。无论是大型公司还是小型公司，它们通常都会雇用这类经理。从事劳动管理这一职业的人经常在大学教授这门课程，或是给盈利和非盈利公司担任独立顾问。

为了胜任这一职位，劳动关系经理要对他工作范围内的最新劳动法和工资法有充分的了解。人们希望他能给管理层和员工解释有关的政策变化，并解释合同措词和上下文语境。在某些情况下，他被指定向工会代表说明管理层的看法。

通常，劳动关系经理的工作主要是解决冲突。在相对次要的小事件升级为大规模职场投诉事件之前他就要介入调解，避免情况恶化。这种调解能防止工作中断、诉讼或罢工等事件的发生。要做好调解工作，劳动关系经理需要和各方相关人员沟通，包括政府机构、工会、雇员和管理层。

如果劳动关系经理是为地方或地区一级的政府机构工作，他的工作很可能更多地集中在政府雇员的特定问题上。这些问题包括工作分类、劳动法以及其他规章条例。这些规章条例涉及工作场所的安全规定、工资、小时工和公平雇用等问题。一些管理人员还研究经济学、职场沟通和劳动法，并为政府机构编制统计数据。

无论是在私营部门还是公共部门，劳动关系经理的日常工作职责都是一致的。他按要求记录所有的职场活动，包括劳动内容和职场沟通。由于经常被邀请出席员工和管理者代表的会议，劳动关系经理需要在他的观察和报告中保持客观的立场。人们还期望劳动关系经理能提供基于劳动关系活动的统计报告。

成功的劳动关系经理通常是一位好的倾听者，他享有办事公正并善解人意的美誉。劳动关系经理的组织能力很重要，因为他要处理大量的文书文档工作，而其中涉及的问题可能会持续讨论几个星期或几个月。因此，具有卓越的口头和书面沟通能力者有优势。

一般来说，胜任这个职位的人要求具有工商管理学士学位、劳动关系或人力资源学士学位。高级劳动管理职位可能还需要相关专业的硕士学位。具有工会代表或人力资源管理经验者优先。

3. 员工满意度调查

员工满意度调查是雇主探索企业如何以员工为中心来运营的一种方式。这样的调查通常以匿名方式进行，通过对员工的多方面提问，测评员工对工作的满意度。这些问题可能与培训、发展、有效管理、歧视、薪水、工作环境或同事关系等有关。许多雇主很关注这些调查，特别是当他们很难留住员工的时候。然而，他们可能也有兴趣听听有关如何改善员工与雇主之间关系的想法。

调查员工满意度可以采取多种不同的方法。通常，雇主会与独立的人力资源顾问合作。他们实施调查，然后为公司解释调查结果。在线调查成本较低，因为在线调查得出的结论能提供某些预先确定的补救措施。然而，如果公司能负担得起更昂贵的方案，可能会更有帮助，因为这种方案提供的任何解决措施都是为特定的公司及其员工量身定做的。

调查结果是否保密是被要求参加调查的员工最关心的事情之一。最佳的调查结果是保密的，任何担心这一点的人都应该得到保证，最好是书面形式的保证，即保证调查方不能对员工在满意度调查中做出的负面性评论进行处罚。当一个公司真的致力于提高员工满意度时，他们不仅要接受好的评论，也要接受坏的评论。如果只关注正面的评论，他们无法改进。因此，为了得到这些结果，雇主应该使用那些能保证答复机密性的调查方案，否则可能最终只能得到一些不诚实的、不具成效的言论。

员工满意度调查的质量在很大程度上取决于它如何帮助公司提高满意度。当雇主不愿意做出真正的改变时，调查就没有多大意义。员工往往知道他们的同事对工作有什么看法，而且大多数人都能辨别出问题所在的领域，如员工流失率高。如果调查以后，员工并没有在一定时间内看到这些问题得到改善，那么员工保留率可能会下降，尽管其他因素（如就业市场不景气）可能会使员工仍然从事着他们并不喜欢的工作。

虽然员工满意度调查应该能促进工作场所的改善，但员工个人也需要对将要看到的改进情况持现实态度。改善的程度取决于关注共同问题的员工数量。个别员工可能对雇主有合乎情理的不满，但并非所有员工都如此。而雇主未能解决个别员工的问题通常是因为他们正尽力采取措施来满足大多数员工的需求。在工作环境中感到舒适的员工可能会试图与管理层说明合乎情理的个人问题。

4. 提高员工满意度

员工满意度是衡量员工对工作和工作环境的满意程度。保持高昂的士气对任何公司来说都大有裨益，因为积极的员工更有可能产出更多，休假更少，并对公司保持忠诚。为了提高或保持高员工满意度，明智的雇主可以灵活运用许多有效的方法。

员工入职培训。让员工满意的最好方法之一就是确保他们从一开始就感到满意。提供全面的入职培训，确保员工对工作期望持现实态度，确保新员工不会出现一开始异常乐观，继而很快失望的情况。适当的入职培训能培养积极的态度，降低离职率。

积极的工作环境。乐观、积极的工作环境是必要的。如果工作环境不积极向上，那么你就无法期待员工积极乐观。相互鼓励、避免微观管理、给予正面的反馈、确保建设性批评等这些方式都能使公司不仅仅是员工的生存之处，更是他们事业蒸蒸日上的地方。

提供有竞争力的福利。丰厚的薪水很重要，但有竞争力的福利对保持员工的满意度也至关重要。如果福利待遇差，员工可能会在福利更好的其他公司寻找就业机会。除了保险之外，如弹性时间、带薪假期和事假等福利也是影响员工满意度的重要因素。

员工敬业度。那些认为自己的工作无趣或认为自己对公司没有作出贡献的员工是不会积极地投入工作中去的。要让员工满意，必须使他们感觉到自己正在参与更重要的工作，而不仅仅是完成个人的工作任务。让员工参与目标设置，使员工融入公司组织结构中以提高员工敬业度和满意度。

培养技能。每个人都需要某样东西使其为之努力不懈，停滞是空虚的。员工的潜能高于他们目前的职务水平。鼓励员工发挥这种潜能将有助于提高他们的敬业度和满意度。无论是内部培训、辅导、在线课程或外部培训都能鼓励员工提高他们的技能。

表彰与奖赏。赞赏优秀员工对员工来说意义重大，但这并不需要在正式的公共场所来进行。企业应该鼓励主管和经理每天认可并感激员工的工作。同时，在公司范围内实施一个正式计划，以表彰在每一位表现卓越的员工。健康的竞争能鼓舞士气，鼓励员工努力工作，提高员工的满意度和保留率。

跟踪工作满意度。不要坐视不理，却只希望员工满意——相反，要收集一些相关数据，实施匿名在线调查或流动调查，有效地跟踪员工对福利的认可、对主管的反馈以及对有助于员工满意度其他方面的数据。企业可以改善、调整并监控满意度，减少员工流动量，为公司节约成本。

人力资源专家从事的是企业中最具挑战的工作之一，因为他们的工作是考虑其他人的工作、其他人的工作满意度、辞职的可能性，以及他们的态度对同事的影响程度。通过各种措施提高员工的满意度可以使你的工作（以及其他人的工作）更满意，更充实。

5. 劳动纠纷

劳动纠纷是指雇主和雇员之间在集体谈判时有关谈判的条款（如雇用条件、福利、工时、任期、工资等）产生的争议，或在实施已达成条款时引起的冲突。

劳动纠纷是一种冲突，它产生于工会调解下达成的集体谈判协议中的条款。在工会与雇主协商协议时，或已达成的协议被违反时，可能会发生劳动纠纷。如果劳动纠纷升级，就可能发展成罢工，即员工直到纠纷得以解决才会上班。这种情况成本非常高，并可能引起政府强制性的干预。因此，工人、工会和雇主都希望能避免劳动纠纷。一旦发生劳动纠纷，可以采取以下几种有效解决方法：

劳动仲裁。劳动仲裁是一种非正式的裁决过程。劳资双方共同授权仲裁员根据听证会上提供的证据颁布最终的、有法律约束力的裁决书。任命劳动仲裁员的权力由集体谈判协议产生。

申诉调解。绝大多数申诉都在劳动仲裁之前得以解决。劳动管理部门越来越多地考虑将调解作为仲裁的替代办法。我们都是劳动申诉的娴熟调解员，我们调解过许多有关纪律和合同解释方面的劳动申诉。

中立协议。中立协议越来越多地被看作是一种工具。它为工会组织行为制定基本规则。我们认可工会，批准工会选举，检查工会卡，并处理由中立协议产生的仲裁纠纷。

基于利益的谈判。劳动和就业协议的谈判日益复杂。传统的谈判通常是权力的较量，并运用权力相互对抗，而这往往牺牲了更好的协议，甚至关系。我们将利用基于利益的问题解决过程，使谈判员和领导成为共同的问题解决者。在这个过程中，双方都有可能获得利益，只有满足双方利益的解决方案才更为稳定，而且双方应该互助达成建设性的意向。

申诉和冲突是雇佣关系中不可避免的一部分。公共政策的目标是通过建立有效预防和解决劳动争议的制度来解决冲突，促进良好的劳动关系。劳动行政机关通常在国家立法中确立劳动争议程序。有效制度的关键目标是确保冲突各方尽可能通过安抚和调解等协商一致的方式解决问题，然后才通过法庭或劳资法庭恢复仲裁和/或判决。